SOUNDINGS

SOUNDINGS

On Shakespeare, Modern Poetry, Plato, and Other Subjects

ALBERT COOK

 WAYNE STATE UNIVERSITY PRESS   Detroit

95 94 93 92 91   5 4 3 2 1

Library of Congress Cataloging-in-Publication Data

Cook, Albert Spaulding.
    Soundings : on Shakespeare, modern poetry, Plato, and other subjects / Albert Cook.
        p. cm.
    Includes bibliographical references and index.
    ISBN 0-8143-2331-6 (alk. paper)
    1. Shakespeare, William, 1564-1616—Criticism and interpretation. 2. Poetry, Modern—History and criticism.   3. Philosophy, Ancient. I. Title.
PS3553.055S68   1991
814'.54—dc20   90-22103

The book was designed by Elizabeth Pilon.

To the memory of my brother

Contents

Acknowledgments

For ongoing discourse I have profitted from the students in a seminar on Shakespeare, and from the comments of the Brown University discussion group in ancient philosophy. Among the many colleagues who have helped with these essays, I should especially single out Thomas McFarland, Victor Terras, Sam Driver, Christine Brooke-Rose, Peter Baker, Lee Jacobus, Robert Scholes, Frederic Will, and Andrew Sabol. The constant alertness of my assistant Dr. Blossom S. Kirschenbaum continues to be of great help in many ways. And I remain always grateful to my wife Carol for encouragement and support.

I am also grateful to the journal publishers of these essays: *Arizona Quarterly* ("Projections of Measure: The Continued Synergies of Pound and Williams"), *Helios* ("Some Thoughts on How to Discuss Epic Poetry"), *Modern Poetry Studies* ("The Syllabic Module"), *Accent* ("Metaphysical Poetry and *Measure for Measure*"), *American Journal of Philology* ("Dialectic, Irony, and Myth in Plato's *Phaedrus*"), and *Arethusa* ("Equanimity and Danger: The Distribution of Questions and Style of Confrontation in the Four Dialogues around Socrates' Trial"); and to Jeffrey Meyer, ed., *T. E. Lawrence: Soldier, Writer, Legend*, London: Macmillan, 1989 (*"Seven Pillars of Wisdom:* Turns and Counter-Turns"). I should state my gratitude, too, to *New Literary History* for having accepted "Some Observations on Shakespeare and the Incommensurability of Interpretive Strategies."

Preface

L ooking back over the variety of these essays, I feel that it might be acceptable to situate them in the context of some aspects of my own relation to literary and critical theory, rather than to confect justifications or extensions of the principles I variously adopt or defend in them.

"Analytical criticism is already becoming the stock-in-trade of the academic writer on modern literature, while the vital advances are being made in theoretical works like those of Kenneth Burke and others. We applaud this tendency. For literary criticism, focusing as it does the most abstruse problems of ontology, ethics, the theory of knowledge, and their interrelations, is the chamber music of intellect; it has human value only in so far as it is philosophic." So I wrote in 1947, enthusiastically vague on the large hermeneutic interaction between analysis and philosophy that was itself to develop in the intervening years. I was writing in a manifesto for a magazine where I and my fellow editors were to bring fiction and poetry together with criticism in the vigorous continuing mode of the time. A year earlier as an undergraduate I had written my first, and almost my only, fan letter, to Kenneth Burke, congratulating him on *The Grammar of Motives*. The former editor of the *Dial*, poet, novelist, and perennially aspiring composer was not to find his theoretical work taken into the mainstream of academic discourse for another decade or so, and I did not meet him myself till nearly thirty-five years later when we coincided as visiting lecturers at the Buffalo English Department. This was more than a decade after my tenure as its chairman from 1963 to 1966, when I re-shaped it along principles that were already in the process of moving toward the terms of that early manifesto.

One midnight during my chairmanship years, Charles Olson and I were having a drink with a distinguished classicist whose seminar on the pre-Socratics I had taken my first semester of graduate study, around the time of the manifesto. He declared to us that we were lucky to be teaching in a situation with which we could identify intellectually. He had never had that luxury, he said. It was a sobering thought, since he had held a leading pedagogic role in three of the best universities in North America; but I had myself also experienced the elective blindness of classics depart-ments centered on establishing data, a more extreme form of the myopia that was a perpetual threat to departments of modern literature as well. And yet those more restrictedly scholarly goals, too, properly grounded and oriented, were part of the common enterprise, even if at times they would arrogate to themselves the management of the whole.

We were indeed lucky then at Buffalo, and generally during these years in the university, but theory had in fact long before found a home there. It was practiced by the New Critics, who were often philosophical in ap-proach, though they are sometimes now inaccurately lumped with the mere analysts. They also exercised, sometimes curiously, a sense of social interaction as it bore on literature. Such a social, and even a philosophical, approach was exercised in his own way even by Matthew Arnold, and in fact by other philosophical critics from the mid-eighteenth century on.

Indeed, at that very same earlier time, I was having a friend mail me from France a text that was still not owned by Widener Library, Jean-Paul Sartre's *L'Etre et le néant,* which I spent much of the summer of 1948 studying through. I was not the only American academic attending Merleau-Ponty's inaugural course at the Collège de France in 1952–53, nor later was I the only one of my compatriots hearing Lévi-Strauss's course there in 1963–64. Such interests were to sweep through literature departments, as they gravitated toward a gradual dominance of theory, in various manifestations.

Accounts of these developments could justifiably occupy book-length discussions, and indeed they have done so many times. But it can be briefly observed, just from the angle of the reception of French ideas, that the self-questioning of Sartrean idealism continues in the mode of Jacques Derrida as it encourages the theorist to account for, if not to succumb to, the persistent fault lines and contradictions in the works he addresses; a his-tory transformed by the Annales historians but also by the "thick descrip-tion" of Clifford Geertz (who repeatedly, and in his most recent book, acknowledges his deep debt to Kenneth Burke) continues with and beyond the mode of Michel Foucault and Gilles Deleuze to set a standard of adequacy for establishing cultural interconnections; and a transformed psychoanalysis in the mode of Jacques Lacan extends and deepens much literary discussion by enforcing attention to the armatures of depth implication in texts. These richly derived approaches are sometimes fruitfully combined with each other and with much else; they have come to inform the multifarious related theoretical discourses invigorating the profession today.

The essays printed here reflect some of these developments, I trust, and this brief and partial personal retrospect is offered as perhaps more appropriate than the methodological considerations I might have adduced to cover such a variety of practice. Although most of these essays have been written in the past three years, others range through much of my career. The earliest and almost the latest are those on Shakespeare; of those five, four have been written very recently, whereas the piece on *Measure for Measure* was written in 1950. (I have left it in its original form.) It is my hopeful conviction that they will be regarded by a reader as all belonging together, albeit with the looseness inevitable to essays separately written, as separate acts of sounding.

SECTION ONE

Projections of Measure:

The Continued Synergies of
Pound and Williams

Poetry is intrinsically musical, and it calls for a kind of invention that may not be solved by reverting to the tune of some received meter, though that is a solution that contented Baudelaire, Rimbaud, and Wallace Stevens, among others. Rimbaud, however, as a metrical American poet (Hart Crane) reminded himself, did say, "Il faut être absolument moderne," pre-echoing the "Make It New" of Pound and Confucius's bathtub. The imperatives of inventing a live music in poetry can present themselves as problems, and one can too easily ignore those problems by received conventional, or even by received "unconventional," solutions.

To find and invent his music, the poet at all times is called upon to hear and adjudicate among the possibilities before him. These possibilities, in almost all but the most primitive societies, are multiple, and call for a solution, even if, like Lucretius and Propertius and Vergil and Ovid, the poet has made the choice of a single pattern measure, or, like Catullus and Horace, has chosen from among a group of given measures. The solution of all these Roman poets is to exploit special possibilities within their given meters. Unique solutions seem to have been sought, and found, so far as we can tell from the slender evidence before us, by the earliest Greek lyric poets: by Alcman and Sappho, as well as by Pindar.

Chaucer evolved his Mozartian metrical fluency, the most finely tuned for centuries, out of a number of French and Italian possibilities that stood before him, a solution to the English dead end he might have found

17

himself in. It was not obvious at first that the quantities of Stanyhurst and the fourteeners of Golding and Chapman were dead ends. It took the startling efflorescence of the iambic pentameter in the 1590s to unleash the possible modulations of that instrument.[1] And the next decades saw a continuing efflorescence, at the hands largely of playwrights. Milton, facing this multiple situation, reintroduced a version of Latin music as a superaddition to blank verse, subjecting it also to a deep innovation of his own.[2] Skipping over high points in this history of metrical choices, I would note that Wordsworth still further made the resolving choice of diluting the "Miltonic" blank verse of Thomson for the open-ended meter of *The Prelude,* hitting a register that got a slightly different music in the "conversation poems" of Coleridge, which themselves drew, as Wordsworth did not, on some composite of the tonal modulations of Pope and Dryden. Blake found a completely different repertoire of solutions out of the (same) manifold possibilities facing him.[3] Keats, in one mode, made the choice of, as it were, re-Miltonizing Thomson; he took that choice, in turn, and applied it to what might be called a pentameter amplification of Collins's Odes.

Tennyson, come at not from the fatal dilutions of the Georgians but "forward" from the possibilities offered to a follower of Keats, toned Keats down, much as Thomson had toned down Milton. Browning, in this light, roughens up Coleridge, and Matthew Arnold, as it were, Drydenizes Keats, if a shorthand description can be offered for a process that would take many pages of analysis to describe, and so really to justify.

I leave out of this hasty account the super-melodic solutions of Byron and Swinburne, a siren song on which many wrecked. The musical embarrassments produced by Longfellow, Holmes, and James Russell Lowell are aimed clumsily in that direction where William Cullen Bryant had managed some freshness by choosing to attend to Wordsworth for one mode and Collins for another. The solutions of Whitman and of Emily Dickinson were inobvious and fresher, both remarkably original in their rhythms, given all the fertility of the former for later poets and all the self-containedness of the latter. But music is all.[4]

In the past hundred years, the range of possibilities has never been greater, and the range of viable solutions is correspondingly wider. As always, most solutions are *faute de mieux* and settle for what that forceful inventor of music Gerard Manley Hopkins called "Parnassian verse" (though he meant more by the term than just lazy music). Certainly the opposition of metered verse to "free" sets up too one-dimensional a definition if we were to take it as a guiding principle. Among many options for focusing in this area, it can be illuminating, I believe, to concentrate once again on the Pound-Williams tradition, down to the present, since, special pleading aside, that tradition of embodied solutions does exhibit a fertility nearly equal to that of Whitman himself, who is, of course, also a strong component in the music of both Pound and Williams. And one may find some definitions coming to hand by centering further, once again, on what Olson and Creeley did with the results of Pound and Williams. How Pound and Williams would proceed in, say, 1917 was not obvious at the beginning for either, nor was it simply obvious for Pound that the troubadors would provide a way out from, so to speak, choosing Swinburne on the one hand or Whitman on the other. Pound would seem to have chosen Browning, but that choice is not so obvious or so simple. It should be observed that it did not really do the job for him either. What did, interestingly, was not the meter but a metrical counter and resistance to a sort of opposite meter in another language: his solution was to produce a Whitmanoid pastiche of Propertius's elegiac distichs. Pound's achievement continued from there.

The inspired, very different solutions that Olson and Creeley had arrived at by 1950 began with ascertaining that, of all the imposing presences on the living horizon of achieved poetry, a vein of specially accessible vitality was to be found in Pound and Williams above all—though not to the exclusion of a great deal else. That combination in many ways has proved a main fertile avenue of solutions to the present, if not the only avenue. It is exactly rhythm that distinguishes both Pound and Williams from all their contemporaries. Both go far beyond the free verse of Whitman, and also of Stevens, Eliot, and H.D. What distinguishes these two poets begins with their evolution of a measure, and the Olson-Creeley letters remain full of discussions about measure, as by 1950 Olson had characteristically found the abstractions for "Projective Verse" by extrapolating from measure back and forth to epistemology and metaphysics.

Now it took ten years and more for Pound to find his measure, the melopoiea and logopoiea to match the phanopoiea that imagism had given him. Imagism, really, would resist entering the Vortex. The "vorticist" epic would become possible only after he had first stretched his measure into the long lines of *Homage to Sextus Propertius* and then condensed it for "Hugh Selwyn Mauberley." By this time he was able really to start the Cantos, which even as late as 1917, and with all his theory behind him, he kept botching into blurred versions of Browning's and even Tennyson's blank verse, as evidenced by the strangely clumsy draft of the "Three Cantos" in *Poetry,* June 1917;

> And all my chosen and peninsular village
> Has made one glorious blaze of all its lanes—
> Oh, before I was up—with poppy flowers
> . . . .

As well begin here. Began our Catullus:
"Home to sweet rest, and to the waves' deep laughter,"
The laugh they wake amid the border rushes.
This is our home, the trees are full of laughter,
And the storms laugh loud, breaking the riven waves
On "north-most rocks"; and here the sunlight
Glints on the shaken waters, and the rain
Comes forth with delicate tread, waking from Isola Garda—
Lo soleils plovil,
As Arnaud had it in th'inextricable song.

The sensibility here is even softened by audible Tennysonian echoes. These echoes are not just the verbal and thematic ones of "waves' deep laughter," "peninsular village," "Isola Garda," presented in a tone that is nearly indistinguishable from Tennyson's filtering of Catullus. The echo is also rhythmic; Tennyson's "dying fall," though loosened, is still audible here, especially in lines 1–3 and 6–10; and consequently through the whole passage. It lacks, in fact, the toughness of Catullus, and even the formality of the "Ave atque Vale" of Catullus's poem about his brother.[5] And as for the Lago di Garda of these lines, Pound refers to the Sirmio of Catullus, but he has also not left Tennyson's Sirmio very far behind:

FRATER AVE ATQUE VALE

Row us out from Desenzano, to your Sirmione row!
So they row'd, and there we landed—"O venusta Sirmio!"
There to me thro' all the groves of olive in the summer glow,
There beneath the Roman ruin where the purple flowers grow,
Came that "Ave atque Vale" of the Poet's hopeless woe,
Tenderest of Roman poets nineteen-hundred years ago,
"Frater Ave atque Vale"—as we wander'd to and fro
Gazing at the Lydian laughter of the Garda Lake below
Sweet Catullus's all-but-island, olive-silvery Sirmio!

One can match the meditative voice of these Ur-Cantos, also to the voice of Tennyson's Ulysses:

I cannot rest from travel: I will drink
Life to the lees: all times I have enjoy'd
Greatly, have suffer'd greatly, both with those
That loved me, and alone; on shore, and when
Thro' scudding drifts the rainy Hyades
Vext the dim sea: I am become a name;
For always roaming with a hungry heart
Much have I seen and known; cities of men
And manners, climates, councils, governments,
Myself not least, but honour'd of them all;

And we should not forget that there is a Tennyson who anticipated Imagism:

> Now sleeps the crimson petal, now the white;
> Nor waves the cypress in the palace walk;
> Nor winks the gold fin in the porphyry font:
> The fire-fly wakens: waken thou with me.
>
> Now droops the milk-white peacock like a ghost,
> And like a ghost she glimmers on to me.
>
> Now lies the Earth all Danaë to the stars,
> And all thy heart lies open unto me.

But this takes us far afield, and in any case Pound has left imagism before these first-draft Cantos.

So he gets no equivalent for Catullus here; he will take details, but no measure at all, from this scrap heap of decaying gestures. Much later, in Canto 29, he will reinvoke Lago di Garda, with only a glance at Catullus.[6] The Tennysonian sigh is retained in phrases of his own that are culled from poems much earlier than "Near Perigord," but these phrases are now purified, ideogrammatized, stripped, and juxtaposed:

> Pearl, great sphere, and hollow,
> Mist over lake, full of sunlight,

The six syllables of the first line here are matched, through its heavier stress pattern, to the eight syllables of the second. And that heavier stress pattern simultaneously makes them a mismatch—though there is so much variation that no iambic or anapestic foot is firmly identifiable as a norm, and that variation leads us in the direction of Greek cola, whose rules for an entire line allow for substitutions that would make these lines, by this analysis, variants of each other.[7] These are close to being dactylo-epitritic lines, but at the same time they exist in a context where other, English norms are also operative. So we also note the variation of caesurae in these two short lines, two marked caesurae in the first line, echoed and matched by two possible ones in the second, "Mist/ over lake,/ full of sunlight." But it is only the matching that tips the first caesura of the second line toward identification, and the lines are also mismatched, with the stronger first caesura in the first line, as the commas firmly indicate. Though still writing here about Lago di Garda, the *miglior fabbro* has left Tennyson far behind.

These two lines could almost have been written by Creeley; not, I think by Williams, and not by Olson: there are too many modulations within the line, though in this particular pair of lines Pound observes the isochronicity that Charles O. Hartman has well characterized as an attribute of much good verse, free and other. The definition is a suggestive one, "isochrony . . . a beat or pulse—not counting the accents but equalizing the time between them." As Hartman reminds us—and it is a basis for all the metrical practise I am considering here—"all linguistic stress, in speech as well as verse, is relative stress."[8] If this possibility holds, it will guard against asserting simple derivations, Creeley from Williams and Olson from Pound. Indeed, Creeley emphasizes the earliness and persistence of Pound as a reference point for himself: "But it is again the sense of *measure,* and how actively it may be proposed, that I found insistently in Pound's work."[9] I am saying that these lines of Canto 29 could almost have been written by Creeley because they contain modulations that it would be hard to find anywhere else in English before Creeley. But the glancing observation cannot be pressed into a perspective, still less, I believe, into a scansion system or anything more specific than a general characterization.

The imagist, the vorticist, and the theoretician of Gaudier's planes, are all assertible even of these two lines from Canto 29. Yet as late as the draft Cantos, none of these is anywhere to be perceived; the measure is an only mildly modified version of Browning's rough blank verse. This is also true of the measure of "Near Perigord," of which the draft cantos are an ill-focused imitation.

At almost exactly this same time, mid-1917, Pound is already discovering the anti-Propertius in his translations of that Roman poet. A new, discursive measure, far crisper than Whitman's, is unleashed to rebound against the tight and precisely counted elegiac distichs of Propertius. And if the lines of the Roman poet are close to being isochronous, then lines of "Homage to Sextus Propertius" are notably not so, anticipating the nodal breath-clusters and superimposed meters of the Cantos in their range of metrical possibilities. Again, in any case, as Hartman says, "If lineation helps to enforce attention, it serves as a prosodic device, whether the line is metrically organized or not."[10]

In "Near Perigord," which does offer mostly isochronous lines also in its sense as well as in its structures, the *fin amor* of the troubadors has been ingested so as to brace the similar but, of course, far weaker pre-Raphaelite languors, which by the time of Mauberley, partly through Propertius's satiric tone, Pound will have learned how to satirize. In the Cantos, further, he will be able to set satire on love, the theory of love, and the sharp effect of the passions, all into their own logopoietic vortex, through the melopoeia he will have learned not from imitating Propertius—as he had been trying to imitate Browning, Arnaut Daniel, Rossetti, and the Elizabethans all together—but by inverting Propertius for a measure that allows the adaptive voice its amplitude, and with it a flow of comment:

> And in the mean time my songs will travel,
> And the devirginated young ladies will enjoy them when they have got
>   over the strangeness,

> For Orpheus tamed the wild beasts—and held up the Threician river;
> And Citharaon shook up the rocks by Thebes and danced them into a
>   bulwark at his pleasure,
> And you, O Polyphemus? Did harsh Galatea almost
> Turn to your dripping horses, because of a tune, under Aetna?
> We must look into the matter.
> Bacchus and Apollo in favour of it,
> There will be a crowd of young women doing homage to my palaver,
> Though my house is not propped up by Taenarian columns from Laconia
>   (associated with Neptune and Cerberus),
> Though it is not stretched upon gilded beams:

And this varied cadence continues for seven more lines. It pushes, as it were, against isochrony—the isochrony of Pound's own Imagist and blank verse poems, of Whitman, for that matter[11]—and of Propertius. Nothing could be more foreign to the measure of Propertius, the single meter of the elegiac distich that he wrote all his life, though lines 5 and 6 offer audible approximations of an inverted elegiac distich. The closest approximation to Propertius is not Whitman, of course, but Pope. Not even Whitman is as ample or as controlled as Pound manages to be in these lines, where the range of the Cantos is already audible, though not yet in the syncopations that he there attains, the laminations of meter upon meter:[12] Here is heard the elegiac distich's end-stopped click, along with the further click of the dictated caesura at the end of the sixth syllable of every second line.

> Carminis interea nostri redeamus in orbem,
> gaudeat in solito tacta puella sono.
> Orphea detinuisse feras et concita dicunt
> flumina Threicia sustinuisse lyra;
> saxa Cithaeronis Thebas agitata per artem
> sponte sua in muri membra coisse ferunt;
> quin etiam Polypheme, fera Galatea sub Aetna
> ad tua rorantis carmina flexit equos;
> miremur, nobis et Baccho et Apolline dextro,
> turba puellarum si mea verba colit?
> quo non Taenariis domus est mihi fulta columnis,
> nec camera auratas inter eburna trabes.

That is the sound of Propertius. Mauberley's measures have equivalents for that, but the "Homage" does not. It extends the logopoietic invention of Propertius into an amplified melopoiea. This amplification can be heard, perhaps, in the single locution "devirginated young ladies" for "tacta puella"—the opposite of "intacta," as we are reminded. That five-syllable word is remarkable for distributing its accents ambiguously, "de-virginated"; whereas "young ladies" is sharp and contrastive—as well as plural for Propertius's generalized term, "non-intact girl." "Tacta puella," on the contrary, like all Propertius's locutions, is precisely distributive, metrically emphasized by coming right after the caesura, as one dactyl and two-thirds of a second.[13] Pound's rhythmic invention here buoys up the logopoietic sweeping away of the troubador and pre-Raphaelite love mystique, but tenderness also invades the satire through Pound's assimilation of Propertius's involvement: neither poet, indeed, can be called the detached spectator exactly.

Still, to point one other detail near the end of what I have quoted, Pound amplifies the simple "Taenariis . . . columnis" of Propertius into a large mouthful: "Taenarian columns from Laconia (associated with Neptune and Cerberus)." This scholarly aside heavily modulates its jumbo line by steep accentual differences within the line, pulling it, as it were, together, and then by the necessary shift into a softer voice when the parenthesis is appended to the long noun phrase. Pound the scholar offers us an amplified gloss that Pound the inventor of measure pours into this startlingly long line. As always this (mis)matches the neatly framed line of Propertius. Moreover, within a poem the gloss does not function simply as an informational footnote. The "Laconia" is scholarly for the Roman region of Sparta; the "Neptune" and "Cerberus" by association get the open chaos of the sea and the ominousness of the underworld into Pound's poem, notes that are controlled by Propertius but of course not present in his lines, since Pound has added them. In adding them, he is already on his way not just to the measure of the Cantos but, correlatively, to their thought rhymes and condensed thought ideograms. Looking back from them we can see that the Neptune of Latin poetry, the Neptune of English poetry from the Renaissance through the Victorians; and the Cerberus of both, as well, have been assimilated by being named and blocked by the logical—and rhythmic—gesture of the scholarly aside.

Olson too is not just a bookish poet but a scholarly one, and he too uses scholarly investigation as grist for his deep systematizing, using his measure as a divining rod. And both poets are notable for what they omit, Olson going right to Pound and Williams, ignoring all the rest of the complex modern tradition, just as Pound has omitted, for all practical purposes, the whole complex modern tradition from Baudelaire through Valéry, to say nothing of Rilke and the expressionists, or even the Crepuscolari, who offer a still more purified version of his pre-Raphaelitism, and still less the *Blast*-like Futurists, and the beginnings of Montale and Ungaretti (even though Marinetti is a figure in the Italian-Fascist Canto 72). But before long Pound will break through into those overlaid meters I have described elsewhere,[14] which clamp a new kind of tightness onto the discursive voice of his Propertius. We have the four-dimensional harmonics of the Cantos.

Williams, too, began with blank verse, hard as it is to believe. And he occasionally had recourse to it. The theory of *Spring and All, Kora in Hell, Instigations,* and so on, though of probing mastery, does not really do justice to the abstractness of the meter he discovered could be achieved by the radical but simple procedure of attending to the ongoing modulations of the voice, one he encouraged in himself by inobviously highlighting the obvious, that it was American. His early associations with abstract painters, at the same time, brought him to give his metrical intent also an abstract expression: "The feeling is of words themselves, a curious immediate quality quite apart from their meaning, much as in music different notes are dropped, so to speak, into repeated chords one at a time, one after another—for themselves alone." "Poetry . . . as in all machines its movement is intrinsic, undulant."[15] Williams's voicings went through various developments, up to his late triplets, which he mysteriously termed a "variable foot." As Hartman says, Williams's variable foot . . . seems to have meant that each of the three staggered lines of his stanza should be thought of as one foot, the whole stanza thus becoming a sort of trimeter line" (66). (The line itself, or more properly, the triplet, had been devised in a modernist context by Williams's friend Conrad Arensberg, who published samples as early as 1917 in a little magazine associated with Marcel Duchamp.)

Williams's metrical discoveries, however, go far beyond simply being free verse, and they also go far beyond our ability to label them "American." Indeed, one could give the geographical dialectal designation to the intonational patterns not only of Williams's asserted American cadences but those of Emily Dickinson as much as those of Whitman. And the contrast of Robert Bridges with, say, Edwin Arlington Robinson, or the Robert Frost who was also a theoretician of the American spoken voice, would highlight the American stamp of the latter two. Frost's sense of the "colloquial" matches and parallels Williams's, as Jerry McGuire has defined it: "[Words] shift with their contexts and create the possibility of throwing off old significations and discovering new nuances and shadings of experience . . . (through) formal organizations that Frost called 'sentence sounds.'" And McGuire quotes from a letter Frost wrote in 1918 along these lines, at a time when Williams was developing his own parallel theory: "I suffer from the way people abuse the word colloquial. All writing, I don't care how exalted, how lyrical, or how seemingly far removed from the dramatic, must be as colloquial as this passage from 'Monadnoc' comes to. I am . . . sure that the colloquial is at the root of every good poem."[16]

Harvey Gross has pointed out the effect of immobility gained in the "Objectivist" slant to Williams, by seeming to isolate and arrest individual words.[17] Then, given such interactions through partial arrest of the voice, there emerges, through all this time, the possibility of several ranges of complementary expansions. As Hartman says, "Williams's poem derives much of its rhythmic interest from a more complex counterpoint, changing the relation between its isochronous lineation—comprising both interval and pace—and its syntax. In this it resembles highly enjambed blank verse."[18] But it also differs crucially from blank verse in the inescapably primary attention-arresting strategy of inverting the relation between design and instance.[19] The contrapuntal effects of line against voice pattern, design (even if arbitrary) against instance, are to be found in any poetry whatever: one zero case is arrived at in end-stopped lines, where the counterpoint reaches a total convergence.

All this expands Pound's "sequence of the musical phrase"[20]—as Pound himself expanded it, beginning with "Homage to Sextus Propertius." This is his pronouncement of largest import on meter, and virtually his only one bearing on the practice we are discussing that carries through all these discussions. Again, the word *sequence* points to instance, and *phrase* points to design. And taken together, they assert the primacy of groupings within a line, "the musical phrase," over what it contributes to, the music of an overall line, metered or "free." And one can postulate, listening to Olson, a play of the eye immobilized in a short line and the ear moving vivified through the inescapable progressions of sound. Creeley, of course, preserves and polishes this rhythmic inheritance, jazzing it up with an insistence on syncopation, the rhythmic counterpart of minimalization. As he says, speaking of Zukofsky but by implication also of Williams, "people speaking (at least in American speech) do exhibit clusters or this isochronous pattern of phrase groups with one primary stress; so there is a continuing rhythmic insistence in conversation. But this possibility has been increased in poetry."[21] Thirty years of Williams will be passed on in the intensifications of Creeley:

THE DISAPPOINTMENT

Had you the eyes of a goat,
they would be almond, half-green, half-

yellow, an almond
shape to them. Were you

less as you are, cat-like, brush
head, sad, sad, un-

goatlike[22]

Here an initially short line is powerfully varied, and it is tonically resolved in a final line, "goatlike." This line is as close to a spondee as an English word can be, and it is further highlighted by consisting of a single word that is a component of the somewhat larger single word, its negative, from which it has been severed. This extreme enjambment itself resolves the other chief device in the poem, the variation of strong caesurae within the lines, throwing rhythmic (and therefore semantic and syntactic) emphasis on each word as it comes out in the heavily modulated sequence.

II

Measure leads to vision, Olson always prophetically insisted, that being the common denominator of his various formulations.[23] In "Projective Verse" Olson forcefully defines "composition by field" in terms of measure: the "kinetics" has two halves, and the two halves are

the HEAD, by way of the EAR, to the SYLLABLE
the HEART, by way of the BREATH, to the LINE.

These are, respectively, almost the abstract metrical design for line and the individual instance of articulation for the syllable, because it is clear Olson means one syllable in its pull against another when he speaks of "the swift currents of syllable," which would be another way of saying the instances of the flow of the voice. And his "line" virtually coincides with "design"— that is, with lines in their pull against one another—since he calls line "the threshing floor of the dance," speaking of "the law of the line" and of "stretching conventions." Further, he speaks also of "stave and bar" when he quotes, not Pound or Williams whom he does mention, but rather the opening of *Twelfth Night*. The typewriter is evoked, precisely, as a delicate aid to transcribing live metrical effects. It is almost as though line is the "high energy construct" and syllable the "high energy discharge" he speaks of before making these definitions. The definitions themselves, as they couple head and ear to syllable, heart and breath to line, bring Olson's human universe into view here, as always, though our attention at the moment is not directed to the governances and stretches of his metaphysico-psycho-cosmology.

At about the same time, though, while throwing such large systematic definitions within which we can locate both the voicings of Pound or Williams and the regularities of Shakespeare, Olson is encouraging his own live development, we may say, by refusing Pound recourse to the very breadth he has here defined. He would reject Pound's recourse to the possibility of metrical regularity—a Pound who is at that very time continuing and refining the intense metrical integers of the cantos:

the dross of verse. Rhyme!
when iron (steel)
has expelled Confucius
from China. Pittsburgh!
beware. the Master
bewrays his vertu.
To clank like you do
he brings coolie verse
to teach you equity,
who laid down such rails![24]

The equations here, perhaps, do not quite add up, but in their valiant spanning of whole cultural epochs and synchronic civilizations, they use the use of measure as the criterion for special perception. The single revelatory criterion as a measure is a notable Poundian gesture, and here Mencius-Olson remains a pupil of that master in his very apostasy. As a corollary, in fact, Olson might here be trammelled in rejecting such gestures of Pound's close to this time as the final couplet of the "Pisan Cantos," or of such runs in them as the three Rubaiyat quatrains at the climax of Canto 80:

Tudor indeed is gone and every rose,
Blood-red, blanch-white that in the sunset glows
Cries: "Blood, Blood, Blood!" against the gothic stone
Of England, as the Howard or Boleyn knows.

Indeed, there are alexandrines as well as blank verse lines, and generally an iambic regularity, in "The Moebius Strip."[25]

In Olson's fullest range of voice and most assured measure, in *The Maximus Poems*, I have always been convinced that the largeness of breath, through well-managed pauses, governs the syllable even more than it does the line (though one perforce leads into the other, half to half). In any case there are effects that combine Williams's energy of variation with Pound's assuredness of cadence, and something clearly in their vein and clearly new is heard from the beginning, in the first Letter:

(o my lady of good voyage
in whose arm, whose left arm rests
no boy but a carefully carved wood, a painted face, a schooner!
a delicate mast, as bow-sprit for

forwarding[26]

This allows the range of the "Homage to Sextus Propertius" long line, but it reins it in and breaks it up. The bold isolation of "forwarding" is an effect that indicates a broader register than the Cantos. (I am not declaring Olson to be the better metrician but simply to work on a wider scale.) This is the end of section 2. Section 3 has a comparable range, but section 4, in its variation, pulls suddenly into isochronic regularity, three four-line strophes, where the syntactic and syllabic and accentual regularities of the last serve to highlight the semantic leaps:

> of a bone of a fish
> of a straw, or will
> of a color, of a bell
> of yourself, torn

What does "torn" go with? It goes with everything and nothing, or with all together, since "torn" of "yourself" would have to be metaphorical, and "of yourself" could in turn be either subjective or objective genitive with the other six nouns, two to a line; but it could also be parallel with them, the key seventh among bone, fish, straw, will, color, and bell. The iso-chrony evens all this out, substantiated by the minor variation of two bisyllabic words among eighteen monosyllables, and also by the strongly anaphoric syntax here.

Pound himself enters into "Letter 6," as the subject of Olson's visit with his first wife to St. Elizabeth's. The poem opens with a four-syllable two-line strophe unpunctuated, that forces a change of voice volume in the third word and fourth syllable, a very different rhythm from Pound's, though still notably on Poundian principles:

> polis is
> eyes

After Pound's appearance, toward the end of the same long section, the terms are repeated, reversed, made part of a longer strophe rather than isolated, and modified by the capitalization of "Eyes" and by an ampersand for "and":

> Eyes,
> & polis,

Moreover, two commas have been added, one at the end of each line. The simplicity of the four syllables has still permitted, within its small compass, the addition of no fewer than six delicate modulations.

More boldly still, Olson randomizes and totalizes his effects at points in the ongoing poem. In Maximus III (438) one whole section consists of two crisscrossed lines, an effect that dimensionalizes the simultaneities beyond Apollinaire (or beyond the mere arbitrariness of Cummings).[27] This is a whole section, and a more complex later section, "This is the Rose / of the World," both illustrates its subject and simultanizes it in the super-Apollinairian and trans-Mallarméan turning round and round at the same time outward (or inward), connecting and separating the central beginning-ending "This is the rose of the world," with the spiralling outer initial-final proposition, "Migration in fact (which is probably as constant in history as any one thing" (479).

From just this range of examples, it is fair to say that it is in Olson's own verse that one hears what he attributes to the late Shakespeare, the "aerodyne" of managed quantities.[28]

Williams and Pound go beyond free verse. That beyond is a beyond in depth, which forces the voice not only to syncopate, as in the "Slow flow heat is silence" of Eliot,[29] but to force the syncopations so that they register gaps or silences. These gaps themselves work ambiguously to seal accented syllables closer together—insofar as the unaccented syllables are omitted—and to force them farther apart, insofar as there is no overall design of meter to measure which syllables exactly have been omitted. The effect of this doubt is to throw emphasis once again onto the accented syllables for a sort of super-syncopation, stronger because the voice is left alone, and the individual syllable is reasserted in its isolation. This effect cannot be achieved by free verse alone, or the negative suppression of regularity. Nor is it to be heard even in superbly controlled open free verse cadences like those of Whitman, or, differently, those in Pound's Mauberley. An intuitive system that scores the syllables into vibrant place is called for. That means, coming from Williams's direction, starting with the cadences of a normal voice unaligned to any metric design, and then structuring gaps or pauses into that, so totally that the line cannot escape into a free verse looseness. These intensifications, of course, already govern the early Cantos and Williams's poems of the twenties. The effect can be heard variously in Zukofsky, in the later Basil Bunting, and in Reznikoff, as also in Lorine Niedecker. The Americans offer a keen variety:

> Arnold heard the blowing of the whistle:
> the train was coming.
> The only light was that of a small lamp
> behind the shutters of the station,
> and it gave at best
> a weak light on the platform.[30]

> Something in the water
> like a flower
> will devour

> water

> flower[31]

> towing of earth on earth
> dwarfed mimosa has shut—sleeps:
> flood'll lull nations windrows: oak-ilex
> holm: the rushbottom chair legs
> shortened accord seat and back
>
> cushions—2 crewel threads flowers,[32]

In the first of these passages, Reznikoff takes the convention of alternating shorter iambic lines with blank-verse lines, permutes it with end-stopping, and forces these two devices to flatten into a paractactic deliberateness by dwelling on the accents, forced the more markedly into verse emphasis by the fact that the narration is so even and "unpoetic."

In the second passage, Lorine Niedecker takes the opposite tack of heavy enjambment and internal echo so dense that it throws rhythmic emphasis, and a rich musical slowing, both on the four echoing substantives (water, flower, devour, water) and on the fifth that is distinct for not offering echo (Something). Such internal echo, combined with caesural slowing and a sort of American-colloquial shorthand version of the Miltonic packed syntax, livens the third passage, where Zukofsky makes these crepitant rhythms both even out and swallow up the particulars he names. This modulation, where the instance of the voice is brought to bear heavily on the design of the verse, continues into the work of Oppen and even Rosalie Moore, as well as many other places. It is alive and well as a resource, even in places where one would not expect to hear it.

The whole effect was called by Olson, somewhat metaphorically, the breath unit. Pound early felt his way toward breaking the line down into more discriminated clusters than usual by typing larger spaces between words, as Kenner points out for "In a Station of the Metro."[33] Olson's vergule in the middle of a line, not only heard but gestured by the hand at his live readings, systematizes Pound's contrapuntal inner-line organization. Of course, such an organization is heard magisterially in *The Maximus Poems* at their most vibrant. It is also heard, very differently, in Creeley from early on, though, again, we would not want to make the over-assertion that Olson develops Pound, Creeley Williams, since each of them takes the depth-cue from both of those poets, as well as from many others, including the Mallarmé of the much syncopated late sonnets, to whom Creeley wrote an homage. And it is an uncertainty before other possibilities that perhaps led Olson to recoil before the very different neoconservative measures of Pound's *Confucian Anthology*, wherein Pound was continuing his lifelong adaptiveness of poetic developments on a base of scholarly interests; but the Arnaut Daniel-cum-Campion and Waller of the "Envoi" to Mauberley is one thing—even though it could never lead to *The Cantos*. The Englished quatrains of the absolutely syllabic archaic Chinese poetry is another. Olson, working out his own deep version of how the archaic can center a poetic voice, does not want to accommodate the "clank . . . " of the *Confucian Odes* as a legitimate development in Pound.

In the many projections of possibility here, one can pick up the cue of Williams's insistence on an "American" voice and see how it combines. It should be remembered that these metrical possibilities are not exclusively American. The example of Pound may be used to pull powerfully at sonorities that approach the conventional:

> Drip—Icicle's gone.
> Slur, ratio, tone,
> chime dilute what's done
> as a flute clarifies song,
> trembling phrase fading to pause
> then glow. Solstice past,
> years end crescendo

Here is an English voice, the Bunting of *Briggflats*. (Hear the rhythm in the very title, "Briggflats"!). It moves also in a rich ground-tone, slowed down. In these features Bunting's British voice is recognizably akin to an American voice in the late work of one who was early a kindred poet, the Louis Zukofsky of "80 Flowers":

> A look at it hale
> looking airs fragile bud green
> looks thru catkin borne erect
> bract flowers naked gold before
> leaves unfold full osiers cure
> headaches weaving lancets white gray
> bark with thyme blown seacoast
> basket the life pussy willow[34]

Bunting in these lines of his talks about what he is doing to its rhythms. His rhythms are also recognizably akin to another English voice, the still fuller-lunged voice of Dylan Thomas:

> Never until the mankind-making
> Bird beast and flower
> Fathering and all humbling darkness
> Tells with silence the last light breaking
> And the still hour
> Is come of the sea tumbling in harness.[35]

The last line in particular can be heard as recognizably in the register of the nearly contemporary Bunting, and Thomas was free enough with his syllables, for all the incantation, to draw criticism from his auditors for not keeping regular meter—astonishingly, perhaps. The difference, of course, is crucial. Bunting does rhyme, but he allows the voice to break, the phrases to cluster and press against the line rather than to pull forward into an ongoing surge. He offers, so to speak, certainly not the music of Pound but as though the music of a Thomas fascinated by Williams—to put the whole complex development in parable form. If we return to the abstract side of these possibilities, we see that Creeley, freed by Williams, abstracts him, in sound:

WAS

The face
was
beautiful.

She was
a pleasure.
She

tried to please.[36]

Once again, Creeley is to Williams as Mallarmé is to Baudelaire. The lightness and improvisatoriness of jazz has here been imitated, and a monodic note so simple, so elemental in its verbal resources—even to call it a diction seems affected—that is exceeds the plain style. It is pre-plain style or post-plain style, the way jazz declares its sound to exist in an even domain not bounded by levels of classification. But at the same time it is low-key, complicated in mood. It changes its modulations, its beat, at nearly every syllable, whereas jazz works on its 4/4 base in a way this does not try to emulate—except in coolness, the inevitable word that one must apply even if it is un-cool to apply it:

REFLECTIONS

What pomposity
could say only—
Look
at what's happened to me.

All those others
surrounding
know
the same bounds

Happiness
finds itself
in one or many
the same—

and dead,
no more than one
or less
makes a difference.

I was thinking
this morning
again—
So be it.[37]

"love"

The thing comes
of itself

                    (Look up

to see

                        the cat & the squirrel.
                                    the one
    torn, a red thing.
                            & the other
somehow immaculate[38]

The practice, of course, admits of still wider variation and modulation.
Here is Robert Kelly's music about music:

IN MAHLER'S SLEEP

an archaic austerity
comes out of the ground

(bird skeleton, snake skeleton,
no redundancy)

comes out & confronts the sea.[39]

Here is Charles Doria's assimilation of isochronous syncopation to a range
of poetic assertion that has an epic largeness:

the tree flies

the bee gathers honey with our tongue

        they live undefinedly

death feels the flash

> thousand suns at once

> "I am become death"

> diadems maces discus immeasurable[40]

And here are the minimalist late offerings of Gary Snyder, where the gaps in predication are matched by the pauses in the brief lines:

> The white spot of a Flicker
>   receding through cedar

> Fluttering red surveyors tapes
>   through trees, the dark woods.[41]

Kelly's variety of word-lengths, and his variation between repetition of phrase and large-voiced change of phrase, counterpoint against the isochronicity of his lines, in which also three of the five lines lightly rhyme and the other two have a nasal and a dental in varied echo (nd/ton). Doria, like a condensed Pound, starts out with a line as long as an alexandrine at its climax but varying around a tonic short cluster, as short as three syllables in the first of the lines quoted. The effect is to isolate the individual lines for internal echoes that are always audible but never so pronounced as to throw just that line into prominence. They are as colloquial as Williams, while at the same time as suspended as Mallarmé. A similar double process occurs in the matched compound noun phrases, with participles attached, of Snyder's nearly isochronous, multiply inter-echoing couplets.

   Moving to a larger and vaguer area of speculation, if we return to the tangent of the components "American" and "British" in a poetic voice, it would be hard to provide a long, systematic, and empirically detailed description of the differences between British and American English. It should be remembered in this connection that Williams was fighting a British pull in his own background: William George Williams, his father, was a Spanish-speaking Caribbean Englishman who retained his British passport to the end of his life. William Carlos was raised by an English grandmother as well as by a mother from the Caribbean who spoke Spanish and French better than she did English.[42] Still, we can observe in general that differences between British and American—to say nothing of Caribbean—English would obtain most deeply not just in minor variations of diction[43] but in overall *rhythmic* patterns—of superfixes and the like—since the grammar of the two versions of English, and almost all the diction, is virtually identical. Then we could continue to notice mixes of various sorts—the tendency toward "British" patterns in Americans—

even, I should say, young ones. These traditionalists-come-lately have been acculturated to the so-called common style, which is nothing but the British Attic style developed in the eighteenth century.[44] Further, more interesting hybrids could be remarked—T. S. Eliot, a conscious imitator of British speech as well as a resident in Britain. Some British discursiveness is still audible in the early Denise Levertov, who had published a first book of poems in regular measures before leaving England for an America where she adopted the style of Williams in a way distinct from that of her early associate Creeley:

> Below the
> darkening, fading
> rose
> (to which, straining
> upward, black
> branches address them-
> selves, clowns of alas)
> the lights
>
> in multitudinous
> windows
> are
> bells in Java[45]

One might hazard a guess that a person like Jonathan Williams, long resident in a part of Britain more conservative in speech than metropolitan London, would show some traces of the British in his American voice. Pound himself carried off successfully the creation of a character-persona who is satirically made to satirize British-patriotic doggerel, Alf:

> Was I started wrong as a kiddie,
> And would my old man have been smarter
> To send me to work in Vickers
> Instead of being a carter?[46]

Here the speaker derives from a class, and it is a class that in some features may sound more like the English working class than does the British upper class usually mimicked in poetry. So Ed Dorn's *Geography*, written to some extent in Britain, as the title "North Atlantic Turbine" tells us, carries out a discursive voice that owes something to a British undercurrent, as well as to the achievement of Pound's *Propertius* (itself, in this connection, a hybrid British-American product, written after a decade in London):

> (The central difference between Medieval
> and Renaissance is simply expanded commercial enterprise,
> isn't that the "spirit of the age?"

> Ghiberti's doors are the doors
> to the biggest bank, and bank doors
> may be "the gate to paradise". The Baptistry
> is clearly a bank (those doors
> would fit the Chase Manhattan as well)
> tourists have never mistaken that—
> the iron grating was put up
> to protect the gold being rubbed off
> by their inquisitive fingers.[47]

Here the open-ended Olson parenthesis is accommodated to the discursive flow that is still within hailing distance of "Homage to Sextus Propertius."

The possibilities abound; Pound and Williams, Creeley and Olson, have multiplied them. Olson has gone one step further than Pound by insisting, for simplification and for complication, on the full inclusion of his measure in the expanding circular universe of his cosmic vision. That such assertions stand at the border between mystification and insight does not prevent our crossing the border in either direction. And the superbly flexible monody that Creeley has made of Williams's measure will accommodate many polyphonies, as well as many angles of vision—while itself only a salient case in the considerable range of modern metrical actualizations.

Some Thoughts on How to Discuss
Epic Poetry

Propp, in his book on the Russian heroic epic, puts it neatly—
perhaps too neatly—when he stresses the "heroic character in the
content" of epic poetry.[1] In terms somewhat different from his, we
have become accustomed through Milman Parry at one end and Marshall
McLuhan, Eric Havelock, and Walter Ong on the other to seeing the code
of the hero as expressing the total, self-enclosed conception of the world not
far from tribal society.[2] In Greece, for example, Homer offers us a commu-
nal society founded on *timé, areté,* and *aidos* that the hero at once ornaments
and exemplifies, overseen by the Olympian gods who are organized in a
comparable system of checks and balances. The society of these poems is at
the same time complicated: it is seen nostalgically through a retrospective
lens. It suppresses, or at least passes over, more primitive layers of myth still
alive at the time, as Rohde and Nillson[3] have pointed out.

The centrality of the hero in such poems does legitimate our passing
over such qualifications, at least provisionally, and we can move in our
concern continuously from the smallest unit of the formula or the metrical
staple to the largest question about the world vision of the poet. As
Charles Segal puts it, when he focuses on likening Homer to Plato rather
than contrasting the two: "Homer's formula, like Plato's language of the
Forms, creates a world. Their allegiance is not primarily to the particular,
but to a large vision of reality, to a heroic universe. . . . The epic stresses
the typical, the immutable; . . . it is here where the poet and philosopher,
for all their differences, overlap: each seeks to arrive at the timeless and

essential quality above the particular and to view human life against the vision of a coherent, ennobled ideal which embraces the whole of reality."[4]

I shall move back round to the implications of that last statement. To look at the smallest unit first, the formula, our discussion of it shows no signs of abating, as the large studies of Michael Nagler, Berkeley Peabody, Gregory Nagy, and Norman Austin show,[5] and the alert attention of the papers presented at the Michigan Conference on Oral Literature and the Formula in 1974 is an additional testimony.[6] There the application of precise questions about the formula was extended to Anglo-Saxon poetry, for example, by Robert Creed and John Foley, as William Whallon and L. D. Benson had done before; such applications as this, or Joseph W. Duggan's to *The Chanson de Roland*,[7] only carry out the comparative principle of Parry himself, who was inspired at a Slavic scholar's lecture heard in Paris to go and test on that comparative ground the hypotheses he had already adumbrated in his master's thesis on Homer. The formula, a staple conjunction of sound and sense, has persistently posed questions of definition, questions delicately demarcated by Joseph Russo[8] and others. And the question of definition—what the formula is—leads to the question of how the formula works—how it is used—in the construction of a poem. Berkeley Peabody offers a series of matrices to explain the function of the formula, and Michael Nagler expands the notion somewhat to delineate generative family resemblances among groups of phrases, borrowing the idea of "sphota" or "burst of poetic ideation" from the Sanskrit grammarians. In this connection, through more than analogy, Gregory Nagy follows the lead of phrasal congruences and connects the sound-sense conjunction of the formula, and then on the meter in which it occurs, to Indo-European patterns.

Another way of asking how the formula works in the construction of an epic poem is to ask how original the phrasing may be. It will not really solve this problem just to say that the phrasing may be traditional and the use and/or the combination original. There is in poetry generally a tendency toward traditional phrasing, toward poetic diction, in any case. The problem is neatly posed by the discussion between D. L. Page and Kenneth Dover apropos of the diction of Archilochus, where the former maintains that it is overwhelmingly formulaic and the latter protests that it still breaks definitively with the epic tradition.[9]

The formula typifies what it designates. This feature of the formula links it in turn not only to poetic language generally—to a poetic diction—but to such specific uses as simile, metaphor, and the kenning, which may itself be seen as a sort of formula. In overall theory these remain very much live questions. Can any formula be called truly metaphoric or akin to live metaphor when it is drawn from tradition? In the form of epithet the metaphoric character of "ox-eyed" Hera may be qualified in a society much closer than we are to a sharing of numinous functions between gods and animals. Since the epithet is applied to others than Hera in tradition, and to women collectively by the *Iliad* (3.144; 7.10; 18.40), it approaches the status of a dead metaphor—to a greater degree, perhaps, than other formulas. But whether there are degrees to the deadness of metaphor in a formula, as there certainly are in language, is not clear. Nor is it clear how such a question would apply to the metonymy of "bronze-greaved Achaians" or the near-synecdoche of "white-armed Hera."

How, too, would such usages relate to the extensive use of seemingly systematic abstraction in the *Mahabharata*—not only in the *Baghavadgita*—but, I read, in the last quarter of the poem? There are accretions in the *Mahabharata,* of course, and it is not certain there are none in Homer. To speak of accretion is to imply periods of history. But there, too, we are confronted with problems. Often metaphor and simile are rudimentary, or have a firm visual base, in early epic poetry. But it is hard to account for the kenning in this light, to say nothing of *Gilgamesh,* a millennium earlier than any of these poems (though at the same time from a civilization possibly somewhat more developed). *Gilgamesh* contains series of metaphors more direct than anything in Homer. Are these metaphors themselves in turn formulaic? Do they, as well they might, resemble a litany of praise in some way?

In this connection, turning from the small detail of the poem to its overall conception as these mirror each other, it is well to remember that epic is not our simplest or earliest literary form. *Fuerunt ante Homerum poetae.* The rough and ready typology of the Chadwicks, derived largely from elements entering into the Eddas, is still serviceable.[10] They offer five kinds of early poetry: (a) narrative poems, (b) poems dealing with situation or emotion wholly or mostly of speeches, (c) poems of didactic interest, (d) "celebration" poetry, elegies, and panegyrics, and (e) "personal" poetry. The earliest kinds are (b) and (d), poems of situation and of celebration, but all these kinds are to be found in that developed composite we call the epic poem.

There is, of course, always a continuum between form and content. The actions of the hero that the poem describes correspond to type, as do the phrases of the poem and the kind of address in which it is cast. Beyond the large characterization of such poems as oral, by Albert Lord, Ruth Finnegan, and others,[11] and beyond the simple adherence of the hero to the code, his actions themselves fall into the patterns that Aarne-Thompson classifies,[12] in a series that defines him as a "hero" on the checklist of Lord Raglan.[13] Still another matrix of equal experience for the hero is proposed by Dumézil.[14] He finds a tripartite division of roles—the ruling-priestly, the warring, and the commercial-agricultural—to underlie the Indo-European societies for whom our most elaborate evidence tends to be the epic poem. For *Mythe et epopée* even so diverse a poem as the *Mahabharata*, his chief example, reflects these functions: epic illustrates myth, as for Havelock epic serves to encode myth.

The comprehensive picture of a society that an epic poem tends to give brings Dumézil within the purview of our topic, though he is mainly concerned with Indo-European society rather than with the nature of poetry. Those concerned, however, with the nature of poetry are brought to address epic as a chief example: this is the case with Emil Staiger,[15] who defines the type as offering *Vorstellung*, a foursquare representational view of the world. It is also the case with Walter Muschg,[16] who assimilates the epic poet to the general type of the inspired bard, a counterpart of the hero. Such an approach is implied in the typological studies of Thomas Greene[17] and many other investigators into the strictly literary, rather than simply mythological, typifications enlisted by the epic poet in his delineation of the hero.

II

The subject tends to spread, we keep seeing, into adjacent domains. Our study of epic illustrates in a secondary way how comprehensive, how fertile in connections with the society it depicts, an epic poem may be. This broadness may be taken to sponsor the two further questions I would like to raise. They are not new, but they are not settled either.

First, how do erotic motives and developments govern the epic poem? Dumézil's functions are all busy ones, of peace and war, and epics do center on military action. Just the same, many epic poems contain the erotic motif in some deep, if tangential, manner. Even in the *Iliad* Helen serves as a remote cause and present wonder, Briseis as a proximate cause. The erotic is a strong force for Odysseus on the sea and at home. Aeneas, who moves under the protection of a mothering Venus, begins his political adventures with a fateful love and ends them with a dynastic one. Matchmaking is at issue at the center of the *Mahabharata* and also of the *Ramayana*.

If medieval poems do often concentrate almost exclusively on military action—if they can be *chansons de geste*—the universe of erotic subtleties in the troubadours expands in the *Roman de la Rose*, a poem whose large conception and whose allegorical tendencies assimilate it at least in some degree to the line from the *Odyssey* through the *Aeneid* to the *Metamorphoses*. It lacks a jousting hero, but not a quester.

Is the epic simply "a long poem" then? That is part of our question. Or consider the medieval German tradition, of a time when the Minnesänger had taken up from the troubadours. The *Nibelungenlied, Parzival,* and *Tristan und Isolde* all pivot on doughty military action. The love interest is deep, however, in all three. The disasters of the *Nibelungenlied* are occasioned by the second match, not a first, and by a woman's fury at her family's betrayal of her beloved husband, the hero Siegfried, who has disappeared through death early in the poem. Love hangs over *Parzival*. It dominates *Tristan*. The hero of that poem is at the same time a notable, indeed peerless, military hero, in the pattern of Achilles. Among these poems there obtains a hierarchy of engagement with the love motif, reaching a peak in *Tristan*.[18] There is also the hierarchy of subtlety toward love, ranging from the relative crudeness of the *Nibelungenlied,* to the sensitivity expressed in *Tristan,* on a par here with the troubadours or the Minnesänger—but, again, in what relation?

> Love appears fairer than before.
> And in this way does it endure.
> Were love to seem just as before
> Then would love soon disappear.

> Si dunket schoener sît dan ê.
> da von sô tiuret minnen ê.
> gediuhte minne sît als ê
> so zergienge schiere minnen ê.

(11875–78)

Does a hero who turns his attention from military prowess to perceptions of which such lines as these can be drawn remain a hero? That is the question.

The second question has to do with the persistent philosophical component in epic poetry. Hesiod is a contemporary, or even a predecessor, of Homer; he begins one of his inquiries by mounting a definition of truth, in a powerful tripartite form that has considerable generalizing power, as Piero Pucci has analyzed it.[19] A systematic mythology, a systematic anthropology, and a systematic guide for the conduct of social interaction and agriculture, all are to be found in him, at least incipiently. If Xenophanes saw himself as departing from a Homeric base, would Empedocles and Parmenides have seen their verse as wholly divorced from the Homeric enterprise? If indeed a real lost poem lies behind the attempts to Charles Doria[20] and others to reconstruct from Kern's fragments the narrative of an Orphic cosmogonic epic, then such a poem would provide another link in this chain of poetic repertoires aimed at a lengthy exploration of "the nature of things," to translate the title of a still later long, speculative poem.

There is much that amounts to philosophy in the *Mahabharata*, and the Poetic Edda leans heavily on the powers inherent in wisdom. A chief figure in the *Kalevala* is a seer, and a poet who is also a seer as well as a hero figures largely in the *Mabinogion*. Extending this strain into more sophisticated time would allow us to include the poems of Ovid and Dante among the "philosophical" epics, to say nothing of Blake's prophetic books. Noticing that all three of these "truth" poets present theories about the force of love would close the circle by joining my first question with my second.

Finally, then, it will not do simply to define the epic hero in a circular fashion as the military hero. "The long poem" may well be the more adequate category, since we find military heroes more purely in ballads, in byliny, and in short epics like *The Lay of Igor's Campaign*. Since all long poems present amalgams, we could simply say that a military campaign may serve as one organizing principle for the amalgam.

Again, we have either left the epic hero, or we have extended him. To know which, we would have to know what ground we were on. I would submit that we are still finding out.

Prophecy and the Preconditions
of Poetry

E specially in the prophets, but generally in poetry, an overriding tendency in expression leads toward recursions of sense, and these recursions are often easily classifiable, with Lévi-Strauss, into structures of binary opposition, which can be taken as further evidence for the bones of the skeletal structure that undergirds myth. This is true for the oppositions and identities in the parallelism of Hebrew verse, and also for the elaborate pairings of Trojan and Greek, wartime and peacetime activities, persons, and divine powers, presented in the *Iliad* and differently in the *Odyssey*.[1] The recursions must be identified by sense, and they may also be identified by sound; but there are features in the sound and in the sense that tend to carry beyond the recursions. In poetry, though, it is the sound that carries the feel of myth and enlivens it. Myth "grips" a society, or an individual in it, as well as schematically expressing their conceptions.[2] And what enlivens the myth is not just sound, not just the absolute repetitions of ritual, but the inventive sounded repetitions of the bardic voice: myth in all cultures carries its integrating and integral onus through the structured sound of the poetic utterance. That is its large precondition, which is preverbal, so to speak, as well as perhaps universal.

Religion for Isaiah and other prophets is at once a context and a focusing subject, one that links a whole people to a Supreme Being. This religion defines politics in a way so constantly changing in its dynamism that even a term like "theocratic" would be somewhat misleading. In the "triangle" of forces envisioned by a prophet in this tradition, the side of the speaker determines what the side of the people will mean (and the other way, too), whereas both are determined not just by the presence but by the action and the reaction of Jehovah. These conditions, if they are coded into words, are nonverbal in the sense of working prior to words. In the theological situation, which is also a political and a dialogic one, the poetry is founded on a life-and-death urgency that also enters into repetition of its central subject, repetition of the dire threat against the people from invaders, of their dire need and a possible transcendence of it, of the omnipotent and potentially dire vigilance of God. Repetition, in the form of thought-rhyme or parallelism, is the defining form of the utterance as well. Its semantic and rhythmic base can thus be taken as an echo of its context and content. Yet at the same time the set of the prophet-about-to-speak brings him under the pressure of his utterance into a speech that finds fulfillment as it presses itself beyond the formal and logical antitheses he codes into his poetic lines. He carries forward into overriding hopefulness, or (in the mode of Jeremiah) into overmastering grimness.

The Hebrew prophet would seem to bring all these features into condensation and amplification under pressure of his "burden," and at the same time to retain more distinctly the bard's "original" priestly function, as a consideration of the preconditions of utterances in Isaiah may demonstrate.

> Arise, shine, for thy light is come,   1
> And the glory of the Lord is risen upon thee.
> For, behold, the darkness shall cover the earth,   2
> And gross darkness the people:
> But the Lord shall arise upon thee,
> And his glory shall be seen upon thee.
> And the Gentiles shall come to thy light,   3
> And kings to the brightness of thy rising.
> Lift up thine eyes round about, and see: 4
> All they gather themselves together, they come to thee:
> Thy sons shall come from far,
> And thy daughters shall be nursed at *thy* side.
> Then thou shalt see, and flow together,   5
> And thine heart shall fear, and be enlarged;
> Because the abundance of the sea shall be converted unto thee,
> The forces of the Gentiles shall come unto thee.
> The multitude of camels shall cover thee.   6
> The dromedaries of Midian and Ephah;
> All they from Sheba shall come:
> They shall bring gold and incense;
> And they shall show forth the praises of the Lord.
> All the flocks of Kedar shall be gathered unto thee,   7

The rams of Nebaioth shall minister unto thee:
They shall come up with acceptance on mine altar,
· And I will glorify the house of my glory.
Who *are* these *that* fly as a cloud,   8
And as the doves to their windows?
Surely the isles shall wait for me,   9
And the ships of Tarshish first,
To bring thy sons from far,
Their silver and their gold with them,
Unto the name of the Lord thy God,
And to the Holy One of Israel, because he hath glorified thee.

(Isaiah 60.1–9)

Against the evenness of the parallel members of sound and sense here, there is a corresponding unevenness working as a sort of countercurrent so that the oppositional patterns are swept forward. These mark the pressure that has thrust the prophet forward to make his charged utterance in the first place. As Benjamin Hrushovski says, "There is an overlapping of several such heterogeneous parallelisms with a mutual reinforcement so that no single element—meaning, syntax, or stress—may be considered as purely dominant or as purely concomitant"; and, as Robert Alter says, "there would seem to be some satisfying feeling of emphasis, for both the speaker and his audience, in stating the same thing twice, with nicely modulated variations."[3] And as Alter goes on to quote Victor Shklovski, "The perception of disharmony in a harmonious context is important in parallelism."

The immediate syntactic parallelism that governs the repetitions of the members here spreads outward and backward, evenly and without classificatory emphasis, into a swelling "staircase" parallelism through this whole passage, where in the afflatus of the prophet's voice all members exhibit some basis of equivalence to one another as well as becoming cumulatively more emphatic, to the point where past and future merge in a "prophetic present." The first two verses set the perfect present ("is come," "is risen") against a paralleled future ("shall cover"), an effect condensed here but expanded later in the sons who come from afar, the daughters who are supported the way a nurse would support (*teamanah*). Seeing is coordinated with flowing (or shining)[4] and fearing with broadening (*rahav*). "Abundance," "force," and "multitude" converge in their objects and in their attributes. The forward motion of the poem here energizes and integrates, as well as subclassifies, its "antithetical" members of people and Gentiles, into the ground of "identities," between people and prophet, people and God, people and Gentiles, sea and land, past and future, light and dark, fathers and children, kings and people, animals and men, close and distant, name and actuality. All these categories crop up in this passage, but also spread forward and back throughout the work of "Third Isaiah" (post 536 B.C.), as here.

This thematic matching carries through that presumptive individual prophet to "First Isaiah" (740–701 B.C.) and "Second Isaiah" (550–540 B.C.), other individual prophets from recoverably different times who had to have written before "Third Isaiah" could be born. This writer assumes an "Isaiah mode" as the set into which he forms his utterance. So, for example, John L. McKenzie finds[5] that the second verse here "echoes 9.1, which describes the darkness just before the birth of the messianic prince," and that the third verse "sees the fulfillment of 2.2–3," Kedar is repeated from 42.11, and many more specific echoes could be tabulated, to prophetic work that is datable before the time of "Third Isaiah," who was classified by the canonizers mistakenly through scantness of historical information, into what can still be correctly classified as an "Isaiah" key signature, and therefore seen as a group of coherent echoes in the same book.

Even in all the prophets, there is a limited stock of themes to which they return, and which they recombine so pervasively that almost any utterance can be taken as parallel, by echo partial or whole, or by antithesis partial or whole, to any other. Just from "First Isaiah," one can gather further echoes of these lines. Verse 5.30 dwells on the contrast in the movement from dark to light, as does 9.1–4. And 5.26 speaks of coming from the ends of the earth, as the last five verses above effectually do. Verse 6.12 speaks of "a great forsaking in the midst of the land," with which these lines are in full antithesis. The mention in 8.7 of "the king of Assyria in all his glory" touches on the theme of the majesty of the peoples who here are said to converge upon Israel. "The earth shall be full of the knowledge of the Lord / As the waters cover the sea" (11.9) puts this convergence in another way that touches on the sea theme here as well. In 11.10, as here, the Gentiles seek the rod of Jesse, and the four corners of the earth are mentioned. There is a whole series of the "burdens" of the large, near nations that are seen in a brighter light here. Tarshish and its merchants come into play in chapter 23, and Midian has again been mentioned in 9.4 (as, from "Second Isaiah," Kedar is mentioned in 42.11). Yet the emphases are different. "First Isaiah," in his references to Assyrian domination, leans on a hard future, "Second Isaiah" expands on the imminence of a restored one. "Third Isaiah," here quoted, broaches fulfillment.

These are, in a sense, preexisting attitudes conditioned by a political present toward which the prophet is expected to take a God-centered future orientation. The pattern type of a "tribal" society (and any society, like that of Israel, will offer variants of the pattern and divergences from it) that first differentiates a priest-king from the group and then splits those leadership functions would find echoes in every society's assignment of roles to a poet, even the modern one. Shelley's jejune notion of poets as the "unacknowledged legislators of mankind" would thus find a complex grounding in social practice, where for "unacknowledged" one would read "skewed" or "conflated." Nor is it just the priestly function that the poet fulfills, though mainly that. Saul was a king so little known as a prophet that his role as one must be asserted,[6] and David and Solomon were differently accorded a poetic function along with the kingly one.

The prophet in Israel drew not just on his own personal charisma but on the expectation that he would have a charismatic function to fulfill by virtue of his exposure as a channel of a divine message. That exposure carried with it the dangers of stress, exhibited variously by Hosea and Jeremiah, among others. And it also carried the danger of invalidation: there were such things as false prophets, and the true prophet could at any time be maltreated by being accounted one.

Poetry assimilates to religion in earlier traditions, and, albeit obscurely, in later ones as well. Homer's function within Greek society includes a religious dimension, though one distinctly different from the place of the Rig Veda in early Indo-European society, where the priestly families were almost bureaucratized; and certainly, in neither Homeric nor Vedic society, was the poet exposed to the danger of the Hebrew prophet. Hence Homer's utterance began under the precondition not of risk but of validated security. For all their differences, there is a certain relaxedness in the conditions available to Homer that enables him to produce an expansiveness and comprehensiveness in the verse narration of pattern stories. The role of the poet within the Homeric poems has the relaxedness of such variety: of Demodocus and Phemius in the Odyssey, and in the Iliad the Linus who provides the harvest song fixed, as it were, on the Shield of Achilles.[7] The rhapsode seems freer than the skald, and the extraordinary breath of Homer's poems rises to the openness of that precondition. This situation does not change deeply for the philosophical poems of Parmenides and Empedocles. The social conditions that produced Wisdom literature, by contrast, resulted from a more marked transformation. The prophet's danger has faded, and the wisdom of Proverbs and Ecclesiastes keeps focussed in a practical, social orientation. The very continuity of the Greek poet's foregone security implicitly licensed him into far-reaching systematic speculation. Hesiod is inspired on the lonely mountain, but he returns to make an unthreatened public utterance. And these characteristics inhere not only in the poetry of Pindar but, arguably, as conditions of utterance that transcend the presence or absence of meter, in the pattern-stories that constitute Plato's dialogues, though they take within them a severe and complicated attitude toward poetry. At the same time, Greece offers (in this as in other ways) a repertory of models. In a complex situation that for each poet has many common features, a different interaction with the circumstances bodied forth in the poetry (and not just a difference of personal vision) is projected by Archilochus, by Alcman, and by Sappho, and then again later by Pindar and Bacchyllides.[8]

II

Erving Goffman's fine-tuned discriminations of the social constraints on normal oral interchange throw into relief not only the richness of poetry but its strategic exclusion, whether it be oral or written, of cues noting those constraints.[9] Suspended in poetry is Goffman's "footing," which does not have to be established in poetry between poet and auditor since it exists as a precondition. "Set alignment" is not shaken in poetry, though it may be shaken in ordinary discourse. "Projection" for poetry is always much longer than in conversation, and the "continuity" does not shift adaptively but remains immobile. There is no "bracketing of liminal roles," and there is no two-person arrangement improvised. A liminal role can be set up, however, in a poem, as the addressee is pulled rhetorically and fixedly into the poem. Here poetry formalizes a fixed version of the two-person interchange with just one person speaking, in the epistolary form from Theognis through the Renaissance to Thomas McGrath's long, fixed "Letter to an Imaginary Friend." A version of the epistolary rhetoric can be enlisted as a support for the ontological implications of the poem, as in Whitman's "What I assume you shall assume," Ashbery's shifting personal pronouns around a fixity of rhetorical set, and the "general" intimate "du" of Rilke's *Sonnets to Orpheus*. This last elides and comprises the reader-auditor, the poet, and the archetypal legendary poet, Orpheus himself.

If we may continue to see the conditions of the poem by throwing them into relief against Goffman's descriptions of ordinary talk, there is no small talk as such in a poem, though the modern poem may assume small talk into itself, which thereby gets magnified in the prior act of cuing into a poem. And there is no code shifting in the poem, or none that does not metalinguistically call attention to itself as code shifting and so submit the code-shift to a prior assumption of fixed framing, of a meta-code preexistent to its individual utterance, in which the shift is itself recoded.

Goffman's principles apply *a fortiori* to Homer. If much communicative extensiveness is structurally edited out of a written poetic presentation, something like an equivalent condition would apply to oral performances as well. The public, live reading or performance by skald, rhapsode, Vedic priest, or modern poet would in all these very different cases have to mark its difference, and even its heightening, of ordinary speech by an abandonment of kinesics other than those rigorously pre-programmed, of random intonation, and adaptive situational cueing. The kinesics would be dictated by the context of the situation: there would be gestures appropriate to just recitation that would mark it as recitation. The structuring of meter or thought rhyme would remove the randomness from intonation, and so would (further) mark it as no longer random. And the situation would be a given, a fixed place into which the poet stands to utter, rather than adaptive to an ongoing series of cueings. The respondents would not be responding but listening, and their stillness would create a void, a sort of zero state, of cueing around the reciting poet. It would create the expectation of a special vocabulary and a special subject matter, because poetry does have a special vocabulary, and, in the Zuni performances studied by Dennis Tedlock, a special expectation of the kind of story and the structure of the story.[10]

We cannot even be sure that Homer did recite, though his case is complicated by the clearly recoverable features of marking for recitation in the "oral" poems. Yet they have written features too, the so-called Pisistratid redaction. And adjudicating, with an inevitable arbitrariness, between the oral and the written elements would still not result—except by what amounts to the fiat of a Parry—in reducing all the components to one or the other. The presence of both oral and written elements in Homer makes his case more complicated, and just for that reason less fully recoverable, than the cases (themselves distinct) of poets cued firmly into recitation with musical accompaniments—Sappho, Pindar, Alcman. But poetry inescapably begins by emphasizing the oral component: it must be recited aloud, even by a "silent" reader. That is its precondition. Yet in Dante's context this silence itself becomes a constituent element in the inexpressibility trope of medieval poetics. Poetry builds into itself a par-ticipatory sense of what it cannot express, and this paradoxically contrib-utes, as an assumption, to its "ineffability." As John Scotus Erigena says, "The good Cause of everything . . . can be expressed with many or with few words, and also together with silence."[11]

By Dante's time the performance of secular poetry accompanied by music had withdrawn to the sort of optional formal occasion in which the musician Casella participated. And in the religious tradition, hymnody was still vigorous; some of these hymns are quoted within the *Divina Commedia*. Still, when Dante spoke of poetry as a *fictio rhetorica musica composita*, "a rhetorical fiction composed with music," the term *music* had only recently become metaphoric, as it is here, where it refers to the sound of the verse and not to a musical accompaniment. The troubadors were finished. The metrical matters that concerned Dante can be seen to interact with his constructive vision, and the sound structures of his invented form reverberate with expressions and analogues of his intellectual structures, as these are coded through his "pragmatic" social anthropological conditions, in his own time and place, and across time to the fundament of Indo-European practice. This condition is of course true for poetry generally, but markedly so for poets who set a redefinition of the love relation at the center of their work—the troubadors, Cavalcanti, and, late in the many English transmutations of such conventions, John Donne, who moves them into the light of the striking condition of an attention to the particularities of a nearly conversational voice.

The *dolce stil nuovo,* prepared by and hedged for defense in the *De Vulgari Eloquentia,* perpetuates the troubador's choice of vernacular utterance but divorces it from the necessarily accompanying music. At the beginning of the *Purgatorio,* music faces two ways, as is appropriate for this intermediate and purgative realm. On the one hand, it frames and gathers up the unanimity of the souls crossing under the guidance of an angel to this shore of the other realm—"They were all singing together in one voice," "Cantavan tutti insiemi ad una voce," and what they sang was a psalm (114) that Dante in his prose discussions has already taken as the type of his allegorical method, "In exitu Israel de Aegypto." They are not singing it in the vernacular but in the Latin, which for the Roman church is still the language of the scripture, here quoted.

This is one way that music faces here, the voice-collecting, wordless ground for holy words communally sung. But we soon hear of another music. The first soul that greets Dante on this shore and tries vainly to embrace him is the musician Casella, waiting here because he was indolent in life. He corrects this fault by enjoining alacrity and by "leaving off singing" ("lasciar lo canto," 131).

The initial discussion quotes the group on the new bank as plural, but when Casella breaks off he undertakes on his own an individual exchange with Dante:

> Ed egli a me: "Nessun me'è fatto oltraggio,
> se quei, che leva e quando e cui gli piace,
> più volte m'ha negato esto passaggio:
> Chè di giusto voler lo suo si face.
> Veramente da tre mesi egli ha tolto
> chi ha voluto entrar con tutta pace.
> Ond'io che era ora alla marina volto,
> dove l'acqua di Tevere s'insala,
> benignamente fui da lui ricolto.

A quella foce ha egli or dritta l'ala;
però che sempre quivi si raccoglie
quale verso d'Acheronte non si cala."
Ed io: "Se nuova legge non ti toglie
memoria o uso al'amoroso canto,
che mi solea quetar tutte mie voglie,
di ciò ti piaccia consolare alquanto
l'anima mia, che, con la sua persona
venendo qui, è affannata tanto." (2.94–111)

And he to me, "No wrong is done to me,
if he who lifts it when and for whom he pleases,
has denied me this crossing many times.
for of a just will is his own will made.
Truly for three months he has taken up
whoever wished to enter with all peace,
Whence I who now was turned to the shore
where the water of the Tiber takes its salt,
benignly was gathered in by him.
To that mouth has he now set his wing,
because always there are gathered here
those who do not sink down to Acheron."
And I "If a new law does not take away
memory or use of the song of love
that once was wont to still all my desires,
with that may it please you to console a while
my soul, which, in its own person
coming here, is so much out of breath."
(Translated by Allen Mandelbaum)

The prelude to Casella's solo singing of Dante's earlier song is itself hedged with a theological caveat and surrounded by this discussion, in which the narrative, the confrontation, and the theological definitions interweave, as characteristically in the whole of the *Commedia*, with an ease that takes the preconception of its own role, the personal expression of the post-troubador lyricist melded with the overarching system of the versifying pilgrim-encyclopedist. All of these gestures can be extrapolated into a multiplex allegorical reading of Dante's relation to music, and by association to the poetry that for him it accompanies. Dante's soul is "tired," or literally "out of breath," "affannata," and so he is physically unready to sing himself, for all the singing he has listened to. But there is a charitable substitute for singing himself. Indeed, Casella, notably set one of his own notable poems, "Amor che nella mente mi ragiona," "Love that is discoursing in my mind," a line that undergoes intellectual exposition in the *Convivio* (3.1). He is said to sing it for Dante on this occasion, a song that,

like the encounter itself, has the double face of a rememorating delay and
of a love-charged quickening of personal collaboration. Casella himself,
indeed, breaks off the group's "negligenza" in listening so long, whereas
the recounting Dante has already said he sang so sweetly that he can still
hear the sweetness ("Cominciò elli allor sì dolcemente / Che la dolcezza
ancor dentro mi suona," 114–15). Instead of simply enlisting music,
Dante memorializes music, provided with the occasion for doing so in the
precondition of the "long poem," which since the time of Homer has not
been set to music, though in Dante's own time shorter poems, like the
very one he quotes here, were so set. The effect of the *De Musica* of Saint
Augustine, the organization of perceptions through number, has been
complicated by itself being subjected to the sort of philosophical ratiocination in which Augustine participated. This poem's ratiocination, in turn,
in its new style, is presented in the simple integers of a colloquial language,
what I have elsewhere called "the refined style."[12] And this new style has
the same sweetness that Dante here attributes to music, a "dolcezza." It is
the *dolce stil nuovo*.

Whitman originates the platform of his own preconditions, a new
framing, a new footing, and a new set of ritual constraints, based on a
redefinition of the system-contact between the speaking poet and his
readers:

1.

I celebrate myself, and sing myself,
And what I assume you shall assume,
For every atom belonging to me as good belongs to you.

I loafe and invite my soul,
I lean and loafe at my ease observing a spear of summer grass.
My tongue, every atom of my blood, form'd from this soil, this air,
Born here to parents born here from parents the same, and their parents
    the same,
I, now thirty-seven years old in perfect health begin,
Hoping to cease not till death.

Creeds and schools in abeyance,
Retiring back a while sufficed at what they are, but never forgotten,
I harbor for good or bad, I permit to speak at every hazard,
Nature without check with original energy.

Here, in this opening of "Song of Myself," Whitman goes the ideological
fusions of Wordsworth one better, so much so that the invocational definitions of Dante, or even of Milton, are completely lost. And yet Whitman's
abstractions declare him to be on a terrain he will just evoke like a Fourth

of July orator or the writer of newspaper features which he was before he
broke into this poetry. The equivocations about uniqueness and identity,
which are implicit in the arrogation of total agreement between himself
and the reader, appear in the changes this passage went through, especially
in its title. Untitled in 1855, it assumed in 1856 the title "Poem of Walt
Whitman, an American." From 1860 to 1881 it was called "Walt Whitman," finally changing then to "Song of Myself."

This returns the Wordsworthian self to the bardic representational
function, and without declaring or formalizing into Blake's "Hear the
voice of the Bard." At the same time it is radically different from the
precondition of the Hebrew prophet, the gist of whose national identity it
tries to borrow by fiat while declaring that "creeds" are "in abeyance"—an
impossible statement for a biblical prophet, and indeed even for a Blake
who wishes to use that tremendous authority while redefining it. Whitman posits an authority derived from an audience that has been proleptically transformed by the poems written to celebrate and create it, "democratic vistas" of identification that resemble Blake's quotation from the
book of Numbers (11.20): "Would to God that all the Lord's people were
prophets" (*Milton*, "Preface"). In Blake's prophetic future the realization
of a deeply recreated convergence and personal identity would arguably
result in an abounding access to such poetic possibilities on the part of
every revivified superman. In Whitman's, the invigorated citizenry would
converge upon the capacity to center the poems of Whitman as their
utterance. Once he is under way with "Leaves of Grass," Whitman gives
that book the ongoing definition of a sort of open canon, into which he
can insert future poems and constant rearrangements and redefinitions.
He absolutizes, in effect, what he could not have known was the expanding framework of *The Prelude;* and by writing no other poems than are to
be included in it, he gives it a de facto coherence that is coterminous with
his life, which then becomes emblematic as the guarantee and source of the
poetic utterances.

As he says in "Inscriptions," as the last line of his poem "To a Historian," "I project the history of the future."[13] He links Democracy with
Religion, capitalizing both: "As there can be, in my opinion, no sane and
complete Personality—nor any grand and electric Nationality, without the
stock element of Religion imbuing all the other elements (like heat in
chemistry, invisible itself, but the life of all visible life,) so there can be no
Poetry worthy the name without that element behind all."[14] The floating
theoretical basis for his identification with his audience also floats in the
poems:

> See, projected through time,
> For me an audience interminable.

> With firm and regular step they went, they never stop,
> Successions of men, Americanos, a hundred millions,
> One generation playing its part and passing on,
> Another generation playing its part and passing on in its turn,
> With faces turn'd sideways or backward towards me to listen,
> With eyes retrospective towards me. . . .
>
> O such themes—equalities! O divine average!
> Warblings under the sun, usher'd as now, or at noon, or setting,
> Strains musical flowing through ages, now reaching hither,
> I take to your reckless and composite chords, add to them, and cheerfully
>   pass them forward.[15]

In such a situation Whitman can touch base on ineffability without theorizing it ("The words of my book nothing, the drift of it everything," "Shut Not Your Doors," 13). And he can speak not of singing but of his assimilation of singing: "I hear America singing, the varied carols I hear" (12), pulling the varied carols together by fiat in the amplitude of his voice.

Silence is a marker for the poem, whether for a reader or recoverably in the recitation of a troubador, a rhapsode, or a Zuni storyteller. The larger silence of beginning and ending sets it off.

The Indo-European pattern, and the conjectural tribal base for the priest-poet-spokesman, has still retained many of its initial features while undergoing marked differentiation in the traditions that have come down to us. The member of the Rigveda priestly family works out a hymn, addresses it to a specific god, and fixes it into its chosen staple pattern rhythm and even its precise wording, so that it can be memorized and repeated verbatim on other similar ritual occasions. Pindar and Bacchylides compose victory celebrations that are aimed at a specific Olympic victory and are addressed to the sponsor of the actual athletic victor (who is sometimes a contestant himself). They refer to the gods tangentially, and at the same time integrally. And the poems, recited once, are then part of the literary corpus. The skalds, from the account of the life of Egil Skallagrimsson (to take that example), are impelled to shape the poem as a focusing and intervention at a moment of stress in their own power or family interactions.[16] The addressee is placated or exalted by being celebrated, and the result is a concrete change in the relations of the skald, who draws concurrently on the magic properties of the coded utterance and on the magic that (separately, as it were) inheres in the mechanism of coding, the runes. The kennings are a constant reminder of this process; their farfetched riddle-like coding differentiates them from the normal, simple formulas of heroic verse. The large number of possibilities for stable properties—such as for the sea—emphasizes the improvisatory power, and also the memory (but not the verbal fertility) of the poet. The most extravagant kennings seem to refer to the gods, and to poetry, and *a fortiori* to Odin as a source for poetry.[17] In centralizing such repetitions of reference, they close the circle by both touching on the poem's preconditioning source, as Homer does when he invokes the Muse, and at the same time using the kennings of the god-given heightened language of verse, as Homer does not claim to do.

With all the differences among these traditions, the poet in them begins with a preconception of how the sound and sense will harness their recursions—a conception that is pragmatically linked to a form of performance and so larger than just the verbal conventions he will enlist when he moves from silence into utterance.

The Syllabic Module

In metered verse the design of the lines as a recursive pattern dominates the instances of the statements, which flow along by the process
of natural language. In free verse this balance is inverted: the process
of instance dominates, and the recursive pattern of design, present in most
cases from the mere fact that verse orders its words into lines, takes on a
random character, even when the relation between design and instance
grows very complex, as it does for Pound. (See my *Prisms: Studies in
Modern Literature* [Bloomington: University of Indiana, 1967], 93–98.)

But the sense of contemporary verse is often organized on variable
axes, and its sound should be developing further in a corresponding direction. Theoretically, we should be producing metrical modes, analogous to
the structure of serial music, in which the randomness of instances in free
verse is subordinated to audible patterns without returning to the simple
recursions of meter. For all the structural openness and thematic complexity of *The Cantos,* and *Paterson,* the meters in those poems retain the
random character of free verse. The rhythm of the *Maximus Poems,* for all
its crispness and pitch, remains just an especially supple free verse. The
breath-unit serves as a module only by a kind of metaphor; the raw livening of the discrete utterance is simply declared to have a special character.
Syllabic verse, too, is itself just a form of metered verse based on syllable-
count.

Now the randomness of verse instance can be subordinated to recursive patterns without being made to conform to a simple linear meter. The

internal rhymes and crossing assonances of skaldic verse constitute such a
recursion. And Pound's printing of Cavalcanti shows that even the design
of meter can be reordered into another, translinear metrical recursion,
where syllabic isochronicity and caesura are given a determinant role:

> Donna mi priegha
> > perch'i voglio dire
> D'un accidente
> > che sovente é fero
> Ed é sé altero
> > ch'é chiamato amore
> Sicche chi'l negha
> > possal il ver sentire
> Ond a'l presente
> > chonoscente
> > chero
> Perch i no spero
> > ch om di basso chore
> > > *(Literary Essays,* London, 1954, p. 163)*

The strophic series in the odes of Pindar are based on such translinear
recursions, tightly formalized ones. The fixed strophes, corresponding
from one to another line by line, have their sequences fully laid down after
the first group of strophe-antistrophe-epode has been given. The alternatives are closed as soon as the pattern has been presented. Thus the odes
offer a "vertical" pattern, to adapt a musical term, for counterpoint against
the "horizontal" bars of the individual line.

Rhyme itself, by no means a usual feature of verse, developed almost
contemporaneously in the Western tradition with musical polyphony. It is
added, as a vertical element, to counterpoint against the horizontal regularities of meter, which are a usual, and arguably a necessary,[1] feature of
verse. But rhyme, as a vertical element, occurs only at a set point, and the
rest of the line up to the rhyme remains vertically random though horizontally determined.

In the principle of the syllabic module, as exemplified in the poems
that follow, every syllable is enlisted both horizontally and vertically. In
Midway, for example, every line has a syllable-count, one of seven horizontal possibilities. But in addition every line stands as a function of the
module "3"; and so every line has a vertical relation to the other lines,
through permutation rather than through identity. Instead of moving on
from identical line to identical line, and instead of flowing ahead pro-
cessively as in free verse, the poem has its syllable-clusters "rhyme" with
each other vertically.[2] Here is the beginning of that poem:

MIDWAY

No one
Is like
Me, I
Am like
Everyone.

Stolid and still at ease,
Bewildered as you please.

Birds on the thickets of
Aerials
Under water towers.
Dioxyde skies.
Ailanthus trees.
Adhesive-taped
Radios.

Compacted eyes
And ears, flesh and quick blood
Learn the thousand syllables.

Adhesive taped onto
A mirror's
Crack, smudges black, the glass
Smudges cloudy.

Softly, softly
They return, a
Common experience.

The breathing of
Osiers comes clean

Horizons sharpening
Illusion-charm.

Lifetime growing pains come
For someone ill at ease.

My toes
Have sung
And the
Strings of
My arms,
My whims.

Every syllable is part of such a cluster, and the ear collocates all the syllables vertically as well as accumulating them on the horizontal line. In such a system even a run of two or three identical lines has the functions of "rhyming" its modules, as well as repeating its meter.

The line unit is bound both horizontally by syllable-count in the line and vertically by recursive series from line to line. At the same time, the line, within its limited number of syllabic alternatives, remains free, as free verse is free, to choose, at every point, the particular alternative for the particular line. This practice, of course, is only analogous to musical counterpoint because several notes can be sounded at one time, but normally only a single syllable.

In the syllabic module the lines are all syllabic lines. But in addition they are subjected vertically to a series of recursive rules that totally determine their function in a larger pattern, one that retains the processive freedom of free verse because the alternatives are never closed. In *Midway*, for example, every syllabic line is a variant of the base module, 3-syllables. The recursive delineation becomes strictest at the outer boundaries (2– 12), whose stanza-pattern is most often determined as soon as one two-syllable line has occurred. But the recurrence of "2:6 plus 12" stanzas is itself random. In *Due Dates* the progressions among the three variations of syllabic module are determined by rule, but alternatives still exist: a four-syllable line; it may not be followed by an eight-syllable line, nor may it follow one.[3] Here is a run that may illustrate the rhythmic progression of *Due Dates:*

> If the wrong bell has rung,
> Ingorge strong medicine.
>
> Parties pour out
> Scotch taken neat, ice cubes,
> Little boulders
> In a wash-flashing sea
> Of stringent stuff,
> Me and my friends
> Gone in on the selves won
> For sweet losing.
> Crack those discrepancies.
>
> Feeling one's own blind way
> Of codified yesterdays, builds
> The black switchboard into
> Roman triumph.
>
> The hunching houses devoured
> Us pale and oversize,

Heroism melts
In fantasy,
Hope's fair remonstrances
Jockeying for
What I whistle down.

Jollied and apprized
Before a son be born,
I take salt air.
Purple transparencies
Of jellyfish
Go sticky in my hands.

In *One-Way Mystery* the vertical pattern is a total one: every stanza must contain no fewer than twenty-four syllables, and no more than forty-eight; every stanza must also be divisible by eight.[4] So every line moves further toward closing out possible alternatives. But the stanza-progression remains open to alternatives, and hence it does not lose the aleatory character of free verse, for all its elaboration. The lines are open too: a line of three syllables must be followed by one of five syllables, but a five-syllable line may be followed by one of three, five, or seven, as a nine-syllable line may. Pairs are determined, but at every point in a stanza there are alternatives of the succeeding pair.

The effect may be heard not only as recursive but as somewhat totalizing. Here is the beginning of *One-Way-Mystery:*

Mystery
Charging a mirror
One way ungainsayable
Through time, it does not give back a view.

The lover
Has not bungled when
A white flank shines suspension.
She in stalled thought prevents herself
From losing
Heart at one failure.

The packing
Of teeth has an end.
The waving
Of trees rustles on.
Love blunts a warning,
Hoping it will disappear.
Damp at her hair's roots,
The fidgeting girl will wait.

A voice deep as a grave mouth
Comes back for more. Love maintains itself
Through vicissitude, aging,
And spreading depression's fell assault.

The pilot
Takes his assignment
On trust for
A number of lives.
That, in its precarious
Air-sealed series, will include his own.

Not every echo in verse is audible simply because it is patterned, and one can argue that the fan-out rhymes of Dylan Thomas's "Author's Pro-logue," for example, are too distant to be audible, especially since they consist of a single recursion not begun to be picked up until line 52 of that poem, with a spread between its outer rhymes of 104 lines. This is too far to be heard, the more when it occurs only once.

But syllables, issuing as the irreducibly significant phonological ele-ments of the verse's sound, coming in a sequence one after another by recursive rule, must be heard as entering the patterns of their ordering. In music a "logarithmic" progression will be heard, we can argue from Boulez' implications, though the musician cannot control that progression without a computer: the listener picks up a drift where the player would lose one himself. (Boulez, *Penser la Musique aujourd'hui* [Mainz, 1963], 93–113.)

Poems written in syllabic module should be heard, then, not just in the line, which sounds like free verse until horizontally similar lines have established themselves. The syllables should also be heard to undergo a vertical livening. This can happen only when variation occurs. The prin-ciple of the module must apply to varied lines to be felt as more than just a simple linear meter. So in haiku, a sort of molecular syllabic–module poem, the second line is heard as "5" syllables plus the largest count possible less than half of "5" rather than simply "7," only when the third line recurs as identical with the first. The power of the stanzas used by Alcaeus and Sappho, and then by Horace and Catullus, derives from the total syllable count of the stanza as well as from the strict variation of the lines. The syllable count amplifies endstopping and enjambment because the line, at the sensitive point of its ending, is a place-marker in the module variation of a syllable sum as well as the boundary of a metric unit.

My poem "The Widow's Future" (*The Charges*, p. 58) draws the rules to a nearly maximal strictness, being written in four-line stanzas rhymed a-b-a-b with just four syllables to each line. But it remains monodic, on a simple linear plan:

It slides and flows
Sloppily right
Through these eyes,
The grey of the night.

Until it turns
Fathomless black.
My light is on.
I can't turn back.

A further feature of these syllabic-module poems consists of their being "shadowed" by the standard meter of English, iambic pentameter. One identifies meter by expectation, and also by cultural context. One has to have read two lines at least before he can confidently expect that the poem before him is in the given meter, say, iambic pentameter. An English reader, before he opens a book, knows from his cultural context that he stands a fair chance of encountering some iambic pentameter, just as a Roman one had a fair chance of encountering dactyllic hexameter. English "poem" may be said to imply "strong possibility of iambic pentameter," just as iambic pentameter may be said to imply not just "five foot-line with the beat predominantly on the second syllable," but also "ten-syllable line." This being the case, any ten-syllable English line, whatever its pattern of accent, will suggest "blank verse." And any five-syllable line will suggest "half-line of blank verse," as (even more) any six-syllable French line will suggest "half an alexandrine." In English twenty syllables will suggest "two blank verse lines." Now, the module of *Midway* is shadowed by the absence of blank verse. No line of that poem, and not most combinations of three lines or fewer, can fall into the pattern of ten syllables as a count. Thus the poem constantly has a shadow of blank verse running across the lines.

In *One-Way Mystery,* however, the shadow is not blank verse but the module itself, 8. This is a double module; it governs each couplet (which must be either divisible by eight or, if not, succeeded by one that is also not), and it governs each stanza (which must be divisible by eight). Yet eight-syllable lines are excluded from the poem, as are 4-syllable lines—the four modular possibilities stand as bounding those two numbers (3,5,7,9).

The syllabic module, then, offers a structuring both more inclusive than conventional linear meter and more free, since a given line is often chosen from a set of alternatives rather than dictated by the meter. But the alternatives, being always a definable set, avoid at every point the randomness of free verse.

Given the features I have just described, the principle of the syllabic module is capable of a wide range of variation, even within a fairly simple set of prescribed rules. And it will—audibly, I am convinced—accommodate quite an elaborate set of rules, as in *One-Way Mystery*.

A form of the syllabic module is used in my long poem *Modes*, which has ninety-three sections. *Modes* is written on a simple set of rules. The syllabic module is three syllables. Lines are permitted only of twice the module or three times the module: of six syllables or of nine syllables. Progression from one line to another, as in *Due Dates*, is only permitted with a difference of one module (three syllables) between the two lines. (That is, the progressions 9-3 and 3-9 are not permitted.) The ruminative expansions return every single one of their syllables to the module while remaining free as to progression:

> It all *fior*
> *del verde*
>
> Brown needles
> under the evergreens
>
> A snow-shadowed branch casts a shadow
> a stream under thin ice
> catches light
>
> Skate as over crystal
> though dark ice
>
> Remember grimed buildings
> sandblasted
> to a soft version of
> their original white
>
> Slab on slab.

Of course, a great deal of variation is possible within these syllabic limits: of word length, pitch, intonation pattern, stress, enjambment, and so on. And for an individual section, further limits may be added to the simple rule, as triadic progression of sixes and threes:

> Piero
>   Della Francesca's squares
>   Angels and open stalls
>
> Klee's lined clowns
>   More human than human
>   Who have dreamt
>
> Are dreaming
>   Are drilling, squaring off
>   A blue haze

A further rule of rhyme regularizes it further, as in the section of six-syllable *terza rima:*

> Presses to be combined
>
> While the toll fills the air.
> Lost faces learn aplomb.
> The pitch is in the fire.
>
> Wanderers coming home
> To roost, sigh and resist
> A further martyrdom,

Still tighter is a version of three-syllable *terza rima:*

> If I learn
> when the slow
> griefs clear out
> time will turn
> inside out
> the eddy
> of their tow
> graces hard
> to come by
> will have come
> to hand, guard
> down, sleight-palls
> of peach bloom
> show benign,
> waterfalls
> vaporize,

In another direction is a section of nine-syllable lines, prevailingly with "Anglo-Saxon" alliteration across the caesura:

> When thriving fails and fathers are through
> In the gathering stress of stored response
> The child who fathoms gleamings of choice
> Out of wide hoardings and gutterings
> Knows in his bones what harm is to come
> When leavings vanish and lore is vain.

Closer to the fuller tonic freedom of *Modes* is a section simply of nine-syllable lines:

> Caught in the steamy purlieus of their
>   painful pasts, the men will not resist
>   vegetating and a deep motion

in the soul evades intelligence
dooming them to groaning depths of play.

The nine-syllable line, of course, is almost a blank-verse line. As such it "shadows" the blank-verse line, and it suggests the ruminative progression, which itself is the main thrust of *Modes*. Sections with special extra rules are the exception; generally the sections flow along in indeterminately bounded units of three, six, and nine syllables, as:

Looking into the lacks
you were born to grow out of, win from,
by incorporating
a readiness of transformation
at a date late for overbuilding
windowless schools glass homes,
hexagonal buildings,
gridded streets,

What you don't want it to
be, it already is,
hole streaming its dark flecks

Wing of stone spume of the winter sea

TM, meditations,
of waters of valleys, what have you,
sourceless and objectless.

The past as a window on the past.

The whole long poem "Midway" will illustrate the method of the syllabic module as it works through an extended unit:

MIDWAY

No one
Is like
Me, I
Am like
Everyone.

Stolid and still at ease,
Bewildered as you please.

Birds on the thickets of
Aerials
Under water towers.
Dioxyde skies.

Ailanthus trees.
Adhesive-taped
Radios.

Compacted eyes
And ears, flesh and quick blood
Learn the thousand syllables.

Adhesive taped onto
A mirror's
Crack, smudges black, the glass
Smudges cloudy.

Softly, softly
They return, a
Common experience.

The breathing of
Osiers comes clean.

Horizons sharpening
Illusion-charm.

Lifetime growing pains come
For someone ill at ease.

My toes
Have sung
And the
Strings of
My arms.
My whims,
And the wall will not remand the old distances,
And the alley arrives, the empty hall reminds
Where we have learned the trance.
Over the longest separation comes the call
That liberates and blinds.

Trapping the immovable
A sleight of hand
Not worth a slice
Of a light hour.

The divine
Will will have computed
Me at my reckoning.

Windfalls just dissipate.

What I would have done is
Idle thought.

Going away find me
Close. The roar
Of suspending engines
Will not have devoured the pure
Silences.

Memorial Day, asphalt
Would melt before the open
Space between the stone Grange
And the Bandstand.
On the screened piazza
The old rocked, hair
Wholly taking light,
While I played
On mica flakes
In a burning air, ran
By the rapid, iron-
Tint, clear stream.

The inner ground
Is falling away.
The surrounding
Vapidity appals
And nullifies.

Musk through gnarled elms
On a cold midnight hill,
We wrapped up in a kiss.

The whimperings
I may have dreamt I heard.
Sunflower sun.

Rigidity, stay with
Me, I would be rid of it.

My life is
White on white, I
Ease into remonstration
Easily.

The suffering
Black man deprives
Both of us when I say
What turns away
From his plain
Difficulties for these
Syllables.

Windows in desperation
Broken, the child
In the shadows glums his soul
Brothers and slows.

The mallard duck's copper-
Green neck band shines
Over the ruffling waters
Under the russet leaves.

To stroke the
Down on a leaf.

Visible instances,
Audible confirmations.

The whining pain midway
Of sundering a love
Facing whatever music
Will combine.

Rosin for a violin,
A bow of white gut string.

Happy the lappings of
A future of water.
Dire the combustion of
A coming fire.

The green
Budding
Haze is
Defining
Abundance.

Tear the poor calendar
Of holy days.

Fish are thrumming their way
Through the weighty waters.

The acreage of sadness
Is bombed out, desolation.

The husked wedge
Of a seed
Is blown in this
Chaff-blowing,
Frail, hair-starred, white
Milkweed-billowing, dust-
Blowing air.

You abide at the center
Of my world whom I want
To live at the bright edges
Holding time.

The interchange
Of persons broadens out
Though they may narrow down
The remaining spaces.

Raspberries
Cling to the bush, the time
Of ripening is
Another day.

To start divining
Where I could be becoming
Twofold, threefold,
Fourfold and one
Polished, free,
Love-energic,
Perceptive, slack
In tension lithe.

I wish I knew.

Les moments musicaux, place
Conjoining time.

Les monuments
Musicaux.

A season
In the fields.

I have been there,
Have heard, then
The trickle
Of water
In a brook,
Exquisite,
As someone French
Enamoured of Japan
Imprints a print
On his desire.

Sun-disk illuminated
Void over parting branch, fruit
And green lawn.

Build and
Rebuild
The shining
Silences
And behold.

Of a cloud the blowing,
Of silk the sheer,
And the shoring of waters
In a daze.

Search the strong fog.

Swooning for
The blue rhythms of windows,
The eden of a shore,
Where he has
Been he knows.

The bean vine grows
Leaf on waxy leaf, is
Curling around the pole.

And will be
Yellow, yellow, yellow.

Red, red
Orange, oranging
All I might arrange
In and through and by
Enrapturement.
Glass, cigarette smoke, Venetian
Blinds, a dense hour.

The full gaps of the loved
Dead are shining.
The gaps of my love ahead
Shine less, I
Will be shiny, my sorrow
Can overcome anything
But where I am
And changing.

Darkness proves
Such new light.

To favor and be free
A little while.

The time
Ripples
Around
The life
I can survey.

And the stone resolves into its rugged facing,
And this love can reside immobile and absolved
Of sharpening a sting.
He who was not in the least for fear to be known
Is pacified to tug.

What I have written down is
What I have taken down, midway.

Holding on to
The soon-to-be
Deathly sun's
Own perihelion

Flinging my moth-
Velleities into
The city's lit glass shield.

A stone Byzantine angel
Glistening on the round
Of an arch, wings.

Hilarity
Sets the tone.

One sapphire concentering
Lights more brilliantly than
A million
Inter-reflecting gems.

The soft mind
And the soft skin join, whose
Raptures now and to come
Leave him stunned, the man I
Thought to be.

Youth in its course
Breaks the charm
And what remains
Will set the style
For what follows.
Decrepitude,
Vigor, radiances,
Fulfillment.

The window
Offers another place
For sheering
Sight down to
What it can clearly hold.

White-fuzzy
Green thorn leaves
Grace my pots.

This mindwarp
Tells its own grain,
To flick and fleck
Ends of desires.

A pool not limpid enough
Of spreading words
Wherein I declare to be
Gazing to see you and really
See me wholly hoping
Not to fall in and die
To the appeals
Of responding
Time upon time.

A machine draws
The foamy
Odorous
White liquor off
The cow's dugs.

The whinings of a bell,
Obliterations of
A forest
Here in an absolute
Calm, aspirations
Do not take hold. They float
Loose of redeeming time.

Hedging my purposes
I take little less away.

The still
Room of
Your home
Holds the hour
In its press.

And they are straining gaily where the least
    have come.

For nothing else to see, and do not run away.
Touched with fire and calm
They give their ears the power to take a refrain
And let it ring its best.

His head went down
Into the files of others
And did not come up till
He was so tired
He could not care.

Creamy love,
A Boucher cloud
Pearl pink and whitish and
Puffing the gold
Wind for all it is worth.

To be moving
Toward you
Remains profound.

The terrible
Wisdom of afterthought.

Lovely is this ringing
In my ears.

Midway, tawdry
Circus's red and gold
Power to excite, excites
A dawdling child,
Gold and red silk
Uniforms flick lively.

The pocket mirror is
Smudged from children's candy,
The handkerchief crumpled,
The baby's face
Is pink with cotton candy.
Everyone is tired. The car
Smells. Interlude.

The rain-swept highway shines,
The factories are shut.
Someone on the back seat,
Sleeps. Relax.
At the wheel.

It was not the inkling,
Not the remonstrations.

White stones
Blue sea
Gold sky
Banish all
That presses.

Midway, murk
Of fall, musk.

Kyrie eleison
Kyrie.

And one year
Melts into another.

The leavings
Are brought into a bright
Aspiring.

The wedding cake of air.

Where is room for
Your darksome eyes?

Dithering and bothering,
Weathering, withering

Behindhand
Midway with
Charity
Meaning poor, and should be
Bountiful
Body is
Binding on soul,
One earth-grey

Light on, one
Darkness, one
Hollow of necessity
Throws it back
Upon one.
I am here.
Time is up.
Here I am.
Up is down
In the Greek's reckoning
Who must have seen
More seas than rivers, have been
"Behind," meaning
"Ahead in time,"
From the time of heroes on.

Snapshot cuts
The moment
A movie does
So many frames
Per second.
Frames lost and found.

A needle
Column distancing the
Flat glass "behind" my head.

A beveled
Column, hieroglyphic-
Engraved, set
In a square
Comes to its point
Above me.
In the glass of the shops
Surrounding, I am offered
Necklaces
For my love,
Bracelets,
Wrist watches,
Gold rings, round things,
Listen, listening, to lose
Sight and tap a white cane
Would be no worse
Than to find
Yourself not
Wanting somehow.

The Sodom of muffled ties
Is making angels weep.
The Rome of
Repletion
Will not hold you
To numb the name
Of its Jerusalem.

Ghostlied, grim
The split of mother and
Father heals
In the shadow
Of my grasp.

Father, Son
Holy Ghost.

Wrenched as I darkly craved
From a craving
For a fuller light.

Dong, ding dong.

And here is one the wind
Of the prairie had driven
To balance
Loneliness in the mien
Of an elegant guest.

I have looked through the slick
Green blades of reeds
And lain on a leaf-mould
Musty ground.

I have eaten with the confused.

Broken faith
Unwittingly

Reverted
To an earlier drudgery
And taken a craven
Comfort therefrom.

Now come back
To my deepening places I
Am taken for the very man
I have yearned not to become.

A shaken
Man, broken
And made whole
His own host.

Surrendering the sense
Of warp seconding woof.

Flitting, driven,
Up. Down. Fleeting
Encounters, and I turn out
To be staying for life
For what it is worth.

The craze touches
Everything I can touch.

To see the clear platform
Of another

Leap, to leave the grasses of
A future farm.

An increase
Stiffens and
Elaborates
My defect
Of response. Do not
Listen to the contrary.
It is folded in anyway.

Expiring
Fanfares lose
Dimension of
Jubilation.

Die the two deaths
Turn the one life
Inside out
Leave it be
One unyielding
Eye. Manumit.

The long hum
Of passing cars fails to drown
Sharp chirps of birdsong
A droopy day.

Hear the Han
Bronze bell's green bosses
Ring silences.

The lizard scurries from the baked stone.

Dew on a wilting blade
Will whiten.
Visible structures, audible
Confirmations.

Better to pat
The shaven dog
And steer clear
Of embroilment.

The neolithic
Corpse huddles
In foetal
Position.

Blithe, blithe and
At home in the fleece of light.

The scar had burred
Dried blood chips stuck in her hair,
And soon is clean.

The death hovers
An elsewhere.

The legs strained
From pelvis down
Up to torso
For dancing
Taut in their own
Affirmation—
Denial of others,
Dance all the same,
Dance and are true
Beyond those falsities,
Powdery skirts
Of lace, footlights,
Bows and entrechats.
We watch. We are
Watching in them,
Open lips moist.

The lost places
Are what they
Have been for a green while
And the found times are spread.

Filling to
The brim a
Glass of water
For a thirsty
Man in dust.

True enough
The map of hell
Lays out hate.

And Purgatory soon
Does its recompenses.

Slumbering by embers,
Who would deny his peace?

The dead masks
Glare on a wall
Cleared for them, the
Pullutations
I subserve make for clean
Breaks, illusions.

The child I was
To be, is
What and when, how and why,
Single way.

I will be
Braving the tough
Dreams of the open eyes,
Whirring ears,
Silences,
The tender
Dreams of eyes closed
Slumbering.

The body's
Core opens.
The spirit of someone
Else enters
The two shudder
Together.

Torsions of bliss
Down into melancholic
Labyrinths.

Passion apparently
Spent is turned
Into more nourishment
With no shadow
Of turning.

The Modified Modernism of
Anna Akhmatova

A nna Akhmatova (1889–1966), as few poets have done, both lived and reflected in her poetry a quintessentially exemplary Russian woman's life.[1] This situation, as much as her modernist associations, provides a ground for her poetry, which is autobiographical in ways that popular poetry often is. Deeply intuitive in its enlistment of image and sequence, it remains unusually conservative, and in its last expressions uncertain, for the work of so important a poet.

In her life Akhmatova ran a course from the lively *dyevushka,* the seductively appealing and gifted girl or ingénue, to the deeply sorrowing *babushka,* the sad-faced and bountifully kindly grandmother. As a *dyevushka* she met her first husband, Nikolai Gumilyev, when she was barely fourteen and married him at twenty. With and through him she began publishing in her teens, became one of the most celebrated poets in Russia by the time she was twenty-five, lived the artistic life at places like the "Wandering Dog" Café, and traveled festively abroad, where she befriended Modigliani and savored the excitements of nascent modernism. She lived in the thick of poetic projects and amorous intrigues, great poet and femme fatale all in one, a star.

But the shadow of suffering fell early with the execution of Gumilyev, in 1921. This haunted her even though by then they were already divorced. And as a *babushka* she was to continue suffering, through the long ban on her work, lifted only intermittently the rest of her life until her last years. In her personal life the sufferings were equally protracted: her only son served two heavy sentences in a prison camp. To the oppressions of the war—the bombings of Leningrad, exile in Tashkent—were added the torturing uncertainties of a helpless mother. Later, after her son's second long sentence was finally over, he showed her the troubled evasiveness that is typical of modern sons. Moreover, through the quarter century during which she became a *babushka,* she lived in the atmosphere described by Nadezhda Mandelshtam, the terror that brought Mandelshtam and others to sudden arrest and horrible death. For the celebrated national figure and generous literary sponsor she became in her last years, the sufferings remained a resonant and validating undertone.

In stanzas more resoundingly classic than anything of her American contemporaries Sara Teasdale and Edna St. Vincent Millay, the *dyevushka* brought to nearly proverbial expression the many ins and outs of her love life. Later, in popular poems, the *babushka* celebrated her patriotism, and the devastations of war. She expanded on her own personal devastations in three long poems: *Requiem,* which lists a stark, even crude, series of sorrowful blows; *The Way of All the Earth,* which recounts sorrows in the persona of a legendary *babushka;* and *Poem without a Hero,* which resurrects the rococo or *Art Nouveau* note of her youthful milieu to invoke a ghost and run through a panorama of sorrowful remembrances. It is impossible to read these poems without some hush before what their writer has suffered—but also, for myself, without some uneasiness before allegories too simply assumed. If these poems are indeed the partial failures I find them to be—verging on a gripped oversimplicity in the first two and a quasi-modernist gigantism in the last—then they testify to one of the most chilling effects of totalitarian rule, its ability to succeed in cramping and distorting the most determined and gifted voice.

Fortunately that voice was not quelled. The *babushka* brought it all together in several poems, the joys of the *dyevushka* as they merge and transfuse into the later sufferings, and most notably in the *Northern Elegies.* This sequence of six meditative poems, to use English comparisons, strikes a register somewhere between Tennyson and T. S. Eliot.

The poems of the legendary *dyevushka,* too, need sorting; the charm of a female Byron must be resisted; as for the later poems we must assess what is poetic and what simply evocative in the solemn piety they command. Still, the charm and the solemnity, at this poet's best, fuse fully in the high ring of the revelatory and the inevitable.

The restrained simplicity that Akhmatova distills in her poems derives from the style of Pushkin and his successors. Her steady and composed understatement keeps her vein closer to the romantic one than to the vein of those with whom she was personally associated among her contemporaries. Reading her poems by themselves, and particularly her early, limpid ones, we would never link her to her fellow "Acmeists" Gumilyev and Mandelshtam, though as Sam Driver points out in his book on Akhmatova, her economy of image and her indirectness of presentation can be derived from their program. Still, there is little in her style that fulfills the modernist aspirations of the Acmeists, other than an austere economy of expression. Gumilyev is somewhat more abstract, Mandelshtam considerably more. Still less does she match the iconoclastic stridency of Mayakovsky, the deeply structured if muted involutions of Pasternak, though in "Boris Pasternak" she does imitate his kind of image formation:

> In the lilac gloom backyards repose,—
> Platforms, timbers, leaves, clouds.
> Whistle of an engine, crunch of watermelon rind,
> In fragrant kidskin a shy hand.

> It rings, it thunders, it grinds, it beats with breakers,
> And suddenly it goes still. It means that he
> Timidly picks his way over pine needles
> So as not to frighten the light sleep of space.

All these poets abjured the Symbolists, but even Balmont and Blok exhibit a more programmatic modernism than Akhmatova. They break more definitely with the line of Pushkin, Tiutchev, and Nekrasov. Balmont and Blok invent a more saturated version of the Verlaine whom Akhmatova and Modigliani recited to each other, but whose metaphoric coherences she never strongly adopted. Some of the qualities of her style can be derived from the delicacy aimed at in *Art Nouveau,* as Alexis Rannit has shown (in an essay prefacing the second volume of her collected works). Yet, finally, she derives far more firmly from the classic simplicities achieved for Russian style by Pushkin (usually with rhymes impossible for the translator to catch directly).

Take, for instance, this poem:

A DRIVE

> The plume brushed on the carriage roof.
> I glanced into his eyes.
> The heart pined, not even knowing
> The causes of its grief.

> An evening windless and bound in sorrow
> Beneath the vault of cloudy skies,

And as though sketched with India ink
In an old album is the Bois de Boulogne.

A smell of gasoline and lilac,
A peace that holds itself on the alert—
He has touched my knees anew
With a hand that is almost untrembling.

This fills out a nuanced moment in a relationship with the sort of haunting detail found in the fiction of Tolstoi or Flaubert, Turgenev or Chekhov. The first two lines present something like a momentary equivalence. The perceptions are psychological, and the fine image of the plume brushing the carriage roof locates the speaker as at once enclosed and expansive, a mysterious association of traits her companion is discovered to share only in the climactic detail. His hand just barely trembles as it touches her knees, and we learn that enclosure, psychological rather than physical, impinges upon his expansiveness. The other details are loose. They are registered impressions, and they cannot be given much metaphoric force—a containment away from figuration that actually strengthens the poem and keeps it moving along. The second, middle stanza is only de-scriptive, skies in the first half and trees in the second. The description of the skies might have come from Tiutchev. The comparison of the Bois de Boulogne to an India ink sketch approaches the deep focusing of Rilke, and yet the sequence of novelistic details "randomizes" it away from the Rilkean crescendos. One catches the Rilkean note in the Rilkean subjects of such poems as "Lot's Wife" and "Rachel," but again the persons are more active than such poems of his, and the images correspondingly so, for all the similarity:

LOT'S WIFE

And the just man went behind God's messenger,
Huge and shining, over the black hill.
But loudly a demand spoke to the woman.
"It is not late, you may still take a look

At the red towers of your native Sodom,
At the court where you span,
At the empty windows of the high house
Where to your dear husband you bore children!"

She glanced—and, bound by a deadly pain,
Her eyes were able to look no more;
Her body turned into transparent salt,
And her rapid feet grew into the ground.

> Who will shed tears over this woman?
> Does she not seem the less because of her loss?
> Yet my heart never will forget
> One who gave her life for a single glance.

The overall experience of "A Drive" is drawn from the psychological universe already mapped out in *Eugene Onegin,* where Pushkin also offers haunting detail after haunting detail for his "novel in verses." Akhmatova's resolute understatement markedly matches Pushkin's, a poet whose work occupies the bulk of her small critical-scholarly output. Understatement is the tonic note, indeed, for the long tradition she epitomizes, a note most clearly sounded in English by the poetry of Robert Frost (a poet she happened to meet at a long ceremonial luncheon during her last years). Other analogues would be hard to find in our century; perhaps the Pavese of *Lavorare Stanca* for the *Northern Elegies.* To match those late meditative blank-verse poems, we would do better, again, to look to an earlier time for more appropriate analogues—to Wordsworth or Foscolo, Musset or Mörike. And at the same time, early poems like "A Drive," ringing rhymes and all, are in touch with a spirit of sensitive amorous reflection not wholly different from what may be found in the lyrics of Cole Porter or the blues, a similarity that would help explain her great, rapid popularity.

A psychological register comparable to that of "A Drive" may be found often in Pushkin's lyrics, as in this typically composed vignette:

> Bitterly sobbing, a jealous girl scolds a youth.
> Leaning on her shoulder, the youth suddenly dozed off.
> The girl at once stilled, cherishing his light sleep,
> And smiled at him, letting her silent tears flow.

Here, as in "A Drive," the poet centers the poem on the complex conjunction of a man and a woman who undergo small, revelatory interactions while courting. Both Pushkin and Akhmatova have other poems where they look in swift retrospection at the whole course of a love affair. In this quatrain composed of two elegiac distichs, Pushkin, like Akhmatova, has saved his key reaction till last—and both poets register a bodily impression, the outward sign of inner perturbation. "Hand" (*rukoi*) is the last word of "A Drive," and in that word we finally learn what is faintly atremble. "Letting flow" (*liya*) is Pushkin's last word, and the key summary all comes after the last cesura of the capping pentameter line, "letting her silent tears flow" (*"tikhiye slyoz'i liya"*). Of course, Pushkin's scene is suspended without a single physical detail here, whereas Akhmatova invests hers in the progression of details.

The sequence "In Tsarskoe Selo" neatly surveys through muted detail a place of reality and legend shared by both Akhmatova and Pushkin. She grew up there; he attended the lycée during the years of his formation as a poet. The third of these poems imagines his presence in the park-like purlieus of the place, concluding with the bare mention of a volume by a minor poet he imitated:

III

A dark youth wanders along the alleys
Beside the remote shores of the lake,
And for a hundred years we have cherished
The stir of his steps, barely audible.

The needles of the pines, thick and prickly,
Have covered the low stumps over—
Here lay his three-cornered hat
And a dog-eared volume of Parny.

The volume appears so flatly as not to be quite either synecdochic or metonymic, and still less metaphoric. The dog-eared Parny composes with hat, stumps, and pine needles, for a nearly *chosiste* depiction of a recently visited forest floor. The first stanza imagines a different perspective—the sweep of alleys, the sound of his steps. This echoes more the first poem of the series than it does the last stanza; it too begins with the "alleys." It goes on, though, into remembrances. The three poems comprise an evocative, slightly dissociated series of convergences: I, personal remembrances; II, the self as a statue; III, the youthful male poet of the last century.

These images are the "symbols" they are called by Russian writers on Akhmatova only by virtue of their inclusion in the poem. To be sure, they are set somewhat into contrast, even contrasts still more explicit than those that may be felt by a reader of "In Tsarskoe Selo"—contrasts between a youthful male poet and an established female one, one century and an-other, art and nature, personal life and literary life. Yet these contrasts rarely can be structured into the sort of firm opposition that an occasional phrase may present. The seriality—what some would call the metonymy—of such images is abundantly clear in "He loved three things in the world", where each image is drenched with association:

He loved three things in the world:
Singing at vespers, white peacocks,
And blurred maps of America.
He did not love it when children cried,
Did not love tea with raspberry jam
And feminine hysterics.
I was his wife.

Singing at vespers, white peacocks, and blurred maps of America form no order. Nor do crying children, raspberry jam taken with tea, and feminine hysterics, except as items in a domestic scene with the tea compensating for the other two. Nor does the second triad firmly contrast with items in the first. "But I was his wife," the last line, will cover assuredly the second triad; since the speaker is a poet, it can be made to cover the first triad also. Still the series is random because neither romantic reactions nor domesticity includes the central, complex interaction between male and female. As she says in "Nothing to me are the ode's ranks," a single detail suffices to begin the poetic evocation, followed by another detail:

> An angry screech, smell of fresh tar,
> Mysterious mould on a wall
> And the verse already sounds, fervid, tender,
> A joy for you and for me.

Symbol, though, remains an intermittent possibility, often a climactic one. The poet may have sudden recourse at the end of a poem to a symbolic set that at once lifts the poem's level of figuration and performs an act of closure upon it:

> Under the frozen roof of the empty dwelling
> I do not count the deadly days;
> I read the Apostles' messages,
> The words of the Psalmist do I read.
> But the stars are blue, frost is fluffy.
> Each meeting's more wonderful;
> And in the Bible a red maple leaf
> Is placed at the Song of Songs.

A somewhat schematized love relation, at once arduous and fulfilling, is presented through a sequence of images that are themselves fairly conventional for the Russian poet, their modernity evidenced only in the stepping up of the traditional Russian understatement. In tone, and also in situation, this poem resembles Tiutchev, except that the speaker refrains austerely from commentary. The dwelling is empty, and yet there are wonderful meetings. The speaker finds the days so deadly she cannot count them, and she both compensates and rises to a new level by reading Old and New Testament. Color comes only in line four, blue stars and fluffy frost. It matches the wonder of the meetings in this winter that contains within itself, finally, not just the emptiness of the first line but the fullness of the last. The red maple leaf used as a place marker for the Bible's one love poem evokes the seasonal cycle, and also the summer of the biblical poem, otherwise not mentioned. The single color of the leaf holds, signifies, marks a place, and serves synecdochally for the course of the seasons, preserving the peak of autumn in the dead of winter. It also serves metaphorically for the live, though strained, love for which the Song of Songs is at once a definer and a mouthpiece, superseding and presumably including the Gospels and the Psalms, as the leaf includes the year and the year echoes the urges and fruitions of the lovers. This entire metaphorical system is moderately classical; only the compacting into this simplicity is unclassical in its modified modernity.

Often Akhmatova is more ample than this in setting a scene and running through it:

> Yes, somewhere there is a simple life and a light,
> Transparent, warm, and full of joy—
> There a neighbor talks across the fence with a girl
> At evening, and only the bees hear
> The conversation tenderest of all.
>
> And we live solemnly and laboriously,
> Honoring the rites of our bitter meetings,
> While with a gust the foolhardy wind
> Tears off a speech that has barely begun.
>
> But for nothing would we exchange the splendid
> Granite city of glory and vexation,
> City of broad rivers, shining ice,
> The sunless, gloomy gardens,
> And the Muse's voice just faintly heard.

Or this:

> How can you look at the Neva?
> How can you go out on the bridge? . . .
> Not for nothing do they call me sad
> From the time you came in a dream.
> Black angels' wings are sharp;
> It will soon be the Last Judgement;
> And the crimson bonfires,
> Like roses, flower in the snow.

Here we are given a series of quite conventional romantic effusions only slightly heightened and purified by understatement and condensation. Only in the last three lines are the pyrotechnics of something like modernity set off. In conjunction with "Last Judgment" and "roses flower in the snow," we have an apocalyptic ending that involves both fire and ice. "Malinovi" means "raspberry" as well as "crimson." Taking this hint, we may note that raspberry bushes have thorns, and a fire of crackling thorns invokes a node of religious images. Still, the thorns are not the thick ones of religious association; a raspberry bush is too thin to serve well in that way. It remains a raspberry bush. And anyway, it is not said that the bonfires were actually burning raspberry bushes; they may be only the color of raspberry. Roses do offer thick thorns, but they are firmly locked into a simile, "Like roses, flower in the snow."

The manipulation of understatement by the mutings of a terminal image, the preservation of an air of open signification by the evasion of interlocking metaphors—these strengths are adopted for the discursive style of the *Northern Elegies,* which easily flow in and out of something akin to surrealism. In these masterly poems the revelatory detail and the summary reflection conjoin for a deep harmony:

> And in Staraya Russa there are splendid gutters,
> And in little gardens rotting pergolas,
> And the glass of windows as dark as an ice hole
>
> . . . .
>
> As though all things which I within myself
> All my life struggled with, had gained a life,
> A separate one, and were embodied in these
> Blind walls, in this dark garden
>
> . . . .
>
> The laugh has still not died, the tears are streaming,
> The inkstain darkened, not rubbed off of the table,
> And like print upon the heart, there is a kiss—
> The only one, in farewell, not to be forgotten . . .

The vision of the poem transmutes the "epochs of remembrances," gathering up the kiss "like print upon the heart" for a meditative calm so all-embracing it can assimilate amorous transports at one end and harrowing troubles at the other. Understatement, direct statement, and the dexterities of near hyperbole here merge in a single, unique style.

NORTHERN ELEGIES

> *All is in sacrifice to your memory*
> Pushkin

I
Prehistory

> *I now live elsewhere*
> Pushkin

The Russia of Dostoevsky. A moon
Almost at the quarter covered by a bell-tower.
Bars are doing business, cabs are flying.
Five-story buildings are springing up

On Gorokhovaya Street, at Znamenya, near Smolni.
Everywhere there are dancing schools, money-changers' signs.
Next door, coiffeurs: "Henriette," "Basile," "André"
And splendid coffins for sale: "Shumilov senior."
But anyway, the city has little changed.
Not I alone but also others
Have noticed that it sometimes has the power
Of looking like an old lithograph,
Not a first-class one, but one quite decent,
From, it would seem, the eighteen-seventies.

                Especially a winter before dawn
                Or at twilight.—Then outside the gates
                The harsh, straight Liteini Prospect darkens,
                Not yet put to disgrace by the Modern,
                And vis-à-vis my home Nekrasov lives
                And Saltikov. . . Both of them on a tablet
                Of memorial. O how fearful it would be
                For them to see these tablets! I pass on.

In Staraya Russa there are splendid gutters,[2]
And in little gardens rotting pergolas,
And the glass of windows as dark as an ice hole,
And it seems so much has happened there
That it is better not to look; let's go away.
Not in every place can an arrangement be made
So that it might open up its secret.
(And in Optina I shall be no more . . .).
The rustling of skirts, checkered plaids,
Frames of walnut wood around mirrors
That are wonder-struck by a Karenin beauty,
And in narrow corridors those wallpapers
With which we were enamoured in childhood,
Under a yellow kerosene lamp
And the same plush on the armchairs . . .

                Everything egghead, slapdash, no matter how . . .
                Fathers and misunderstood grandfathers. The lands
                Mortgaged. And in Baden—the roulette.

And a woman with transparent eyes
(Of so deep a blue that you could not
Not remember the sea looking into them),
With a most uncommon name and a white little hand
And a kindness that for a legacy
I, as it may be, received from her—
A needless gift in my cruel life . . .

The country shivers, but the Omsk convict[3]
Understood it all, put a cross on it all.

See, now he mixes it all up,
And he himself, at the primeval chaos,
Like some spirit soars away. Midnight strikes.
The pen is creaking on and many pages
Are redolent of the Semenovsky drill field.

This is when we got the idea of being born
And, unerringly measuring time,
So nothing would be left out of the mysterious
Sights, we said goodbye to non-existence.

II

And in no way was it a rosy childhood . . .
Of little freckles and teddy bears and toys,
And kind aunts, and fearful uncles, and even
Friends among the pebbles of the river.
As for myself, I began from the start
To see me as someone's dream or delirium
Or another's reflection in a mirror
Without a name, without flesh, without a cause.
I already knew the list of crimes
That I was obligated to commit.
And here I was, stepping out, a sleepwalker;
I stepped into life and life frightened me.
It spread out before me as the meadow
Where long ago Proserpina took her stroll.
Before me, without kin, clumsy as I was
The unexpected doors opened up.
And people issued forth and cried out
"She has arrived, she has arrived herself!"
And I looked at them with consternation
And I thought, "These people have gone mad!"
And the more strongly they gave me praise,
The more strongly the people delighted in me,
The more fearful it was for me to live in the world;
And the more strongly I wanted to awaken,
And I knew I would pay a hundredfold
In prison, in the tomb, in the insane asylum,
Everywhere it is decreed for such as me
To wake up—but the torture of happiness endured.

III

In that house it was very fearful to live,
And not the shine of the patriarchal fireside,
Not the little cradle of my son,
Not the fact that both of us were young

And full of intimations
Lessened this feeling of terror.
And at all that I learned how to laugh
And I set out a little bit of wine
And a morsel of bread for whoever at night
Like a dog might scratch at the door
Or took a look into the lower window,
At the time when we, staying still, were trying
Not to see what was going on behind the mirror,
Under whose paces growing ponderous
The steps upon the murky staircase groaned
As though praying for mercy piteously.
And you said, smiling in a strange way,
"Whom on the staircase are 'they' taking away?"

Now you are there where they know all, tell us:

What was living in this house besides ourselves?

IV

Here it is just so—this autumn landscape
Which I have been so afraid of all my life:
And the sky—like an abyss ablaze,
And the city's sounds, as if from the other world
They had been heard, alien forever.
As though all things which I within myself
All my life struggled with, had gained a life,
A separate one, and were embodied in these
Blind walls, in this dark garden . . .
But at this moment at my shoulder
My former house has still been following me
With a squinting, unfavorable eye,
That window I have always in my memory.
Fifteen years—and it is a though they simulated
Fifteen centuries made of granite,
But I myself have been as though of granite:
Now say a prayer, torment yourself, call me
The queen of the sea. It's all the same. No need . . .
There was a need to convince myself
That all of this has happened many times
And not with me alone—with others also—
And even worse. No, not worse—better.
And my voice—this, it is true, was
Most fearfully of all said out of the dark:
"Fifteen years ago with such a song
You met this day, you prayed for heaven
And choruses of stars, and choruses of waters

That they might welcome a triumphal meeting
With him from whom today you have gone away . . .

Here it is just so, your silver wedding:
Well then, summon guests, rejoice, triumph!"

V

Me, like a river,
This stern epoch has turned aside.
They replaced my life. In another channel
It has flowed on past another place,
And I do not recognize my own shores.
O how many sights I have let slip,
And the curtain will have gone up without me
And fallen the same way. How many of my friends
I did not meet in my life a single time,
And how many cities in their outlines
Might have elicited tears from my eyes,
But I know just one city in the world
And by groping I could find it in my sleep.
And how many verses I have not written,
And their secret chorus wanders round me
And, it may even be that at some time
They will strangle me . . .
The beginnings and the ends are known to me
And life after the end, and something else,
Of which I need not now make recollection.
And there is some woman or other who has
Occupied my own singular place,
Carries my most lawful proper name,
Leaving for me a nickname out of which
I have done, if you please, all that I could.
I will not, alas, lie in my own tomb.

But sometimes the crazy wind of spring
Or the combination of words in a random book
Or someone's smile will suddenly draw me
Into a life that never came about.
In such a year such and such would have happened,
But in this one—this: to travel, to see, to think,
To recollect, and into a new love,
To enter, as into a mirror, with numb awareness
Of betrayal, and of something not there yesterday,
A wrinkle.

But if from there I had taken a look back
At my own life as it is today
I would have learned what envy is at last.

VI

There are three epochs for remembrances.
And the first as though the day of yesterday.
The soul is underneath their blessed vault,
And the body is in bliss under their shadow.
The laugh has still not died, the tears are streaming,
The inkstain darkened, not rubbed off of the table,
And like print upon the heart, there is a kiss—
The only one, in farewell, not to be forgotten,
But it does not keep going on for long . . .
Already no vault is over the head, but somewhere
In the remote suburbs is a solitary house,
Where in winter it is cold, but hot in summer,
Where there are spiders, dust lies on everything,
Where flaming letters are reduced to ash
And the portraits are changing stealthily,
Whither, as to a tomb, the people go,
And on returning wash their hands with soap
And shake a superficial teardrop off
From tired eyelids and sigh heavily . . .
But the clock is ticking on, one spring
Changes for another, the sky goes pink,
The names of the cities are changing,
Already there are no witnesses to events,
And none with whom to weep, none to remember.
And slowly the shadows go away from us,
Which no longer we are summoning,
And we'd be terrified by their return.
And, once we wake up, we see we have forgotten
Even the path to the solitary house
And, stifling out of shame and vexation,
We run there, but (as it happens in a dream)
There all is other: the people, the things, the walls,
And nobody knows us—we are strangers!
And we have landed in the wrong place—my God!
And now when something bitterer arrives:
We realize that we cannot make room
For that past in the boundary of our lives,

   And to us it is almost as alien,
As to our neighbor in the apartment next door.
That those who died we would not recognize
And those from whom God sent us separation
Manage beautifully without us—and even
All is for the better . . .

And the heart, already it does not respond
But my voice, exulting and sorrowing,
All is over . . . and my song is carried
In the waste night, where there's nothing more of you.

(1943–1955)

SECTION TWO

Some Observations on Shakespeare and the Incommensurability of Interpretive Strategies

For interpretation, and particularly for the interpretation of Renaissance drama, a number of hermeneutic strategies have been introduced in the past two decades or so. Many of these, in turn, base themselves on a prior set of philosophical reasonings or psychological inferences, in such a way as to deepen readings, but also implicitly or explicitly to close off other strategies. Their authors tend on occasion to try to act preemptively, so as to present a narrower set of interpretive options than those that can be shown to hold.

In redefining, and perhaps widening, the range of options, we certainly need not surrender the tools of discriminations that have already been gained or are promised through such discussions. Moreover, we should still, and perhaps better, be able to discriminate among applicable, false, and doubtful readings. Still further, I shall argue, we need not rest with treating this rich variety of approaches as a loose repertoire of interpretive instruments. They may, to begin with, be arrayed in a hierarchy for hermeneutic access, allowing for the possibility, which some of them would by falsely exclusive axiom disallow, that they may be brought into syncretic convergence from level to level. This leveling, too, may be carried through without declaring some closed set that would exclude the possibility of still further approaches or, indeed, of other convergences, and even without disallowing the single-track approach which does not itself enter into convergence with other approaches, or not systematically. Some looseness is the normal case. An interpretation need not be grounded by theoretical preliminaries in order to hold. The possible adjudications among Lacan, Freud, Derrida, Marx, and Foucault, for example, do not have to be carried through for the modern interpreter to weave some or even all of these theoreticians into his discourse. Such, indeed, is becoming a normal syncretism for an informed interpretive approach, most notably, with various mixes, in the work of the "New Historians."

It is important to realize that the hermeneutic process, whether applied mediately to texts or "immediately" to life, is not globally subject to the law of contradiction, though of course individual interpretive assertions made within it would be. The law of contradiction does not apply globally because the interpreter can shift his frame of reference the same way that one can discuss the same man psychoanalytically as a bad parent and aesthetically as a good poet. One can discuss language in a play without (necessarily) invoking depth psychology, or vice versa—and this even though Lacan provides a scheme that links language "inescapably" to depth psychology. The same freedom obtains for the interpreted text itself, unless the author of the text has chosen, as Beckett at his limit has done, to play with contradictions in individual statements. The "misplaced concreteness" of a living situation exceeds on principle any formulation, even if the order of a given formulation—Heidegerrian, Lacanian, or whatever—can be imposed on data presented to it. But for such global procedures, one need not defer to the law of contradiction and necessarily choose between Heidegger and Lacan. An aspectual use of them is possible. Not only is an aspectual use possible of systems that claim or axiomatize an exclusive and total approach. Such an aspectual approach has in fact been loosely actualized by being applied, by some critics, to such texts as those of Shakespeare's plays. It remains, of course, to ascertain that, even if arguably supplementary to each other (against implicit claims of totality), hermeneutic approaches may be seen in a hierarchy, or at least in an order of priority. Only the total ones have to be seen alternately, so to speak, in order to submit to complementarity. Others can be used instrumentally, and their instrumentality functions at various levels.

Even without hierarchizing these strategies, we may also choose to bracket some or all of them, refusing to allow them to preempt interpretation either in an endless regress of relativisms or an absolutized measurement of the play by and into a prior totalized coding.

So, for example, at a first level, one may employ the categories of one or more of various versions of speech-act theory descriptively to characterize individual statements within an utterance like a speech in a play, or in an overall utterance like a play.[1] But such instrumentalities resemble those of grammar. They do not condition a statement, a single or an overall statement, so much as they indicate the conditions the statement itself has enlisted.[2] To take a specific case, the validity of Stanley Fish's speech-act reading of *Coriolanus* rests on a first level of observing constituents of the play, prior to its action and independently of the various relativizings and self-qualifications that Fish offers.[3]

To move from one temporally flexed subject—the playwright or the auditor—to the large organization of "interpretive communities" only moves the relativization, of course, to the second degree. But it does not move the speech-act reading from its first-level instrumentality—or out of validity either. Further, as Robert Scholes well says, "No language community is congruous with any interpretive community," and this fact relativizes both.[4] But however much we fragment the interpretive communities or double them over with one another—even if we go so far as to reduce them back again to individual subjects—the possibility of our either referring to them or manipulating the definition of them is neutral with respect to the hermeneutic question-and-answer definition of the hermeneutic act. It is also neutral with respect to the level at which such a constituted reading functions; no definition of interpretive communities can change the set or level of a particular hermeneutic focus. Temporalization, subjectivity, and community-relativism, cannot be taken separately or together as by themselves invalidating, or even as significantly qualifying, a given interpretive act, nor do they have to be adduced in order to relativize it.

Fish's interpretation of *Coriolanus* in accord with speech-act theory is, of course, conditioned, as Scholes points out, by Fish's pre-understanding in such an act. The very fact that he interprets the play, with validity in this instance, has that positive communicative function, as well as the incidental philosophical status of allowing for relativization.

None of this, that is, can be taken to deny "reality in the texts and some freedom in the interpreter." We would want, though, to ascertain where this freedom is leading, and what it implies with respect to other interpretive possibilities. We would also want to know, finally, where it fits in the hierarchy of interpretations, which can be serially defined even if the individual approaches are (as is probably the case) incommensurate with each other. Most interpretations of sense in the action of a play are posterior to the utterances that rise out of and further its actions. So we must move beyond, or up from, questions about language to be able to judge that it would be wrong to interpret *Coriolanus,* for example, as though this character were a tribune in disguise—since there is no evidence for his being so. It would also be wrong to interpret him as having a vision of world peace because he goes over to the Volsci; and it would probably be wrong, though less patently so, to align him to someone aspiring to the equanimity of Augustus and frustrated for not reaching it. In disallowing these interpretations, we must base ourselves on an overall, integral experience of the play and then apply that back to such individual questions. And finally there is no way of omitting this integral experience, for all its own presumptions and subjective conditioning. Hermeneutic adjudications cannot be made just on the basis of separate speech-acts in a play.

Fish's "speech-act" interpretation of the play is not only not the single one possible; it is also, taken as valid, more preliminary than any interpretations, plausible ones or wrong ones, that center on the actions of the play, from the victory near the beginning to the death at the end, or from military prowess through political bungling and tragic decision to capitulation before the mother who was in a psychoanalytic sense responsible for the first three actions. The speech acts are subordinate to, as they lead into, either the victory-death sequence, or the prowess-mollycoddle sequence. Either sequence provides a time-contoured, and also a contextual, definition for Fish's characterization of Coriolanus as someone who "cannot make requests or receive praise." Coriolanus's speeches are relative to the actions that they sometimes—but not always—trigger, on which they are a sort of ongoing comment as well as performative producers of some of those actions. Actions shown or described on stage orient the speeches; and at the same time, one need not produce the speech-act extrapolation for an apt account of the play. Or, in Aristotelian terms, lexis, the speech constituent, cannot directly reach dianoia, the overall thought or idea, without passing through the central mimesis of the play, the imitation of an action.

Fish skillfully points out that Coriolanus's reversal of the act of banishment—"I banish you" (3.3.123)—flouts the important rule of the non-reversibility of words with relation to institutions. However, another failure bears on these words: they do not meet Austin's "felicity conditions" for the illocutionary effectuation of banishment, and Coriolanus is acting foolishly and extravagantly. Even in his words taken by themselves, we have perlocutionary effects of talk, not illocutionary action. Again, what Coriolanus says exemplifies these traits, the context and consequences of which we can then consider in order to produce (one of many, valid or invalid) interpretations of the play, into which the speech acts will feed. To promote "speech-act" to an overall interpretation of the play would be to falsify that constituent by exaggeration, and consequently to frame a question for which there can be no answer. If the question be put "What is Coriolanus mainly about?," the answer cannot be speech-acts, from any point of view, because of the dependence of the speech-acts, both actively and passively, on the "real" acts. We grant those acts reality as the pre-assumption of the play—which can be characterized as "all words" only if such conditions are forgotten, many questions begged, and a sort of improvised radical skepticism be brought to bear upon the play. Such skepticism, if followed consistently, would go far deeper than just to insist on the elusiveness of referents to signifiers and signifieds. Still, if the question be put "How do speech-acts function in *Coriolanus?*," then Fish's reflections become apposite and work well at their level in the constructible hierarchy of hermeneutic approaches.

In one sense, to move to another domain, the question of "How do the Christian elements function in *Coriolanus*" is an unanswerable question from any point of view. If the question is rephrased, "How does this pre-Christian society of the play function when performed before a Christian society?," then we can define our (presumed) horizon of expectation as functioning through exclusion, and sets of answers can be formulated. Coriolanus's son stands to him psychologically as Mamillius stands to Leontes: he is loved and expected to follow in his father's footsteps, but at the same time ignored. But again, one could misphrase questions so as to render the answers false by suggesting (with no evidence) that because fathers in other plays expect their sons to succeed them on the throne, Coriolanus, who hates the people, wishes to restore the recently abolished kingship in Rome, with his son as king. Nor is *Coriolanus* a play about fathers and sons, or about proper succession, as in one dimension is *The Winter's Tale,* and to promote this question to the center of the play would set up a hermeneutic condition that would falsify—and not just relativize—any possible answer.

Philosophical aporiae, in these cases and many others, can all too easily be adduced as bromides, through a false (implied) extension of the law of contradiction to complex areas that cannot be shrunk to series of true-false alternatives. Even the fundamental contradiction, under which all discourse operates, between some form of radical subjectivity and the demonstrated possibility of communication, can be approached from the psychoanalytic, or from the deconstructive, side, or from the side of social conditioning, or some combination of these, to arrest interpretation; in the key of that particular mode, of course, the puzzle of how communication between writer and reader-viewer is effectuated itself enters an endless regress.

If we do not enter such a regress—if we bracket that possibility—we effectually empower ourselves not only to adopt various hermeneutic strategies syncretically but to shift the emphasis among them while either staying within one mode if it permits or moving from one mode to another. Indeed, to move to higher levels or further points in the hermeneutic series is what the psychoanalytic or the deconstructionist approaches do, even if either of them asserts effectually that its explanatory power is so total as to be immune to such adaptation. This is implicitly the case with Lacan.[5]

Psychoanalytic interpretation, or deconstructive interpretation, though they differ among themselves (and though deconstruction utilizes psychoanalysis but not vice versa), operate at the same point of a hierarchy. They subjectivize an act of communication after it has taken place; and in that sense, speech-act theory, and all such linguistic constructs, are prior to it.

They, in turn, are logically prior if applied, though supplemental if not, to such overall social approaches as the superficially similar relativization of groups into "interpretive communities"—if these be taken in their social, rather than their linguistic, dimension. The Marxian approaches, either the tonally tendentious ones of Jameson and Eagleton or the actually tendentious ones of Althusser and Ernst Bloch, are systematic, and for this reason they lay claim to a superior comprehensiveness. This claim would hold descriptively for the social detail they explain; but it would not hold exclusively, since any valid social approach, if consistent, potentially covers all social cases. Still, the Marxian is logically posterior to the psychoanalytic or the deconstructive, which can subsume it only by admitting it; but the reverse is not the case. The "political unconscious" cannot assimilate Freud without changing character; that is, without conflating into the sort of multiply informed hermeneutic syncretism that I am in fact endorsing in this essay. These approaches would even be prior to a value-neutral (*wertfrei*) approach based on that of Max Weber. Indeed, with psychoanalysis, and also with Weber's ideal types, in turn, the actual interactions are imprecisely, let alone exhaustively, describable by a Marxian model. Lacan on the other hand, insofar as he centers Freud on a communicational model, is variously precise but, strictly speaking neither prior nor posterior to him, remaining at that level though making the inadmissible claim of being exclusive. For if this claim were admitted, all other hermeneutic strategies, including those in a given play, would become fully relativized; or else they would be irreducibly preliminary or illusory, "imaginary" in Lacan's terms; if they attained to the "symbolic," it would, within his system, have to be on his terms.

At a level that is arguably of overarching finality, Michel Foucault posits an organizing transformational principle, an episteme, which takes specific and homologous form at the next lower (but still comprehensive) level of the codes of various intellectual or social organizations that are structurally organized by the episteme. The episteme posits relations between the metacode of the episteme and the codes that it may be taken to generate or underlie. There is thus in the episteme a sort of neutrality, and it is open as to the particular manifestations a code may take. Foucault for such intricate interpreters of Shakespeare as Stephen Greenblatt and Jonathan Goldberg provides an advantageous overview and a commanding example that encourages the intrication of codes—of language, political interaction, theatricality, "self-fashioning," and so on,—and the employment of plays as illustrations of such intrications, bolstered syncretically at times by the adduction of Freud or Lacan. For Jonathan Goldberg, who combines the codes of language with the codes of power, "*Coriolanus* is"—among other things, I would insist—"a study in the relationship between power and language."[6] The double terms allow him—with an unfortunate logocentric and theatrocentric drift—[7] to mediate between Coriolanus's power and his language so as to introduce a dialectic about his character, offering therewith also a match he himself characterizes as not exact between the politics of the play's Rome and the politics of James I.

Neither the Freudian nor the Lacanian, in turn, then, is exactly on a par with a Foucault episteme, which as a code of codes, or minimally the projected idea for or assertion of a code of codes, is neutral toward codes within it, subsuming those it inspects, including the Freudian and therefore the Lacanian.[8] In this sense it is more neutral than either Freud or Lacan. But this neutrality has a cost. It asserts a subsumption of other codes—to an episteme. Such a construct clearly comes as a top and final level, to stay with my conception of a hierarchy; or, put differently, an episteme posits itself last in order of a series of logical priorities. But just because of its finality, it is arrested from the possibility of an ongoing, truly dialectical mediation. It can only make global attributions to the episteme, for all the qualifications with which Foucault hedges it. And it cannot really be put into combination with other systems as a hermeneutics, though of course they can be used in loose alternation as honorific modern methods, so that we may look now at the symbolic order in *Hamlet*, and then at its subjection to a Foucault-like episteme involving attitudes toward royalty and power—a use that is oddly both taken for granted and nodally situated in Foucault's own reading of what he offers as the pattern Renaissance painting, Velázquez's "Las Meninas."[9]

Systematically I have discussed four levels—language, construable as a speech-act orientation; psychoanalysis, which can be put on the same level theoretically even if not fully reconciled with deconstruction; the Marxian or quasi-Marxian; and the episteme of Foucault. Related to these are two others that lay a claim to totality and exhaustiveness beyond such levels, those of Lacan (which can, however, be assimilated to the psychoanalytic) and Girard (which is finally a variant at that level, though it assimilates complexly synchronic anthropological data). Since these are, as I represent them at least, subject to a logical series of priorities and so, to one kind of hierarchy, they cannot systematically be combined without ratiocinative adjustments. But one can use a syncretism, or pseudo-syncretism of these approaches "casually," without systematizing. This, indeed, is the dominant mode of "The New History," where an intense eclecticism of alternating attentions may produce rich interpretations, along with mares' nests of misinterpretation. The recent rich vein of feminist studies in Shakespeare potentially, and often actually, cuts across these approaches too, engaging the dialectical possibilities in these plays by radically questioning what lies behind the conceptions and confrontations of gender-determined roles in their representations. So far as political power in Renaissance plays is concerned, a Marxist approach, or one of various Marxian or quasi-Marxian approaches, defines social coherence through a principle that provides "causal" connections—though not at the level of Foucault's episteme, of which as a totalization a Marxian structuring (or the ideal of one; actual ones are hard to find) would be an incommensurate equivalent. The Marxian and the Foucaulvian are incommensurate, as well as set in a sequence or hierarchy, because, though Foucault derives somewhat from Marx, his epistemes will not yield themselves to, or even yield, a Marxian interpretation. The Marxian approach, at the same time, has the cast of, and stakes the claim for, the status of an episteme rather than just of one among many particular codes. A Marxian approach does have the advantage not only of identifying social constituents, however deep, but of setting them into mediation with other factors, as most intricately in the work of Fredric Jameson. Such an approach can suggest mediations, even if the approach is in itself no guarantee of depth, let alone completeness.

The more comprehensive these mediations become, however, the less closely they are dependent on a specifically Marxian framework. When Jameson says, "Marxism subsumes other interpretive modes or systems," he rests on a bare assertion. Or else he depends (unwittingly it would seem) on a characteristic of Marxian interpretation—the capacity to perform subsumptions—which it shares with many other "modes or systems."[10] Marxian convictions may fuel the energy of this writer, but they do not undergird his argument for a specifically Marxian cast to the (always partial) causal matrices he evolves. Even if Shakespeare and Balzac do present such a matrix, they do so without simply anticipating the modern Marxians in particular. This is, of course, to press qualification to the limit, and it remains true, as for Weber and Adorno, that the ascription of the interaction of social institutions, economic and other, with the specific manifestations of artistic expression finds its origins in Marx. But such analyses, if neutralized, lose their tendentiousness, and with it their claim, in any case untenable, to exclusivity.

There is, within the matrix of historical conventions, a sort of counter-current that can be discerned in most Renaissance plays that engage politics. A paradoxical confrontation of dominant codes also tends to come about as the rule of pure power is set into confrontation with the divine right of kings in Shakespeare's history plays and elsewhere. So, for ex-

ample, Leonard Tennenhouse renders explicit the contradictions in the
social order that some plays express.[11] As he says, bringing psychoanalysis
syncretically to bear upon questions of public power, "Psychoanalytic criticism . . . has as its provenance the disturbing or seemingly incoherent
features of a text. . . . Conflicts in matters of economics, religion, government, and relations between the sexes can clearly be seen in various ways.
Elizabethans tended to insist upon those aspects of their cultural self-
image that most contradicted historical fact."

Now Tennenhouse (p. 56) here claims for psychoanalysis, as he applies it syncretically to social constructs, what others would claim for
Derrida. In his reading, the specific values expressed in the codes and
languages of Shakespeare's England, far from stabilizing its cultural order
and beliefs, only highlight its cultural tensions and contradictions. This, of
course, is true of every culture. Here the tool of psychoanalysis is well used
to uncover real tensions of a public sort that can be derived, in *Coriolanus,*
say, from a reconstructible depth psychology of private histories. And
these psychological approaches could be combined, as Terence Eagleton
combines them, with a proto-Marxian reading of the dialectic of class
interests in the play, of failed social actions based in inadequate language.[12]
All these codes addressed to discord in the society operate at a level that is
posterior to speech-act theory (even if Eagleton here subsumes a version
of it) but prior to a Foucaulvian episteme, or even a full-scale Marxian
comprehensiveness. And all such inspection of discords, in Tennenhouse's
reading of *The Merchant of Venice* and in Shakespeare's history plays,
would have to be seen as qualifications of the harmony that is also posited
as a code within the society. The same can be said for orientations of the
plays within a Marxian definition of economic and political groups, as in
Walter Cohen's readings of *King Lear* and *The Merchant of Venice.*[13] On
the same (social) level of interpretation, discord plays off against concord,
in the plays as well as in the society. A notable example of concord is the
dominant obligation in Renaissance society to serve social harmony, an
obligation especially remarkable for us in the strange subjection even of
rebels (indeed, especially of rebels) to the conviction of a divinely constituted royal authority. The harmony that serves as an ideal for this obligation enforces often a subjection to a striking code of capitulation, not
only on characters from Shakespeare's histories but actually in the real
society.[14]

If this ideal of harmony were not in tension with actualities of discord,
we would in fact not be able to detect the presence of such achieved or
missed congruences of play and society.

Coming at these constituents of plays-within-societies diachronically,
the social modes of folklore and myth present a many-dimensional case

that qualifies the logical series, the hierarchy, I have been presenting. These can be taken also just with respect to levels of Marxian and Foucaulvian analysis, or also just at the level of synchronic analysis that is prior to them. Folklore and myth operate as persistent long-range codes. And the typifying or "folklore" component of character and plot must be posterior to the speech-codes on which they draw because the speech codes must exist for them to function, but not vice versa. And they are, though unexamined in their very nature, more comprehensive than the Freudian, which would analyze them, as also than the overall social (Marxian and Foucaulvian) codes that would structure them, or else lay bare their preexistent structures. In the actual application of such questions about folklore to plays, such anthropological approaches in their range are themselves variously applicable to a given play, and assignable to various hierarchies within their level. But insofar as the folk expectation is taken for a determinant of actions and sequences, it is prior to a Marxian dialectic or a Foucaulvian episteme. Then a Marxist structure or an episteme, if adduced, would interpret a folk constituent, one that at the same time either of these hermeneutic systems would have to modify themselves in order to historicize because folk conventions characteristically function on a very long range that would carry them through the periods defined by either Marx or Foucault. Mediations are necessary at all points because of the comprehensiveness, and also because of the taxonomic simplicity, of folkloric and mythic constituents. Other systems do not guarantee effective mediation. And for Shakespeare's incorporation of folk structures, the non-Marxist C. L. Barber provides mediations more delicate, and also more thorough, than does the Marxist Robert Weimann.[15]

An element from a code of folk belief may be deeply latent and faintly influential, like the miming of the Descent into Hell when Hamlet leaps into Ophelia's grave. Such a pattern, because of its latency, functions to provide a kind of mythic template that as a preexistent form has almost the priority of the codes of language. This is so because both the assumed rules of grammar and the unconscious survivals of the Descent into Hell are formal constituents adding resonance and coherence to the play, but not superadded meanings. The omnipresence of these depth structures in folk patterns endows them with a priority to meanings specific to a given play, just as the lexical meaning of the word "fardel" is prior to its use in *Hamlet*. Or again, the structures of folklore may parallel, and therefore be seen as drawing on, the analogous forms in the society, of which the play is a freely combined version on a like armature. Among these social forms would be not only the folk festivals and royal pageants much discussed by writers on folklore, and on theatricality in society itself, but formal processions of royalty and the church, bear-baitings, the span of a church service, and even public executions.[16] The list of what Bacon recommends that a traveler visit, in his essay "Of Travel," contains many items that are analogous to, and hence could be seen to serve as a pattern-source for, the actional foci and contours of a play: formal receptions of ambassadors at court, assemblages of ecclesiastics, displays of fencing and horsemanship, commercial gatherings at "exchanges" and "burses," military exercises, "triumphs, masks, feasts, weddings, funerals, capital executions."

In building the activity on the half-understood patterns of people in social groupings, such folklore-bound interpretations are analogous to a Marxian approach; but at the same time they can be taken as prior to a Marxian approach for lacking a dialectical component. At that same time, in another way they are diachronically posterior to such analyses, or work at a further level, because they cover a longer time span than any dialectic of class struggles can account for.[17] The area of folklore and myth, indeed, because it is itself so subject to mediations through other levels, throws into relief the fact that in order to assert my logical series and my hierarchies, I have really arbitrarily but necessarily restricted these levels for the purpose of discrimination before "releasing" them for syncretic combination. Or, implicitly at the "total" level of a Foucault-like episteme, they may fit sometimes wholly, as the Bakhtinian—or more properly, Frazerian—carnival reversal could be taken to underlie the action of *The Merry Wives of Windsor,* and also the character of Falstaff generally. As C. L. Barber reminds us, however, Falstaff manipulates as well as obeys such folk patterns. Amplifying the gestures of Falstaff out of Nashe's *Praise of Folly,* Barber offers many qualifications and nuances:

> Falstaff repeatedly plays the same game, of course, with much more deftness. . . . In one way he is covering up, by using the moral maxim; at the same time he is flouting morality. Earlier he goes out of his way to get Hal to pronounce another proverb which condemns him. . . . After being so elaborately cued, the prince obliges by recalling the Biblical phrases:
>
> > Thou didst well; for wisdom cries out in the streets, and no man regards it.
>
> Hal displaces the emphasis so that a proverb describing the evil of disregarding wisdom can be taken as a direction to disregard wisdom.

Barber goes on to enlist Freud for further fine discriminations around this behavior, where Falstaff transcends by his dexterity the very folk patterns he is exemplifying.[18] Barber eloquently makes a case for adducing folklore: "So much of the action in . . . comedy is random when looked at as intrigue, so many of the persons are neutral when regarded as character, so much of the wit is inapplicable when assessed as satire, that critics too often have fallen back on exclamations about poetry and mood" (4). Yet, seen at their point in a level of hierarchies in interpretation, "poetry" (taken in its full dramatic impact) and "mood" are in fact posterior to the folk constituents from which they build, even though Barber has quite properly introduced a strategy of refining Frazer, as it were, to the point where the thesis of *The Golden Bough* can be brought to bear in a domain where it had not been introduced with such discrimination, while a rich critical literature had been occupying itself with the (posterior level of) deductions about "poetry" and "mood."

In this light, taken as a figure whose actions are deployed through several plays and in two different genres, the poetry and mood built into and out of Falstaff draw on, and comprise intensifications and tangents of, many areas—power, the Trickster, and even the Trickster Tricked, exemplified by both Gadshill and the end of the *Merry Wives*. This appropriateness of folk patterns to Falstaff would not make them wholly locate him, since he is a figure whose world is a solid and permanent one, celebratory but never topsy-turvy, the way it would have to be in the "Feast of Fools" or "carnival" convention. The contour of his presence in the Lancaster tetralogy includes the famous account of his death and its accompanying vision that fuses paradise (a religious form) with heightened pastoral, which is not carnevalesque: "'a babbled of green fields."[19] The fact that Sir John Falstaff is a knight, as is Sir Toby in *Twelfth Night,* both invokes the definitions of the class structure, Marxist or other, and modifies them somewhat, since such class-bound interpretations cannot allow for the classlessness of Falstaff's, or Sir Toby's, self-indulgences; there is little or no sense that they are parodying or betraying class. Further, Sir Toby is trying to exercise surrogate parental authority over Olivia, as Falstaff tries to modulate between his role of friend and his role of uncle in his relation to Prince Hal.

The "festival" spirit offers a large anthropological area, which is generally present in many comedies, as C. L. Barber has taught us. But beyond that, the spirit and temper of two plays whose titles name specific festivals may be taken to echo the specific festival more precisely. *Twelfth Night* gets the stalled time sense of the age-old intercalary festival in the dead of winter.[20] And *Midsummer Night's Dream* melds hope, sportiveness, celebration, and mystery, in ways that no other festival quite matches—and no single festival, since it fuses Maytime and Harvest, as well as Summer festivals and still more generally a festive presence of Fairies that is peculiar to no specific festival. The Fool, as Enid Welsford has shown us, is a figure who derives from an age-old social history, but that figure appears in pure form only once in Shakespeare: the Fool in Lear.[21] Other figures—Feste, Malvolio, again Falstaff—draw on the pattern but do not fully exemplify it. And of course in *King Lear,* which is no comedy, the fool is at sea under strange, powerful influences.

One may come at these questions still a different way—itself incommensurate with hierarchies—and treat a given code, such as Lacan's, on its own terms as a metacode. Theoretically the metacode only sets constraints of limit, in spite of assertions to the contrary. In its neutrality it may be evoked or not. But the totalizing explanation of Lacan, or of a Freudian code, arbitrarily taken as total, is not neutral and not just relational, even transformationally. It functions as a closed system into which it assumes the individual manifestations of subcodes and also of the coded statement, the dramatic text or script.

The Lacanian set metainterprets a text or script for performance, but it also relegates it to the equivalence of instances of other texts, all of which illustrate, enact, and necessarily elicit his symbolic mode. The crucial question of a text's relation to "the imaginary" cannot ever fully be mediated.[22] In the Freudian sphere Lacan's orders of "symbolic," "imaginary," and "real" are not coterminous with any of the several Freudian sets, which can be used to mount or express the relations to the unconscious of characters or across the stage boundary. Yet the Lacanian orders totalize, and they are on principle exhaustive in themselves. Coming at these explanatory systems simply as items in a larger repertoire allows for the possibility of modulation and variation in the Freudian interpretations; so someone like Paul Ricoeur can base a hermeneutics on its access to, and formulations of, evolutions and modalizations, whereas the Lacanian ones, persuasive because they locate themselves at the exact point of linguistic interchange, are for that reason too powerful.[23] Their algorithms become directly subsumptive of the signifiers, without modulation; hence the accuracy of their totalizing, but self-predictive, formulas about the dominance of the signifier. At that slant of metainterpretation, they cannot be modified or even supplemented, and not even by the transcendences in the work. The transcendences in a play can be asserted by the simple strategy of bracketing the total dominance of the Lacanian symbolic in the first place. Now the Lacanian psycholinguistics both furthers and threatens interpretation, and it becomes a particularly subtle, deep, and treacherous form of the preemptive hermeneutics, even if not loosely (and contradictorily) combined as a sort of academic received opinion with an axiomatization of Derrida and an exaggerated totalization of Foucault. Freudian readings, on the other hand, could be preliminary (if not totalized) rather than exhaustive, though they are also locatable at three points in arguably still another interpretive hierarchy (incommensurate with those I have presented, though overlapping with them): those of the cultural system, the combination of symptoms in the character interactions of a play, and the symbolic response of the idealized auditor.

Joel Fineman's work illustrates the richness that may result from intricating one code, and one level, with another.[24] As Fineman says, "The dramatic revival of the topos required that fratricide be supplied with a new meaning equivalent to the old, one which reversed the explanatory direction of myth. Where the myth instanced universal chaos, political disorder, themes of metaphysical eschatology, with particular fratricides, Shakespeare instead defined the domestic catastrophe in cosmological terms—hence the hyperbolic scope of his rhetoric." Fineman here achieves an intrication of three areas—structures of folklore as they reach down to and up from myth, play manipulation, and rhetoric. He does so in a way that begins but does not end with the Freudian codes. Yet limits, of course, do obtain. And taken by itself, a Freudian reading cannot just enclose "difference," in the fashionable combination of Freud with Derrida, as one looks at maleness and femaleness in the plays, or at least not while remaining Freudian; because, to state the obvious, Freud posits, after differences, a fundamental sameness in the psychic structure of men and women, parents and children. Lacan, on the other hand, can be used to institute difference as a final category because he deals not just with necessary (Freudian) constituents but with the dominance of the symbolic order.[25]

One does not have to opt for the single-track interpretation to approach a play validly, nor does the single-track interpretation guarantee a match to the play, any more than does the entertainment of several at their (various) levels lose applicability because the approaches are incommensurate enough to result in a seeming ambiguity. To apply what E. D. Hirsch says,[26] "Certainty is not the same thing as validity, and knowledge of ambiguity is not necessarily ambiguous knowledge."

Hirsch's grounding of possibilities serves to legitimize further and layered acts of interpretation, though it can also be put at the service of various subjectivizations, which, in their preemptive abrogation of Kant's deduction that aesthetic judgments may be both subjective and universal, would reduce the act of assimilating a text to an atomized sequence, or else to the residuum of a dialogic interchange. There are onstage interactions that would be characterized as dialogic in Bakhtin's sense, and the transaction between the play and the audience also has a dialogic rather than a simply passive character. Insofar as the responses of the audience include, and are even comprised in, the affective, they are susceptible of psychoanalytic interpretation, but they need not be seen from that angle. Instead, they can be seen (in still another set) as a "reception" in the sense of Jauss and Iser, a "reception" that is both prior to and posterior to others as a meta-interpretation—which at the same time has a neutrality that does not put it on a plane above the others. But neither is reception theory at the same level as speech-act analysis just because it depends on language. Nor is it on a par with other reader-response theories, psychoanalytic or not, that are atomistic and therefore deal with constituents rather than with final effects.

These dialogic or reception-theoretical approaches rest on the assumptions of Gadamer, who does not so much offer a method as distinguish between methods of any kind and the "operative-historical consciousness" (wirkungsgeschichtliches Bewusstsein) through which a work is assimilated. For both living experience and textual interpretation, Gadamer asserts, "no assertion is possible that cannot be understood as an answer to a question, and assertions can only be understood in this way."[27] Taking a work (novels, in his instance) as a long series of responses, effectually through the sort of mobile horizon of perception that Gadamer describes,[28] Wolfgang Iser describes the novel as an ongoing dialogue—a fine-sequenced series of answers to questions, as it were, and of questionings of foregoing answers—between author and reader. A particular semantic reality is thereby constructed (eine eigene semantische Realität aufzubauen) in a circle closed by the reader.[29] In Hans Robert Jauss's analysis, the posing of questions by the author in ways that get concretized into the text serves as a beginning for a reader to reconstruct with his own questions the author's "horizon of expectation" (Erwartungshorizont) and to bring about the fusion of the two horizons (Horizontverschmelzung) through the mobile process of Gadamer's theorizing.[30] As he demonstrates, "The historical essence of a work of art lies not alone in its representative or expressive function but also necessarily in its operation."[31] With this insistence on Gadamer's term "Wirkung," Jauss provides a grounding for interpretation, if not also a method, and he provides also a rationale for why arresting an interpretation at one level or another goes so profoundly against the grain; it would arrest the Wirkung, and therefore the procedure by which we can meaningfully get through some set of the questions raised by the work "in its variable experience-horizon of a continuity."[32] Given such a grounding, we are in a position freer toward these theories than we would be toward the others, at whatever level, which would implicitly close off further possibility, or even induce the acceptance of a limited and fixed horizon.

Gadamer, indeed, insists on speech as the key to hermeneutic activity at its ontological base, ("Ontologische Wendung der Hermeneutik am Leitfaden der Sprache").[33] We need not choose between jettisoning these approaches, relativizing them, or thoroughly adopting them. Gadamer carries us this far but leaves problems, as would be the case according to his system. And of course the mediating act of his hermeneutics, while based on language, operates at a level well beyond that of the speech act. There are endless philosophical problems that inevitably arise in accounting for one kind of intersubjectivity and another as between text and reader-viewer or interpreter. But these problems can be bracketed; they need not be interposed as irreducible relativizations of either text or interpreter.

The "mobile" text of reception theory and the more conventional "spatialized" text need not be set against one another either. And in either dimension it is possible to define given interpretations as partial but valid; it is possible, in Gadamer's language, to take the radical question-and-answer of the hermeneutic act and specifically on those grounds to declare some answers improper.

It is clear that the incommensurate hierarchies I have offered are themselves some of several possible ones. In other words, they do not constitute a metasystem, as is implied by my reversion to the enabling hermeneutic strictures of Gadamer, Hirsch, Bakhtin, and Ricoeur, to suggest the possibility of some common denominator among such adduced hermeneutic circles. This combination, in turn, is possible without calibrating adjudications among them. A metasystem, if one were available, would have to order as well as to accommodate the various (partial) metasystems I have treated here, for their special currency of explanatory power in current discourse about Shakespeare. My ordering of them is preliminary, and is meant to clarify, as well as occasionally to adjudicate. It is also meant, of course, to aid and enrich interpretation, which will surely continue to provide new and valid points and conjunctions—or "insights," to use a term that has gone out of fashion but is still useful. The term "insight" has the advantage of allowing any demonstrably valid syncretic observation about a play, as well as the disadvantage of seeming to put on the level of random, one-dimensional, merely intuitive reaction any observation. That is—in still another hierarchy—one extreme (either high if one treats insight as the indispensable quick of intelligent comprehension, or low if one treats it as a reflection of blind adherence to culture-bound automatisms). The other extreme for interpretation would be the metasystems or the metacode of metasystems. These cannot be put together, I am convinced, any further than in the stratifications or nodes of such a work as the *Mille Plateaux* of Deleuze and Guattari—a work that offers proliferations of possibilities so richly incommensurate that is has not been adopted for interpreting Shakespeare, at least yet, and that therefore may serve both as a window on the larger possibilities of multiple mediation for discourses and a warning that at a certain complexity of dialectical mediation the (in the case of *Mille Plateaux* radically unsystematic) branching nodes of formulation may offer combinatory assertions too quickly to be commensurately applicable to such a given act of intense discourse as a play by Shakespeare.

Evocations of Feeling in Renaissance Drama:

Music and Religion

T he immediacy of a dramatic effect, that which most fully comprises the "poetry" and "mood" of a play, can be approached by asking about its use of music and its assimilation to religious feeling, since religion, as William James and others have insisted, always involves emotion, and since the presentation of a play, if we adapt Durkheim's distinction between rite and belief, most resembles a rite (which music often accompanies) rather than a set of beliefs. Music is sometimes easier to identify than religious motifs, since the points are distinct where a play rises to an audible expression above, and to some degree beyond, words: the points of music.

However, the music in a play echoes and extends the words of the play. On both counts the music carries significations that relate to the words, and there are many approaches by which we may understand and formulate, or even codify, those significations. Our ideal might be a close musical analysis of the connection of words and music, which is not my aim, and, indeed, also not in my capacity, to provide. Coming at it from the other direction, I will not be offering any full or true analogue of the "episteme" of Foucault, a metacode that would define the relationship of elements in the code.[1] For music, taken by itself, the signifier and the signified in the connections of the notes converge so fully that it would be difficult to extrapolate them in a way that would ground their relationship. As heard in a play, such music asks to be taken globally so far as its sounds are concerned, though its context would often contain some social cueing

115

that would carry signification, like the lute-song played for Mariana or even the court music played for Henry the Fourth and for Orsino. It would not always carry such cueings; the "music under the earth" in *Antony and Cleopatra* does not, nor does the music of the spheres heard by Pericles. This "musica mundana," to use the Latin term, finds echoes in *Twelfth Night* and other places in Shakespeare, as John Hollander has pointed out.[2]

The matching structures of language in the play, the interactions between words and music that might yield to psychological and social analysis, and the presence of long-range, complex and multiform prior institutions like myth and folklore, might be brought to bear on the effect of the music in a play comprehensively, and they are surely relevant to some degree. In the Renaissance itself a fair amount of attention, especially in Italy but to some degree in England, was given to the possibility of coded evocations and correspondences between music and the emotions, in the discussions of the Camerata of Giovanni de'Bardi at Florence, where the validating connection was introduced and elaborated between modern tonal systems and the Greek modes, with their toning to emotional registers. Vincenzo Galilei associated these revived modes with the affections. Girolamo Mei, a guiding spirit of the group, made the connection between these musical practices and poetry, which was of course widely incorporated in madrigals and song settings, monodic and other.[3]

Comparable complications would obtain for the religious responses evoked in a play, though these can of course also be translated into idea-systems, without extensive attention to dramatic interactions, which is the usual approach to them. Religion, and also the questioning of religion, are pervasive in the Renaissance. And the religious effect of the play draws on but is not, cannot be, wholly formulated in terms of the separate doctrines it may refer to or even enunciate. Nor, at the same time, can the signification of a religious effect in a play be wholly collapsed to its analogue in a rite (and still less can the religious effect be wholly dismissed).

Music and religion, I should like to show, have a special force as foci toward accounting for that in a play which centrally arrests the attention, beyond the constituent structures of other sorts that can be adduced to explain it.

A supplement to current approaches, or at least a shift of focus, would be to center on these two overall features of Renaissance plays, their deep access to, and creation of, states of feeling. These nexusses of evocation enter such plays in their frequent and varied access to music, and in their complex access to the religion, which compelled officially and often actually the allegiances of all members of the society.

As for feeling and affectivity generally, its prominent position in the management of verbal structures is attested to by the large space Aristotle gives the reactive management of various feelings in the *Rhetoric*.[4] Adducing these two prominent but elusive features of Shakespeare's plays, their use of music and their attenuated and qualified enlistment of religious effects and values, one could supplement and even move past (but not abandon) a hierarchy of interpretive approaches.

A play produces, along with and through all its significations, an affective impression on the viewer-hearer. One approach to hermeneutic assessment of the play can be made through the most direct effects it presents, the tunes that accompany songs. Melody strikes directly to the auditor, and initially without the mediation of the words of the song. The directness has a haunting effect in its recursions.[5] So the repetitions of the song are heard to work more directly on the emotions than do the tuneless musical repetitions of the verse meters, and still more directly than the looser patterned recursions of the prose passages. The effect of the music of the song comes through powerfully enough, often, to carry along the sense and orientation in the words of the song as well, and to gather those words up in the emotional effect. The realm of the "affective" in art, of course, is one that might properly constitute the subject of a possibly endless philosophical inquiry. But one may bracket such inquiry and take the effect as a given.

Further, one may distinguish in music generally, and then as music enters a play, several levels: First would be *mimicry,* which is found in Ariel's invisible barking and mewing, the most rudimentary, cacophonous and obscure register of her singing. Onomatopoeia in literature corresponds to the lowest mimicry in music, and the sounds uttered (meows, and so on) by Ariel are such. Further sound patterns would correspond to a higher mimicry, as in the striking case where a writer catches not only one kind of person's specific phrases but his specific intonation patterns. Patterned *repetitions* and *leitmotifs* abound in literature, as do the *abstractive correlatives* of rising and falling movement, both locally in phrases and generally in such large constituents as plot structure. The repetitions of music just as it enters a play can itself function like a leitmotif.[6]

Poetry, and literature generally, defines emotional and intellectual sequences by embodying them. And, at a still further level, literature has been shown, more often than music, to exemplify in Hegelian fashion the whole psychological-spiritual state of an epoch.

Less theoretical than these levels are the categories given by F. W. Sternfeld with reference to music in Shakespeare, overlapping somewhat with the significative functions I have hierarchized: 1) "stage music" (as a serenade or a call to battle); 2) "magic music" (a music that brings about an effect; which, for example, puts to sleep or heals); 3) prophetic or mysterious music (the music under the earth in *Antony and Cleopatra* or the music of the spheres in *Pericles*); 4) music that portrays or reveals character, as when Pandarus sings; 5) music expressive of a mood, like melancholy; 6) music that foretells a change of tone.[7] All these uses of music in plays refer to manner, but there also the coded significances of instrumentation, including the voice.

Music in the dramatic context of a play by Shakespeare is rarely just ornamental or confirmatory. Characteristically it opens the action up and concentrates it in a further range of meaning. In *Hamlet* the songs he sings upon the king's bolting from the play-within-a-play constructs its words, and congruently its music, for a philosophical human overview brought into a conjunction with his purposes, a view not elsewhere exhibited in the play:

> Why let the stricken deer go weep,
> The hart ungallèd play.
> For some must watch while some must weep.
> So runs the world away.
>
> (3.2.282–85)

In asking to "let . . . the hart ungallèd play," Hamlet has here succinctly already resolved to "leave her to heaven," as the ghost later enjoins him, since the "hart" must name Gertrude. Setting this new, sadly reconciled thought to the music of a song must strike the spectator-auditor both with the emotion that Hamlet expresses and with the possibility of coordinating it in the sequence of effects of which the character cannot have an overview and the spectator must. Here the fusion for Hamlet is momentary. This fusion is dropped almost at once in the next song he sings in the same meter (3.2.292–95), where he trails back into the typical sportiveness and distraction of this act.

The play's terminal references to music name a religious salvation it is hard to infer from moments of the action. The statement is based on a hope Horatio expresses that he had not previously articulated: "Good night, sweet Prince, / And flights of angels sing thee to thy rest!" (5.2. 370–71). Here "sweet" assimilates Hamlet to an imagined angelic singing in his afterlife. This music, in the nature of things, can only be echoed dimly and roughly in the actual "soldiers' music" ordered by Fortinbras (410).[8]

The songs at the end of *Twelfth Night* ("When that I was and a little tiny boy") and *Love's Labour's Lost* ("When icicles hang by the wall / And Dick the shepherd blows his nail") open these plays into realms mentioned nowhere else in those plays, as do the two songs in *Cymbeline*, "Hark hark the lark," further ironized by its relation to the singer Cloten, and "Fear no more the heat of the sun," sung out of context for both the supposed corpse and the ignorant singers by her unknown brothers over Imogen disguised as a boy. Mariana in *Measure for Measure*, ("Take O take those lips away / That so sweetly are forsworn," 4.1.1–2) not only ironizes her situation, since she is an abandoned lover and does not want taken away the lips that were indeed "forsworn" but not sweetly. At the very moment of singing, she awaits the Duke, whose rearrival breaks off the song, in order to plan a scheme for the tricky reactivation of a marriage contract that belongs to a different order from the courtly languors and rich erotic pathos of the song's world, otherwise nowhere present in this play, although the mood comes close to Mariana's own sterile pathos of abandonment.

More adaptively still, the music in *The Tempest* constantly operates on the sensibilities of those unaware of Prospero's command and Ariel's agency. It is Ferdinand who hears "Full fathom five thy father lies." "Those are pearls that were his eyes" offers an image of a lustrous and quiet death that ill sorts with the life of shift and stress Alonso has led. This does not modify at all the grief of Ferdinand. When Ariel wakes the rulers with music to protect them from a conspiracy against their lives (3.1.295–312), each one hears it differently, though what the audience hears is just plain words of warning set to music. The scheming Sebastian hears "a hollow burst of bellowing / Like bulls, or rather lions"; Alonso hears nothing; the persistently treacherous Antonio calls it "a din to fright a monster's ear, to make an earthquake . . . the roar / of a whole herd of lions." To Gonzalo, oldest and mildest and most hopeful and charitable of the group, it has come through as a "humming." Gonzalo hears, as it were, a musical version of what is unified into harmony but too distant to be separated for signification, an analogue to the Utopia he has sketched in earlier conversation: "Upon mine honour, sir, I heard a humming, / And that a strange one too." The music is there, but for Gonzalo it is heard as a humming in a dream, imperceptible, undecipherable, but distinctly audible, like the "music i' the air" or "under the earth" when the god Hercules leaves Antony (*Antony and Cleopatra*, 4.3.10–16).

Something of this feeling of meanings fused into the Ur-note of a single musical vocable, as though heard beyond a veil, inheres in Pericles' rapt and shattered description of what he supposes to be the drowning of his wife in a storm at sea. His use of the word "humming" keys this alert, resourceful, much-tested hero into something of the prospective peace of Gonzalo: "the belching whale / And humming water must o'erwhelm thy corpse" (*Pericles*, 3.2.63–64).

Music is connected to feeling, of course, and specifically it is connected, but not confined, to Eros. The proposition is set as a rhetorical conditional at the beginning of *Twelfth Night,* "If music be the food of love, play on." This statement is put in the mouth of an Orsino who is listening to music he has commanded; he says this so he may dwell somewhat passively on the consolations of music, and to keep himself from thinking how really he might activate a love relationship. Instead he goes through motions and contents himself with mooning about a love forever unrealized, a love both expressed and endlessly deferred with the aid of just this music. In Lacanian terms Orsino's desire may be classified as "the imaginary" masking as "the symbolic." But the music itself, and the general maxim, escapes these conditions, as with Mariana. Music is "the food of love" at times; this play transcends the maxim, but does not disprove it. Someone who is more interested in the food of "cakes and ale" than in music as the food of love also turns out at the end of the play to have been successfully carrying on a courtship, Sir Toby. Contrastingly, the song that ends this play mentions love only incidentally as a moment in a life series accompanied unvaryingly by "rain," "The rain it raineth every day." This opening music, through long-range anaphora, participates in the meanings rounded out here, and it cannot be confined, in the ears of the audience, to the illusion it is here made to serve.[9] It carries a kind of haunting echo into the play, and provides a ground for the unforeseen coherences and congruences of a true and possible fruition of loves into marriages, this fragment of a melody the first in a large counterpoint of sounds that mainly works through the words of the play, faintly but crucially oriented to what the music expresses and has to be taken as intimating for its very lack of translatable signifiers—that is, of any accompanying words, since no words are given in the text to go with the music Orsino is hearing and referring to explicitly that, as usually assumed, we in the audience are hearing too when the play opens.

II

In addition to the elusive but all-embracing directness of musical intrusions into the play, any or all of these functions for music can be amplified and qualified by some attention to the religious transactions on stage, which also engage the feelings of the characters and hence of the ideal audience. In this dimension of feeling, the religious transactions themselves resist a simple doctrinal coding, whether in their combination with principles of power seen as the motor for a Foucault-style episteme (the divine right of kings) or with the psychosexual manifestations of the characters as they enter into action. For example, Edmund in *King Lear* is a moral-religious being who makes a deathbed confession. He is an illegitimate son whose brutal verbal treatment at his father's hands opens the play. And he is also an aspirant to power combinations (where for our purposes we can see the "Machiavellian" not just as a single system but as a complex of meanings and gestures the "New Historians" influenced by Foucault have helped us to see). Edmund can be seen in various dynamic recombinations of these elements. To such recombinations one could well apply, for example, a Lacanian symbolic matrix. But all such readings would be preliminary in one way, supplementary in another, to the *feeling* that the dying Edmund evidences and displays while lying on the stage before his brother and others. This feeling is dramatic, whereas the fairly simple underlying religious doctrine is a commonplace idea, and the other patterns are contributory codes but not a final one.

The case of Marlowe throws into relief the necessity of attending to the dimension of feeling in the religious representations of Renaissance plays. Even so schematic a playwright as he is offers us the puzzle of some considerable discrepancy between man and writer, and the discrepancy centers on the feeling evoked in an audience when religious questions are in view. There is evidence that the man was a speculative atheist, a brawler, a secret agent, a wastrel, and a murderer. Marlowe's plays, however, in their actual verbal structures, are for all hermeneutic purposes not demonstrable as in any way modified by such data, any more than the *Morte d'Arthur* in its significances is modified by the criminality of Malory. Marlowe is straightforward in this regard, *pace* both the new historians like Stephen Greenblatt and the older Renaissance specialists like Irving Ribner, who seem happy to enlist an antireligious attitude they find sympathetic to plays into which it cannot be read.[10] Taking *Doctor Faustus* for its doctrinal ideas, we should have to disengage them and then recoordinate their fusions in order to assess the intellectual patterns of the play. To do so we would have to account for the actual gathering force of feeling that the play brings into focus around Faustus' damnation, for character and for audience. As it happens, the evidence in Marlowe's biography for his association with atheistic/scientific circles does not modify the strong forward thrust of this play. The last scenes in particular would be completely sapped of their dramatic impact, and also of their meaning, if they were not accorded the primary religious focus, whatever nuances may enter from Marlowe's convictions.[11] So when Faustus wavers after Helen's entrance, as an Old Man urges him to repent, it would entirely falsify the directness of this scene if the audience were attentive to the supposed skepticism governing the character Faustus (a skepticism for which the actual text offers no cues) or to his supposed victimization. The Old Man is indeed quite direct:

> O stay, good Faustus, stay thy desperate steps.
> I see an angel hovers o'er thy head
> And with a vial full of precious grace
> Offers to pour the same into thy soul.
> Then call for mercy and avoid despair.

Faustus' initial response is to yield; and it has no psychological relevance to see this impulse to yield as itself a torment (as we would have to do on the thesis of a sceptical Marlowe at work here):

> Ah, my sweet friend, I feel thy words
> To comfort my distressèd soul.
> Leave me a while to ponder on my sins.

The repentance does not last. At one speech from Mephistophilis, Faustus, threatened with being torn piecemeal, repents that he "e'er offended" Lucifer and turns the Old Man who had exhorted him over to the devils:

> Torment, sweet friend, that base and agèd man
> That durst dissuade me from thy Lucifer,
> With greatest torment that our hell affords.

Helen has just passed over the stage, and the audience, surely, cannot help distancing itself from Faustus' throwing the Old Man to these wolves. It would surely also register astonishment at Faustus' almost instantaneous shift from this grisly exchange to his absorption in the request to "glut the longing of my heart's desire" with "that heavenly Helen." Not to see "heavenly" as a debased currency in this context, and not to register a dramatic irony toward Faustus, would render any coherent interpretation impossible. The skeptical Marlowe may have existed in life; once again, he is no more present in these concluding scenes than a felonious Malory is in the *Morte d'Arthur.*

When Faustus says "Sweet Helen, make me immortal with a kiss," the line strongly crosses the religiosity of the afterlife with a particular tonality of sexuality. The religiosity and the sexuality both interact with received ideas about the figure Helen, as well as with the psychological relations among Faustus' desire for sexual union, desire for knowledge, and aspirations for the afterlife, coordinated here, if momentarily, to something like a Renaissance version of a "Liebestod" feeling. This feeling is original with Marlowe, and in its fusions it already surpasses the more melodramatic Goethe. Faustus' approach to Helen also underscores the stage he has reached—a nearly penultimate one—in the sequence of his degradation before Lucifer. Lest we be misled by the richness of his aspiration toward Helen, the interposed treachery toward the Old Man underscores Faustus' degradation. In this, later (through the time of the play) is worse, and higher becomes lower. These notions are reflected in his last speech, where Christ's blood streams in the firmament and the clock ticks away toward damnation. Indeed, the "mighty line," the force of aspiration dramatized in the play, and all these extensible intensities out of this story—here mythicized for just about the first time—would give credence to reading the play not as simply Christian (and not simply anti-Christian either). Rather, it seems to succeed at harnessing energies that may also have fueled renegade activity but are here used to infuse with religious feeling an early version of Spengler's reading of the story itself as a key one for the whole culture of the West, for "Faustian" culture from the Middle Ages on.

Here, as nowhere in Shakespeare's work, the doctrinal stands for the main thrust of the play, and the sense of Faustian aspiration runs subliminally through doctrine and against it.

In Shakespeare, again, the doctrinal is itself subliminal and operative as a feeling-tone in the play. The mix of feelings evoked in a play of Shakespeare's not only includes religious feelings but tends to rise toward them by the fifth act. The sense of reconciliation has a religious tone even in a play like *Antony and Cleopatra,* where the values are so predominantly erotic in their juxtaposition to the political-ambitious that the religious tonality is confined to the extravagance of the vision of missed reconciliation between the lovers. It is felt not only in the language but even in the final desperation of the sociopsychic complex that remains unreconciled in *Othello.* Indeed, the feeling of wonder and adventure that accompanies the women traveling in disguise—a motif to be found in *Twelfth Night, All's Well That Ends Well,* and *As You Like It* among others—carries not only an underlying pattern whose closest equivalents are the medieval lives of saints but a feeling of freshness that has a tinge of religious hope about it, above and beyond the erotic purpose behind such voyages, and also beyond the dark shadows of the rough social sanctions invoked at the time against those (especially commoners) who transgress or obfuscate the marked differences between the sexes. Tragedies by Shakespeare—as against those of Webster, Tourneur, and Ford—are rarely shrouded in full gloom as they come to an end. They tend to crest into aphorisms like "Ripeness is all," "The readiness is all," "I have a journey, sir, shortly to go," "Absent thee from felicity a while," and the like. I have been quoting, of course, from *Hamlet* and *King Lear,* dark plays through which the evoked feelings bring a touch of religious light that modifies, without wholly reconciling, the overpowering depressiveness.

A Christian tone of something like reconciliation is achieved in Shakespeare's plays, characteristically, and with a characteristic particularity in each play. The resultant mood is a wry one in *Measure for Measure.* In *Cymbeline* it rises suddenly into full accommodation ("Pardon's the word for all"). The mood is stern in *All's Well That Ends Well;* celebratory in *A Winter's Tale;* relieved in *Pericles;* conciliatorily purgatorial in *The Tempest.* In *As You Like It,* insofar as the play's action operates to bypass both good and evil noblemen through a clever courtship series, the mood is reductive.

But, of course, we could return this particular pietized dimension of feeling, and also the realm-opening dimension of music, from the "direct" transaction through the course of a play—for another round, so to speak—back to all the levels of structure with which the strategies of hermeneutic interpretation, incommensurate though they may be in their hierarchies of level, are well calculated to deal. And then we should return to the play to see what its registrations of feeling mean, with respect to music and religion, and also in other ways. So do the presentational directness and the verbal indirections of these plays feed back to each other and "by indirections find directions out."

"What time th'eternall Lord in fleshly slime/Enwombed was":

Christian Elements in the Action of *Cymbeline*

The recent "New Historians" have gained considerable purchase on interpreting the Renaissance when they apply Foucault's modified but still totalized matrices of coherence for a governing cultural "episteme" to forms of discourse within Renaissance society. Their intrication of codes and represented interactions, in both society and drama, claims that a code of codes always obtains, but actually a given represented existence in Shakespeare may call us back at every turn from assuming of any code or system that it can be characterized in the play's inscriptions by any simple presence or absence of code or system. Rather, a dialectic takes place constantly, and intermodifications abound, many of them provided by a Shakespeare who may also at times wholly draw on the episteme without being totally bound by it, since an original combination can be produced from individual elements that are wholly coded, if taken separately or even if taken together in a different pattern.[1]

In particular, the indirectness and mutedness of Christian tonality, and indeed of the hidden situation in *Cymbeline,* which is set in the same political world and at the same time as the birth of Christ, should not put us off from assessing the pervasiveness, and even the comprehensiveness, of a coordinated Christian vision in the play.[2] It raises, rather, the question of the progression of modes Shakespeare uses to get a religious bearing into a play's statement. The problem of comprehensiveness bears with special force on a code, Christianity in its various forms and emphases, that was regarded in the Renaissance as a code of codes, even if it was subjected at times to the dialectic of questioning.

Although the historical template or episteme governing the relation between a king and the forces around him is manipulated with some consistency in Shakespeare's work, the religious premise is progressively attenuated and sublimated. And at the same time, a temper of what amounts to natural religiosity, especially consistent as it draws on ideals of family feeling, is being centralized, more and more pronouncedly. The move from England in the two tetralogies to Rome or Denmark does not alter the explicitly demonstrated interactions in the public arena, nor does the movement back to early England in *King Lear* and to family within the state from that point onward. The figure of the ruler who is sensitive but withdrawn from power is found at the beginning of Shakespeare's career in Henry VI, and at the end in Prospero. Cymbeline suggests the type, though he also exercises power capriciously like Richard II—until the last scene.

The displacement of Christian concerns, faint in *The Tempest,* as Prospero works through supernatural beings and the classical gods, finds no corresponding displacement in the classical or pre-Christian loci, the Rome of Caesar and Augustus or Lear's England of 800 B.C. These exhibit the forces of power that are in definable respects subject to the same episteme as *Richard II* and *Henry V*—or the Henry VI-Richard III tetralogy and *The Tempest.* But Henry VI functions in an explicit Christian piety that gets modified as Shakespeare goes along. All the way to *The Tempest,* political forces remain much the same, but by that time religion has both gone underground and become pervasive in the "romance" temper. Its functions for Prospero arise subliminally and also shockingly from the austerity of his plans to bring contrition and purgation upon political enemies who are also relatives, as well as to bring fruition to his daughter—a fruition that includes and comprises a displaced political restitution for him. When the classical gods enter, Prospero summons them as an illusion through Ariel, and as a "corollary" (!) (4.1.57). The Juno, Ceres, Iris, and Nymphs of the masque-within-the-play are still more attenuated in the ontology of their illusion and allegory than the Jupiter of *Cymbeline,* while being much simpler. Looked at in the light not of what Shakespeare's personal pattern or derivation of affiliations might have been through the theologically vexed period of his upbringing, but rather of how Christianity functions in his plays, and especially in *Cymbeline,* the Christian codes, if examined in a similar dialectical fashion, would exhibit a sort of openness that refuses to submit its finality to other congruences or deep structures.

The episteme of power, it can be seen, remains the same throughout Shakespeare's career; the religious presence is progressively invested in the action while being buried progressively deeper. *Hamlet* presents a puzzle of the relations among consciousness, sin, and hegemony. At the same time Hamlet, taken just for the assumptions he is shown to exhibit, operates under some explicitly stated theological constraints, as do all the characters in that play. He refers to Christian doctrine from his first confrontation with the ghost to his "fall of the sparrow" speech and beyond.[3] The philosophy student of Wittenberg is most apparent in him when he invokes technical theological points about the status of the ghost (2.2.594–600) or the consequences bearing on the soul at the moment of death (3.3.73–95). In this theological language, indeed, Claudius matches him at once by reversing the speculation, "Words without thoughts never to heaven go." (3.3.97). The "flights of angels" that are to conduct Hamlet "to his rest" announce his salvation in spite of the acts for which some question might be raised in a canon law to which he himself makes reference when abjuring suicide. Further, Roland Frye points out, madness excuses the suicide from damnation in most if not all of the theological discussion of the time.[4] So that the priest who dictates "maimed rites" for Ophelia's body is following a popular, mistaken tradition that is overridden not only by the sentiments of the beholder but also by what turns out to be the play's accurate sense of contemporary theological discussion on the question.

Measure for Measure, with its casuistical straining of the permissible, measures an actual set of manipulated events against a nightmarish law where the state's codes are made absolutely congruent with canon law and the mortal sin of fornication is punished by death.[5] *Cymbeline* can be seen as in some ways an inverse of that comedy. Instead of an absent but active ruler it has a present but seemingly ineffective one who nevertheless manages effectively a large-scale war, oppressing an exiled husband instead of a condemned fiancé. At the end Cymbeline is able, thanks to the constant capacity of his family and subjects, under sudden revelation, to manage prodigies of charitable justice, where in *Measure for Measure* the absent Duke charitably spreads keen interventions throughout the action while his surrogate Angelo acts oppressively.

King Lear works from preclassical gods like "Nature" into a series of Christian-like definitions. The scenes of deathbed forgiveness, a dramatic stand-in for simple conversion, have a distinctly Christian coloring in *King Lear* as well as in *Hamlet*. And *King Lear* itself can be read as an elaboration of ultimately Christian virtues under the most trying and unfavorable conditions.[6] There is something akin to the iconography of Dante's Earthly Paradise in the field of flowers where Lear walks with Cordelia. Of course, his statement to her as he is waking identifies the place where she stands as paradise, whereas in a new deep humility he defines his own sufferings as deserved punishments in the afterlife:

> Thou art a soul in bliss; but I am bound
> Upon a wheel of fire that mine own tears
> Do scald like molten lead.

> (4.7.45–47)

Still more sublimated is the religiosity in *Cymbeline,* where every single main character, except the noble-savage princes, has sinned in some way, but most of them, even Iachimo, have elements that provide a base for their redemption. At the virtuous end of the spectrum, even Posthumus has enough male pride and conviviality[7] to trap himself in the rash bet about Imogen's virtue, to renounce women and plan to murder her on the mere false report of her betrayal. Shakespeare here chose to display persons animated in their best moments by a sort of natural Christian impulse. These *animae naturaliter Christianae* are at the same time burdened extraordinarily with blindness and a propensity for sin. Even Imogen, with her strong motive for anger, has misconstrued the circumstances of Posthumus' order that she be killed; she forgets her correct interpretation of Iachimo's slander on his fidelity (1.7.66–138; 3.6.12–76). The fierce reaction, in both of them, evidences the depth of their love for one another. Their trigger-happy responses perhaps also derive from his orphaning and her semi-orphaning, but also from a human fallibility. It is, in fact, very much like the fallibility under which they all suffer, that of her father. Cymbeline acts decisively on wrong assumptions because of love for his deceptive queen, a figure who combines the wicked stepmother of fairy tale with the Lucretia Borgia–like manipulation of court politics. Yet he acquits himself much better than they do when he perceives his rejection, though Posthumus rises to an emphatic charity in his forgiveness of Iachimo (5.5.418–21). Yet again, Cymbeline takes his cue from this, "We'll learn our freeness of a son-in-law" (421). Like Posthumus, Imogen, and Cymbeline, the virtuous Belarius, too, has impulsively done an act of injustice a generation earlier, by kidnapping the princes in return for a misconstruction (as he claims) of his acts:

> My fault being nothing (as I have told you oft)
> But that two villains, whose false oaths prevail'd
> Before my perfect honor, swore to Cymbeline
> I was confederate with the Romans: so
> Followed my banishment

> (3.3.65–68)

The plot sequence in *Cymbeline* does not derive from the sources, and so it can be taken even more directly as an expression revelatory of Shakespeare's abstract concerns. In one aspect it poses problems akin to those of the Roman plays, but it is unique for being still more general in its scope than they. *Julius Caesar*, seen in the light of nine preceding plays that treat problematic points in British history, removes the political considerations still holding sway over the world Shakespeare lived in to a model empire larger than Britain, and one where neither Christianity nor the divine right of kings, and no direct tradition of succession, can complicate the politics. *Antony and Cleopatra* links with *Julius Caesar* almost as closely as the individual British tetralogy plays do to each other. It expands the ideal empire to its extreme, which is also its opposite, and it also introduces and juxtaposes an extreme countervailing force, the love between Antony and Cleopatra. *Coriolanus* tests the psychic substructure that will produce the Livian ideal of courage as one that will work fatally against the other Livian ideal of governance, and it does so at the early point in Livy (496 B.C.) that Plutarch spatializes into types, paralleling Coriolanus with the Alcibiades who is not mentioned in this play. The role Shakespeare gives Alcibiades in *Timon of Athens* has quite a different contour, even if there is an echo or two of Coriolanus' attitude.

In *Cymbeline* Britain and Rome are brought into massive if short-lived military conflict. The Rome that Cymbeline faces is substantially Rome at the height of the imperial ideal represented by *Antony and Cleopatra*. This Rome, in fact, is still ruled by the same Augustus; he is at a later stage of his life, and so may be thought of as here having ripened into the Pax Augusta. Here too the imperial ideal is inverted not by an exaltation of earthly love but by a quiet presence of heavenly love. Whereas in *King Lear*, the other play set in early Britain, the political situation extrapolates from the familial one, in *Cymbeline* the family situation only impedes and complicates, but then helps to resolve, a political situation that is on too large a scale simply to reflect the reverberations of family. The situation is most analogous to the one in the first of Shakespeare's Roman plays, *Titus Andronicus*, where the very late empire is so impacted that the actions of Tamora can only harry the family of the emperor.

The other Roman plays follow upon British historical plays. And in *King Lear* Britain is brought once again back into the historical picture. In *Cymbeline* it is brought back still more firmly, and juxtaposed to Rome on a nearly worldwide canvas that still retains a rudimentary local, and often rural, character. This king, blinded and circumscribed by his devotion to the queen, does govern, and governs effectively. He does so with the decisiveness and, surprisingly, with the cruelty of the Octavius of *Antony and Cleopatra*.

The pointed diplomacy that is exemplified in *Antony and Cleopatra,* as it appears in the loaded exchanges between Antony and Octavius especially, had been refined through nine history plays and in the public dimension of such plays as *Julius Caesar* and *Coriolanus.* In *Cymbeline* this high diplomatic capability has been further refined into an exquisite courtesy that exudes proportion and considerateness even as war is being prepared and tribute refused. The decisiveness and patriotic self-confidence here transmitted are quite beyond the comparable scenes in *Henry V,* for example.

It was through Rome, of course, that Britain became Christian. Instead of choosing some moment of conversion (and some of these historical moments would have been available in his sources), Shakespeare combines sources to range through a wider extent of the known world than anywhere else. Here he brings together the Roman Empire at the time of Christ's birth and the early England he had already used in *King Lear,* to work toward Christian purgations that are the more remote and mysterious in this romance-like play because at no point till the king's "Pardon's the word for all" (5.5.420) can anyone, including the spectator, compass the action in order to meet it with some plausible version of a fully adequate policy. The Christian coloring in this, Shakespeare's most consistently charitable play, works through subliminal analogue to the tremendous birth at the other side of the empire (referred to here only by the Near Eastern military actions that come up glancingly in the summary).[8] In keeping with the note of remoteness, the playwright has access to no explicit references and no other Christian presence than surprisingly Christian actions defined by a Christian or quasi-Christian vocabulary. These charitable actions, especially surprising in the public arena, culminate in Cymbeline's unprecedented final gesture of granting tribute to the prisoner Romans, the very tribute he has fought them and won to keep from paying. This farsighted gesture, which perhaps derives from Holinshed's attribution to him of a desire not to break with Rome, is not at all mentioned by Holinshed or Spenser. It is capped by a public co-national worship on the altar of the Roman god, a distancing into the classical and virtual religion (as it would have to be, since Christ is alive but Christianity is not yet) in terms that suggest a Christian rather than a Roman atmosphere to the definition:

> Laud we the gods,
> And let our crooked smokes climb to their nostrils
> From our best altars. Publish we this peace
> To all our subjects. Set we forward: let
> A Roman, and a British ensign wave
> Friendly together: so through Lud's town march,

And in the temple of great Jupiter
Our peace we'll ratify: seal it with feasts.
Set on there! Never was a war did cease
(Ere bloody hands were wash'd) with such a peace.

(5.5.477–86)

The antithesis between the contrasted adjectives "crooked" and "blest"
could be made to reflect that between the intricate action of the play and
the mood of the final resolution, as though it had been written to illustrate
the maxim of Saint Augustine, "God writes straight in crooked lines."
Cymbeline's repetition in terminal position of the word "peace" estab-
lishes this tone of blessing. His defensible claim that this peace is unparalleled likewise illustrates both charitable restraint and prudence. It
perpetuates the tone of blessing into a future of mysterious accord with
the civilizing empire, rather than instancing a final subservience or odd-
ness.

This final act of public worship is unique among the plays of Shakespeare. Yet the Christian presence in it is purely subliminal, a mere residue
of the spate of charitable actions fading away into the prospect of a pagan
sacrifice.

Cymbeline is framed with narratives, from the curiously polite and
merely narrative opening by two gentlemen who never reappear to the
succinct rapid-fire dramatic resolutions punctuated by narrative recapitula-
tions of the end. Narrative eases, displaces, and allows for charity, just as
compounded error in the nearly virtuous calls by implication for the solution of grace. Shakespeare wholly invents this conclusion, shaping it on
the rapidly coping spirit of Cymbeline—and invents the rest in the un-
precedentedly complicated combination of the various sources.[9]

II

Until the rapid-fire revelations and testings at the end, then, the play
proceeds and the action is furthered, with characters who live and suffer
under a partial mystery. The contributing partial mysteries lie under the
figure of a total mystery for which the temporal correlation with the birth
of Christ is not so much a solution as a correspondence kept so ineffable
that it cannot be classified under any ordering episteme. We can trace this
ineffability, for example, to the play's music. In the sounds of the play,
which is composed of significant sounds uttered by people on stage, the
pitch of significance, as often in Shakespeare, inheres in the addition of a
free-floating music. Here the music for itself invokes a mood, but for the

action, again as often in Shakespeare, it does not express its mood directly, but rather counterpoints against it.

Whether or not Belarius's "ingenious instrument" (4.2.185) is an Aeolian harp, it has to be set up to play, and it will signal, we shortly learn, the "death" of the drugged Imogen. When we hear the music, however, it must strike us as randomly as it strikes Belarius: "Hark, Polydore, it sounds: but what occasion / Hath Cadwal now to give it motion? Hark!" Music is always a revelation in Shakespeare's plays, and never more so when it is presented without the accompaniment of signifying words, when the sound can reach the audience directly without further mediation and therefore as a reverberation of nothing more than the mood of a sudden, often miraculous and strange, eruption into sound of what is happening in the action.

Shortly, though, these listeners will be singing actual words over Imogen. A religious after-feeling is the effect of "Fear no more the heat o' th' sun." The dense ironies surrounding this song, which I have elsewhere analyzed,[10] operate to displace their rich and equanimous poetry away from the action. The action is felt, however, to be mysteriously governed by a comparably subliminal tone and rhythm. The blindman's buff that the characters, good and bad, go through is finally, if hesitantly, won through their spiritual instinct. Something in them, through what we see and hear on stage, is set proleptically to invoke these songs, but the characters cannot fully participate in what the songs define. Cloten cannot participate at all. He is excluded, for all his critical acumen about the song he sings, by the death he brings upon himself by plotting the sadistic murder of Imogen. He is prevented, and the situation is further obviated and eased through all the confusion at that point in the play, by the mood of acceptance that overarches the play, and at a particular stressful moment in the actual song Imogen's unknown and unknowing brothers bring to her funeral:

> Fear no more the heat o' th' sun,
> Nor the furious winter's rages,
> Thou thy worldly task has done,
> Home art gone and ta'en thy wages.
> Golden lads and girls all must,
> As Chimney-sweepers, come to dust.

The highly wrought song takes over, though it must be as impenetrable to them as this action is. They have learned the words, but where would they who live in the wilderness learn a context for "Golden lads and girls," or for "chimney-sweepers" when they live in a cave? To say nothing of "wages," a metaphor usually applied to sin but here applied to what amounts to salvation. The next uses of "dust" in the refrains will quickly get beyond the black powdery substance that chimney sweepers deal with. In this play, as it miraculously happens—a devastating war is under way— the only characters who "come to dust" are the evil ones, the Queen and Cloten. Even the deaths in the play, then, do not jibe with the benign note about death in this song. And the good characters, as it turns out, will not have to die to "Fear no more the frown o' th' great, / Thou art past the tyrant's stroke." The word "dust" is used only once in this play outside the four occurrences in this song, and then in Imogen's visionary declaration of human equality: To Arviragus' "Are we not brothers?"—when he thinks her a man and no blood kin—she replies "So man and man should be; / But clay and clay differs in dignity, / Whose dust is both alike." (4.2.3–5). Since this exchange comes in the very same scene when her "corpse"[11] is brought in, the word may be heard as calling up the declarations, as well as the mood of the song.

Cloten, who hovers here, sings the one other song in the play, and it enunciates not a weariness and resignation under the "heat o' th' sun" but rather a quickness and delight at a dawn he cannot participate in—he has been up much of the night—nor appreciate other than aesthetically:

> Hark, hark! the lark at heaven's gate sings,
> And Phoebus 'gins arise,
> His steeds to water at those springs
> On chalic'd flow'rs that lies;
>
> (2.3.19–23)

The play is to know only by anticipation or memory, and even at the end, so keen a delight as this song sounds into the play, brightening its mystery in spite of the benighted singer.

When Imogen wakes from being drugged, she thinks she has been dreaming. The sight of Cloten's body in Posthumus' clothes works on her both to purge her of resentment against Posthumus and to put her mercifully to sleep again (4.2.292 ff.). Waked by the Romans, she is restored enough to serve them courageously and duplicitously in a way that will bring her back to Posthumus and to her father. Thus the "dream" of Imogen is juxtaposed to the later mysterious prophecy, and serves the same end, as against the pure illusion of the non-Christian and Celtic eastward-facing "burial" Imogen undergoes (4.2.255) when her brothers sing the song that blends Christian overtones with pagan resignation.

As for the prophecy itself, the tablet of 5.4.109, 138–45 is "real," since it moves miraculously out from the dream of Posthumus to his breast on stage, to be picked up and read. As true in its prediction of the future as the Soothsayer's oracles are, and also as Apollo's oracle in *The Winter's Tale,* it more powerfully initiates an endless regress between make-believe and real, as the masque tradition, which provides the dramatic circumstances of the communication, virtually never does. Jupiter might be "all powerful" in antiquity, but even there he does not reach documents down Mormon-style from the cloud of a dream. Jupiter is a virtualized stand-in for the God in whom Shakespeare's contemporaries, and presumably Shakespeare himself, believed. The displacement from the Christian god to the pagan one, who would have to be allegorized or analogized to be assimilated, reverses the endless regress; the direction is no longer (dream) play-within-a play to real (in the play) but from real god to confected god.[12]

Ironies here operate on the long distance in space (from Rome to England) and in time (at the outside, from one generation to another). For the rule they seal the king off in the dramatic irony that he does not perceive—as we do not on her first appearance perceive the deeply evil fraud of the queen, until Imogen informs us:

O
Dissembling courtesy! How fine this tyrant
Can tickle where she wounds!

(1.2.14–16)

Imogen's outburst, which must surprise the audience this early, and which breaks the tone of courtesy that in fact does dominate the play, correctly identifies an intent that will keep unfolding to control the action, its last strokes not revealed till after the death of the queen. The ironies will the more forcefully converge at the news of her death. This, indeed, is followed by news of which we were as ignorant as the king (5.5). Neither Cymbeline nor we knew that she was planning to poison the king slowly while sweet-talking him to the success of Cloten. Here, as especially at the beginning, narrative serves as both a clarifying and a distancing agent, as in this complexity and big public confrontation there is no way of planning for and controling a situation; grace takes over, or, temporarily, uncoordinated narrative, isolating the persons into the necessity of charitable gestures.

The effect here finally, and in fact throughout, is one of evenness, remoteness, deep peace, and, because outcomes and plausibilities remain hidden from the characters, of a deep holding-back that can be taken as looking forward. The resolution is so full that it cannot be derived from the imposition of an episteme. The Christianity works not systematically, as in other plays, including the history plays, but itself as an effusion out of gestures in the face of the impenetrable, on the part of characters who have mainly their dispositions alone to go on.[13] The constant enlistment of mysteries in this plot toward character-purgation, in such a way as to defuse the merely melodramatic surprise element in the conclusion, differentiates this, and the other late plays, from flat romance.

III

As for event, so for character. Motivation is relegated to the mystery of unfathomability or to general human fallibility even in the best, Imogen and Posthumus. Their fallibility, indeed, serves as a ladder for the audience to reach the deeper contradiction in Cymbeline himself between blind arbitrariness, dotage (tempered by diplomatic adequacy) throughout, and the strong charitable series of the end. Inexplicability dominates everyone but Cloten. He is cordoned off in stupid and tantrum-prone dependence on a mother who has rendered him so by making all his decisions for him. For her too perhaps, the long absence of his father has confirmed her in her duplicitous scheming ("married his place," 5.5.5). At some prior point she has invested all her emotion in the son rather than in her husband, and her distortion of a proper familial pattern, as often in the late plays, induces her to an uncharitableness that shades into darker and darker evil. Imogen and Posthumus, raised together as orphans, resemble the lovers in Shakespeare's comedies, except that there has been no complexity or difficulty in arriving at their union—which makes them the most supremely harmonious couple in all the plays, with the possible exception of Ferdinand and Miranda. And Miranda is willing to defer to her father in ways that Imogen, against the convention of the dutiful daughter, is not. The psychic substructure of orphaning shows up only in their propensity to mistrust, a reaction that betrays a fear of further abandonment, and a fear seemingly (but, through a sort of providence, not actually) justified in these circumstances.

But Cymbeline is a middle-aged lover who dotes as much as Antony does, and he is already well on his way—the over-calculating Queen has no need to poison him!—toward carrying out with Cloten what was Antony's project with Caesarion, of setting the child of his beloved by an earlier union on the throne. Cymbeline's "dotage" (Menenius of Antony, 1.1.1) is never named or other than exemplified, although it is arguably more extreme, and has lasted far longer. It is taken for granted and given none of the play of erotic preoccupation and fullness of expression shown in the earlier play. But it goes all one way; the queen does not share it. Such exuberances and fondnesses are here reserved for Imogen and Posthumus.[14]

Imogen is providentially preserved from the fate of Philomel and Tereus, a tale she has been reading, though her situation dangerously resembles that of Lavinia in *Titus Andronicus,* who has had Philomel's fate forced upon her. Imogen continues in this charmed preservation from harm. The attempt to poison her elaborately misfires. As she wanders toward Milford Haven in male disguise, she need fear encounter with no Goths, and not even with an Autolycus; the very beggars exhibit charity: "Two beggars told me / I could not miss my way" (3.6.8–9). The free acceptance and fellowship she receives as "Fidele" in the company of Guiderius and Arviragus plays between their natural charity and their instinctual response to the presence of an unknown sibling who exhibits some of the charm of a sister without seeming to be one. Even Cloten, strangely and uncharacteristically as he goes on his way to carry out the project of raping Imogen, apologizes for the indecency of his puns ("saving reverence of the word," 4.1.5), touching the tonic note of the play.

Iachimo imposes more heavily, and with a "motiveless malignity" far closer to zero than does Iago's hostility to Othello. Iago steals into no bedroom and spies upon no naked wife to bring back the "mole cinque-spotted" under Imogen's breast.[15] Yet Iachimo repents, as Iago does not, and repents in the process of wandering alone on the battlefield, without the benefit of the sort of shaming confrontation to which Bertram is subject in *All's Well That Ends Well* or Angelo in *Measure for Measure.* Even at the very moment when he is trying to deceive Imogen by feigning a necessity for storage space in her bedroom, he imagines—or else describes; we have no way of knowing—a collective expenditure between a Briton and Romans for a gift to the emperor, which structurally mimes in miniature Cymbeline's final free declaration of tribute:

> Some dozen Romans of us, and your lord
> (The best feather of our wing) have mingled sums
> To buy a present for the emperor:
>
> (1.8.185–87)

Cymbeline is neither Antony nor Coriolanus, and he goes through the Lear-like purgation of his imperceptivity in a few terrible bolts of realization. To these he is so fully equal that he betrays no structure of rage or faltering in assimilating them. He does not go through Lear's long cycle of over-assumption, disappointment, rage, madness, and deep resignation. In the extraordinary courtesy of such public acts that are not within the sphere of the Queen, Cymbeline has already demonstrated that he is quite capable of a full and humble, a Christian, self-integration. Though again, how such deep spiritual capacity can coexist with imperceptivity, and even an over-readiness to cruelty, remains a mystery in the domain of character that is paralleled by the unprecedented mystery in the action, by no means wholly, or even mainly, to be ascribed to the romance constituents with which it began. And Shakespeare, if all the sources hold, has confected more complexity from more diverse bits here than in any other play.[16]

Imogen asks pardon of the gods for the harmless and necessary lie to Lucius (4.2.375–76). Posthumus, under stress, theologizes about the love that may be evidenced by the gods in their invoking or postponing a sinner's death:

> Gods, if you
> Should have ta'en vengeance on my faults, I never
> Had liv'd to put on this: so you had saved
> The noble Imogen, to repent, and struck
> Me, wretch, more worth your vengeance. But alack,
> You snatch some hence for little faults; that's love,
> To have them fall no more: you some permit
> To second ills with ills, each elder worse,
> And make them dread it, to the doers' thrift.
> But Imogen is your own, do your best wills
> And make me blest to obey.
>
> (5.1.7–17)

His injunction to obedience caps a lucid series that may hold but happens to be off the mark of the circumstances he is in, given his ignorance. The disproportion between his pious lucidity and his lack of information sets the tone for the play's demonstration of a necessity to abide the workings of providence in a world that has not yet had the term revealed to it. In a little while Posthumus will be proving his steadfastness in this humble posture by forgiving a Lord who ran away from battle, a circumstance that is again unparalleled elsewhere in Shakespeare's battle scenes:

> *Lord* Cam'st thou from where they made the stand? *Posthumus* I did.
> Though you it seems come from the fliers. *Lord* I did.
> *Posthumus* No blame to be you, sir, for all was lost,
> But that the heavens fought.
>
> (5.3.1–4)

And later in the same scene when the Lord says "Nay, be not angry sir," Posthumus replies, "'Lack, to what end?" (59). The Gaoler who guards Posthumus before his supposed execution in the next scene has a kindly

religious conversation with him and speaks of the Last Judgment in the
neutral terms of an "after-inquiry" (5.4.184), as befits the Roman masking
of these charitable evolutions.[17] In his final prose soliloquy, he wishes not
only that this enemy (as he thinks Posthumus to be) but all men escape the
gallows, in a brief Utopian vision that he would invoke even if it would
throw him out of work: "I would we were all of one mind, and one mind
good: O, there were desolation of gaolers and gallowses! I speak against
my present profit, but my wish hath a preferment in 't" (204–8).

Of course, it is the last scene that provides the spectacular palaestra for
charities. Under the stage figure of what were themselves regarded in the
Renaissance as at best latently Christian allegories—the classical gods—
Shakespeare invents the miraculous delivery of truth about the future. In
The Winter's Tale the classical oracle delivers a truth about the past. In
Cymbeline the message from Jupiter that is miraculously handed down
from dream to (stage) reality contains a truth about the future that is then
set up to validate and define the capital interactions of the last scene.[18]
This takes place under the shadow of that prediction, turned from the
intricacy of the future's unfolding into the stiffness and Nostradamus-like
indirectness of the prediction.

The scene opens with Cymbeline's expression of regret at the absence
of the soldier whom we know to be Posthumus:

> Woe is my heart,
> That the poor soldier that so richly fought,
> Whose rags sham'd gilded arms, whose naked breast
> Stepp'd before targes of proof, cannot be found.
>
> (5.5.2–5)

The king's heartfelt regret and promise frames itself over a quasi-scriptural
setting of poor against rich. An openness and attentiveness we have not
been shown in this king sets the tone for his assimilation of what the play
has shown us would be news as bad as any he could get, that "the queen is
dead" by a horrible death, and further that "she never lov'd you . . .ab-
horred your person" (28–35). His immediate response exhibits a charitable equanimity absent from his personal actions and present only in his
public ones, the clue that from here to the end the new tone will bring
personal and public into a convergence. His clear strength does not prevent him from characterizing her, passingly, as a "most delicate fiend"
(47), even before he learns that she had planned to kill him by slowly
poisoning him. To this, once more, he responds by a rising summation
and extenuation:

                              Mine eyes
        Were not in fault, for she was beautiful:
        Mine ears that heard her flattery, nor my heart
        That thought her like her seeming. It had been vicious
        To have mistrusted her; yet O my daughter,
        That it was folly in me, thou mayst say,
        And prove it in thy feeling. Heaven mend all!

                                                    (5.5.62–68)

The reply to this invocation is—as though to answer his prayer and summon the daughter for more than a just anger about her mistreatment—the
entrance of Imogen, together with the defeated Roman general she has
been serving in disguise, the Iachimo whom we know to repent deeply of
his deceit to Posthumus about Imogen's virtue, the Soothsayer, other
Romans, and the disguised Posthumus himself, the very soldier Cymbeline
has called for. Nearly all are now present whom Cymbeline's instantly
charitable response to his bad news has shown him capable of sorting into
place.

        His next act, as though displacing his new hostility to the dead queen,
is to declare that the Roman captives will be killed for the dead Britons,

                        whose kinsmen have made suit
        That their good souls may be appeas'd with slaughter
        Of you their captives, which ourself have granted:
        So think of your estate."

                                                    (71–74)

This declaration of a military decision, which itself is within the bounds of
rude martial justice, is couched in the language of courtesy and even
religion, especially since it concludes with a Christian-like injunction from
one non-Christian to another; they are invited to prepare more pro-
pitiously for death than did the queen who, it has just been said, "despair-
ing died" (61). In response to this death sentence, an appeal is mounted by
Lucius that Imogen-Fidele be spared.[19] The death sentence will melt grad-
ually in the atmosphere of charity, but immediately Cymbeline grants
Fidele the boon, which is not, as Lucius expects, that he be spared but that
Iachimo say where he got the ring she cannot know he has tricked from
Posthumus back in Rome as payment for the bet about her susceptibility
to adultery—a situation, of course, that itself has brought all three of them
to this point in place and time; and so the purgation of Iachimo and the
reunion of Posthumus and Imogen will result from the most unpromising,
but providentially apt, circumstances (rather than just from the romance
plot of wanderings and surprises). Iachimo declares no Iago-like

bitterness—we have already seen his penitence—but a gratitude that he is given this opportunity for public confession. He then tells the story at some length (132–207)—a story we already know, since the first three acts of the play were mainly occupied with laying it out. And especially in the rapid-fire complexities of this windup, we must take such protracted retelling not for its informational relevance but for its action upon all those present, including the speaker.

That action, I have been saying, is remarkably uniform for purging toward charitable responses, and especially by contrast with the preceding action. This is true even of the immediately following sequence, in which Posthumus, interrupted by the disguised Imogen in the curse he vents on the head of the repentant Iachimo (itself a just purgation for Iachimo) strikes her, a blow that knocks her down at the moment and then power-fully affects and realigns him: "How comes these staggers on me?" (233). His answer will come soon; but it is the king who, at Pisanio's one word "my mistress," perceives and reacts to the correct information, "If this be so, the gods do mean to strike me / To death with mortal joy." (234–35). Waking, she shakes out of hostility not to Posthumus but to Pisanio, whose earlier action she misunderstood, and again the king aligns the action toward reconciliation by identifying her voice, "The tune of Im-ogen" (238). Hearing the true explanation about the drug Pisanio gave her brings her round to so full a sense of herself that she can turn back to the silent Posthumus, whose last act was to strike her, and can joke with him about her disguise: "Why did you throw your wedded lady from you? / Think that you are upon a rock, and now / Throw me again." (261–63). She knows, of course, that it was an interrupting page and not a now restored wife that he struck; and so the banter would include the last, puzzling statement. So her embrace wordlessly says, and the silent Posthumus now speaks again to validate the point of union to which they have returned, as though forever: "Hang there like fruit, my soul, / Till the tree die" (263–64). But there is more to do, and she dutifully kneels to a father who has so unfairly oppressed her that doing so amounts to an act of forgiveness as well as charitable and pious submission.

The account of the death of Cloten, which the king himself respon-sibly seeks out, has the serendipitous by-product of restoring to him the sons he had thought he lost and the counselor from an earlier generation he can now both honor for their recent military role and exonerate. And further, through the delineation of his own joy in terms that meta-phorically assert a transcendence of his very sex, he can carry out the just (but also merciful) act of restoring them to their inherited authority, which he sees as bringing regret to Imogen, and so to him about her:

O, what am I?
A mother to the birth of three? Ne'er mother
Rejoic'd deliverance more. Blest pray you be,
That, after this strange starting from your orbs,
You may reign in them now! O Imogen,
Thou hast lost by this a kingdom.

(5.5.369–74)

And when he hears of Imogen's refuge in their midst, he responds not just
of that but with what can be taken to characterize this whole sequence:

O rare instinct!
When shall I hear all through? This fierce abridgement
Hath to it circumstantial branches, which
Distinction should be rich in.

(5.5.382–85)

In the general gladness of reunion, the way has been prepared and an
atmosphere readied for the Soothsayer's presentation of Jupiter's prediction miraculously delivered to Posthumus in his earlier dream of his parents, read at the bidding of a Lucius who by now has been implicitly
pardoned in Posthumus' pardon of Iachimo. This, as it is spelled out, in
turn, by its being cast in Latin and by its origins in a Roman god, prepares
for, and foreshadows, the surprising spread of charity into politics, Cymbeline's voluntary resumption of tribute payment even though he is the
victor.

Now so much might seem obvious, a pietism easily assimilating a
Christian cast for a romance presented to a Christian culture. Yet there is
much in *Cymbeline*, notably the seriousness of the military action, that is
quite foreign to romance. Most pronouncedly, indeed, the political-
historical situation is too fine-grained and intricate for that popular form.
Shakespeare is sensitive to the epoch in the very early Britain, of *King
Lear*, to a medieval roughness in *Macbeth*, and on the Roman side to the
lateness of *Titus Andronicus*, as well as to the Republican-Imperial centrality of *Julius Caesar* and *Antony and Cleopatra*—as to the robust republi-
can earliness (496 B.C.) of *Coriolanus*. For *Cymbeline*, which is both an
early British and a Roman play, it would be strange indeed if he ignored a
capital epoch that is emphasized in his main sources, by both Spenser and
Holinshed, as they introduce this particular king. Correspondingly, indeed, the workings out of destinies here depend, as rarely in romance, not
just on the pious dispositions of a character, as with Patient Griselda, say,
but on the constantly tested interactions of characters who are defined

only by how they respond to these tests, though they are forgiven grave lapses on both the Roman and the Briton sides (except for Cloten and the wicked Queen). They work in a mysterious remoteness under a providence that, as it happens, is carrying out an even larger action on the other side of the Roman world, the birth of Christ.

Shifts of Tempo, Considerations of Time, and Manipulations of Theme in The Winter's Tale

There are two quite divergent modalities of time set into counterpoint in *The Winter's Tale*. The first operates in the regularity that the seasons and generations order and for which the seventeen-year pattern, the annual festival of the sheepshearing, and the five-act structure, may all be taken to stand. At the peak of the seasonal modality, as we are shown it before Leontes breaks it, the sense of fruition partakes of a slowing and delectating leisure, a sort of paradisiacal version of life in a Renaissance courtly country estate, such as might have been found in the Veneto or Castiglione's Urbino (but not quite yet so fully in Sussex or Yorkshire). Still further exalted is this life of a royalty in a kingdom small enough to be in touch with everything while living paradisiacally unperturbed about the normal business of rule.

The other modality of time is often spasmodic, impulsive, and irregular, and sometimes it is protracted and oppressive in its seeming endlessness, like the "imposition" of Original Sin. This second modality of "spiritualized" time is represented by the gradual or sudden incursions of good and evil, or even by the bends of decision and political interaction, slow or sudden—as in Leontes' nascent suspicion, or Camillo's resignation from his entire career, or Antigonus's shifty deliberation over accommodation to evil that culminates in his sudden, violent death.

An attention to such dual organizational principles will immediately group this play most closely to *The Tempest,* with its fourth-act masque and music, its terminal political reconciliation surrounding a marriage, and its interplay between good and evil in a downplayed politics. There too the cyclic fruition, when the whole action has managed the interposed difficulties, leads to the union of the daughter of one domain with the son of another. *Pericles* too is associable to both modalities of time, the seasonal and the spiritual, with the recuperation of a daughter lost through a mixture of evil and natural forces that culiminates in a marriage, with the restitution of a long-removed queen to her older king, and with the dispersion of political forces. It too deploys its action through kingdoms whose relative lack of geopolitical connection and serial self-inclusion, and whose schematic evil held to the personal side tend to downplay politics in favor of deep psychic interaction.

Made to carry this counterpoint of natural and spiritual time are the four usual sound patterns in *The Winter's Tale:* prose, blank verse, song, and music. The iambic pentameter couplets uniquely given to Time as the allegorical speaker who introduces Act Four might count as a fifth sound pattern, or be seen as a variant of blank verse. These couplets are taken as intermediate between blank verse (with which it then shares the verse design) and song (with which it then shares the framing regularity of echo). In any case, the speech of Time, even with its unusually high incidence of enjambments for couplets,[1] assimilates to a regularity that is unusual in general for speeches. It is a regularity broken throughout this play, which modulates tempo against tempo as the tempo of action feeds back and forth from the tempo of structured utterance. Indeed, the play's tonic note is a kind of regularity, since the well-balanced isocola of the prose of the opening scene are much more balanced, both in length and in internal structure, than are the much-wrought blank verse lines of the next scene after about line fifty, when Leontes is moulting into the gradual dominance of suspicion.

Music is the most regular of these tempos, and it has its own role in each of these late plays.[2] The music is "spiritual" that mysteriously cures and lulls Pericles (5.1.225–31); but in its effect it is reminiscent of the music of the sheepshearing festival in *The Winter's Tale,* as of the music-accompanied masque in *The Tempest*. From this angle the two songs in *Cymbeline* have no resolving force at all: they are at once melioratively suggestive and ironic. And the groundswell of complex development in that play rises from a subliminal, and arguably single, demonstration of the ultimate force of charity in both personal life and politics, a theme with many of the same notes as these other plays transposed into quite a different register.

Another music than song is heard three times in the play, a music not set to words and therefore absolutely measured in its time. The first two of these musics accompany dances, the dance of the Shepherds and Shepherdesses, and then the dance of the Satyrs, in Act Four (168; 343). The third accompanies at first not motion but immobility. It triggers the motion of what seems unable to move, the "statue" of Hermione. This music that awakes her the moment it is invoked juxtaposes that nascent, pure movement with an absolute immobility. The music, a white magic as Paulina explicitly calls it,[3] "turns" the uncanniness of what seems to be a mimetically perfect statue into the living woman it represents. Indeed, it is so mimetically perfect that Shakespeare adduces painting rather than sculpture as the model that its execution matches (5.2.93–99). And it is attributed to a painter rather than to a sculptor, to Giulio Romano, the more emphatically that this is the only mention of a particular painter in all of Shakespeare. There is the further seeming uncanniness that the sixteen elapsed years are spoken of as visible on her face (27–28).

The uncanniness of the statue in deep mythic use is variously evoked in culture, all the way at least to the statue speaking across the barrier of death in *Don Giovanni,* where the words of the statue are set to music. The deep ambivalence surrounding images in culture, whether prevailingly idolatrous or prevailingly iconoclastic, clusters not just toward images but toward representation of the live person in wood, stone, or paint. The uncanniness remains and is arrested, in ancient Greece or a modern city, by the taboo against having a statue of a live notable in a public place.[4] Hermione, however, will come alive; she never was a statue. And this is revealed by a music that, coming from no described source, has its own uncanniness. The conjunction of pure time, the wordless music, and pure timelessness, the supposed statue falls away and reveals itself as a final psychodramatic purgative operation upon the psyche of a Leontes who has already been overwhelmed in the joy of discovering his lost daughter, as the "spiritual" tempo feeds into the "seasonal."

Leontes' physical perceptions are as though mesmerized by his long, psychologically immobilized period of contrition under the guidance of Paulina, who carries through what masks as magic but is almost at once clearly recognized as a final turn of stage-managing, and an extravagant one, to match the extraordinariness of the unmentioned risk involved in concealing a queen for sixteen years in her own kingdom. All these circumstances have a touch of the luster of fairytale, and they happen in the enchanting aura of the play's oblique reference to its title, "A sad tale's best for winter" (2.1.25). This statement seals the play into a sort of pathos that it overcomes, since it is spoken by the boy Mamillius, the one member of this royal house to die, and fairly soon, as a result of what he is here taking a sort of refuge from. These lines late and lightly identify winter as the season with which the play began, an annual measure of time; but by the end it is the winter of life also for Leontes, whose beard is already white at the beginning of the play. The juxtaposition of evenly timed music and immobilized statue caps a recognition that knows no season. It roots the deep perceptions into the seasonal patterns that human beings must accord with, the play tells us, in order to realize personal fruition. Such fruition has both a natural development, going from youthful friendship through marriage to parenthood, and also a risk that psycho-spiritual forces cannot be allowed free rein without undoing such development. The pastoral and the ethico-religious are caught in perilous interconnection, and here the political is seen as itself an echo of both, in the laboratory of a kingdom remote enough and small enough to have almost no associations in the vocabulary of the audience; and even the usual associations of "Sicily" and "Bohemia" are ineffective here.

The actual command for the statue to come to life is given in a doubling of the iambic meter over against a momentary, regular pulling together of the pattern, first a dactyl, then a trochee, and then a single accented syllable as though to begin another trochee (or to conclude an iamb) but cut off as the third foot begins in the accented word of invocation, "Músìc Àwáke hèr, Stríke!"

The person uttering this command is Paulina, who has taken over the strange moral guardianship of Leontes through the generation-long period of contrition. In Sicily's table of organization, she has displaced two men, her husband, Antigonus, who died at the beginning of the period mysteriously as a consequence of his moral hypocrisy,[5] and Camillo, who bolted at the beginning rather than collude. Comic symmetry undergirds psychological rightness in the consequent marriage of Paulina and Camillo, the two good counselors coming together in a marital union whose "rightness" suspends another time question, since they are both well beyond the age of matchmaking, even for the widowed; and the marriage of those who are a generation beyond middle age is indeed fit only for a "winter's tale." Such a marriage would be hard to parallel anywhere in Shakespeare or, indeed, in literature.[6]

The beginning of the play, unlike the abrupt, tense, and mysterious beginning of *Hamlet,* has a relaxed tempo, a leisurely air about it, an air continued as the scene changes for the courteous exchanges between Polixenes and Leontes, between Leontes and Hermione, and between Polixenes and Hermione. This leisurely tone is not only broken in the evenness of its exchanges at the moment of Leontes' deranged suspicion. It is also accelerated remarkably. His lucidity clouds over almost at once, and the irrationality of his suspicion governs the tempo directly, later in the trial scene, and then implicitly in the delay of the whole play.

The displayed foreshortening of presentation here is reminiscent of the much-discussed speed of the opening of *King Lear,* which I have derived from the non-mimetic element of display in the recitative tradition.[7] Here, what seems the casual voicing of a reflection on the polite conversation, "At my request he would not" (1.2.87), turns out not to move evenly in the flow of time but to have a mimetic aspect in its uneven eruption from some depth whose beginnings are wholly concealed. Leontes' departure from balance is marked by a separation from the others on stage, but also by an ambiguous time-marking in this statement, where the speed of King Lear is applied not only to public events—the king's action in public is a public event—but also, and crucially, to the intimate life, as though the interactions of *Othello* were being forced into the public frame of *King Lear*.

Leontes' derangement cannot be accounted for in the temporal cycle, and—unlike any of Shakespeare's other situations—it cannot be accounted for either by some act of evil on the part of Leontes (like Macbeth's derangement) or the others (as in the cases of Hamlet and Lear). Its raw eventuation can only lie in what has to be taken for the very original sin Leontes could almost abjure in the friendship of Polixenes ("The imposition cleared / Heriditary ours," 1.2.74–75). No Iago is by to foment this jealousy, which through Freud we have learned to lie always at the heart of derangement: the unconscious sexual rivalry of one of a sex with another over another of the other sex. Shakespeare's inspired patternings lend themselves, as they would have to on those principles, to Freudian analysis. But here he provides no hinge for such structures in the plot, and he also provides no characterological strategies to serve as some sort of armature for the derangement.

Instead we are given the naked, strange fact, and we measure its strangeness by its extraordinary abruptness, and also its extraordinary prolongations in time, just as we measure the possibility of restoration by the slow rhythms of seasons and human generation, as they actually do come about in this winter, which is therefore a metaphorical winter as well as having some of the subdued glister of a usual one. As Richard H. Abrams says, Leontes' madness follows the pattern of medieval demonic possession without explicitly saying so (as Hamlet at one point does). "Where Hamlet's playful invocation of his madness as 'enemy' leaves off, Leontes' paranoia begins. With terrible literalness, Leontes persecutes his faithful wife, Hermione, as though she were the otherness in himself, his concretized 'enemy.'"[8] We measure the extremity of Leontes' madness by the time its effects persist, by its silent, psychosomatic effect on the young Mamillius, who dies instead of telling the promised sad winter's tale and growing up for the military life he banters about with his father (a military life nowhere otherwise present here), and the courtship that the court ladies tease him about (2.1.1–32). We also measure Leontes' madness by the extremity of his persecution of Hermione at the point of trial and at the point of her giving birth, moments that Shakespeare makes coincident, as though Leontes were going through the deeply evil pattern of some perverse *couvade;* by the commensurate suddenness of his contrition when the news of Mamillius's death is brought in; and by the responses of others through the play. For everyone, indeed, good and evil occur almost abruptly rather than in the measured intrications of the history plays. Responses to evil are as though instinctual, and signaled by the management of time—Camillo's speed of decision: Antigonus's hypocritical dawdling; Pauline's resolute slowness as it is silently matched by the stunned Hermione's; Polixenes' gradual ripening into the wish to heal the breach; the peasants' unrepresented but recoverably deducible patient investment, season by season, of Perdita's treasure; Perdita's gracious subjection to the duties of season, youth, and place; and even Florizel's rush toward the fruition of desired marriage.

The one persistently evil character in the play is Autolycus, who carries out the worst sort of confidence trick by luring the Clown to perform a Good Samaritan act in "rescuing" him so that the Clown can be vulnerable to being robbed. Later Autolycus frightens the Shepherd and the Clown with stories of torture so they will pay him to deliver the "fardel" that proves Perdita's adoption, when they themselves could have delivered it, as they intended. Autolycus's evil, however, is "transparent." Nobody sees it within the play, and it has minimal effect on the action, at best guaranteeing, rather than being strictly necessary for, the delivery of the fardel. That he is given many of the songs in the play, including the first ones, puts him rhythmically, so to speak, out of the action, and at the same time rhythmically in it, harmonizing almost against his will if not against his perceptions—a crooked line proving that God can write straight with him, and the more because his inclusion is a grace note in the plot.

In the emotional correlative that music constitutes, he offers an underlying amoral persistence as well as a greed, and a determination not to be depressed. His song at the end of act four, scene three, asserts this determination, strongly enough to reverse a proverb of the time.[9]

> Jog on, jog on, the foot-path way,
> And merrily hent the stile-a;
> A merry heart goes all the day,
> Your sad tires in a mile-a.

As though in obedience to this injunction, the fourth act picks up with a note of celebratory ceremonial gladness that has not been heard in the play since early in the second scene of Act One, and not for sixteen years, except in the excited preparations of the Clown for the sheepshearing, modified for us (and also for him) by Autolycus's confident robbery. This note, phrased as "Apprehend / Nothing but jollity" by Florizel, (4.4.24–25), will pervade what is by far the longest scene of the play in presentation time, establishing the spirit of seasonal/courtship merriment and fruition that will be expanded by returning to the other, distant kingdom in act five and including the resolution of a sorrow due to royal wrongdoing. In the sheepshearing scene even Autolycus gets caught up, assimilating to the mood of the courtly verse for a song in couplets that dwells on the visual glister of his wares:

> Lawn as white as driven snow,
> Cypress black as e'er was crow,
> Gloves as sweet as damask roses,
> Masks for faces and for noses;
>
> (4.2.220–23)

He will soon drop hawking sensationalistic ballads (265–85) for the uncharacteristic self-subordinating sociability of a simple part-song that he joins with a shepherd and his mistress (297–309).

The opening scene sets a tempo of courteous interchange over the proposed exchange of royal visits, and it does so in a prose further balanced by a balance into isocola. In its subject this discourse opens into a conventional look forward to the orderly succession of generations, closing in the ominous contrary-to-fact condition that will become metaphorical fact under the pressure of the king's subjection to a spiritual equivalent for crutches, "If the King had no son, they would desire to live on crutches till he had one." (1.1.42–43).

The blank verse that takes over begins with a reference to time that speaks of the moon as though it were either a sun or some other star:

> Nine changes of the wat'ry star hath been
> The shepherd's note since we have left our throne
> Without a burden. Time as long again
> Would be fill'd up, my brother, with our thanks;
> And yet would should for perpetuity,
> Go hence in debt.
>
> (1.2.1–6)

In the easy amplitude of this loving banter over the extension of a visit, which dwells on the threshold conventionalities of parting between friends who stand also in the amity of state to state, the participants prove themselves masters of both slowness and a sort of speed, moving in a harmony that breaks with the greater enjambments of Leontes' suspicion. A theological language, invoked playfully, can easily extend this discourse, so masterful do the participants seem, as in the play about "temptations" that immediately precedes the eruption of Leontes capitally ominous aside, "Too hot, too hot!" (1.2.75–108). "Temptation" in this discussion is offered in a sense that deprives it of evil: it is the temptation to marry, and in context it is a recollection of powerful attraction brought forward to provide a gracious compliment to a present and an absent lady in a perspective of time continuous with the more earnest backward look over a still earlier time, the boyhood of Polixenes and Leontes:

> We were as twinn'd lambs that did frisk i' th' sun,
> And bleat the one at th'other: what we changed
> Was innocence for innocence: we knew not
> The doctrine of ill-doing, nor dream'd
> That any did. Had we pursu'd that life,
> And our weak spirits ne'er been higher rear'd
> With stronger blood, we should have answered heaven
> Boldly 'Not guilty', the imposition cleared
> Hereditary ours.
>
> (1.2.67–75)

This overview of Original Sin and its opposite is briefly recapitulated in the last act, when Leontes and Camillo are said to have "looked as they had heard of a world ransomed, or one destroyed" (5.2.14–15). Here the passage conflates the themes of evil and the seasonal, since, strangely, an absolution from Original Sin, as against Saint Augustine and theological tradition, is imagined as possible for prepubertal youths. There is, I believe, no Christian notion that would allow the prepubescent an exemption from Original Sin. The NED gives only this passage to support the meaning "charge" for "imposition." The lack of this sense anywhere else would substantiate the application of other senses, "attach, affix, ascribe" (2) and "inflict." "Ill-doing" is odd for "sin" or "evil," which is sense one in the NED, and it locates the phrase at sense two, "injury," which would socialize the act in the direction of the Machiavellian coarseness in politics that boys may be unaware of. Indeed, children may be ignorant of politics, but children who were inducted into the regular practice of religion that the confessional passingly referred to would imply (1.2.235–38) could not be unaware of the doctrine of Original Sin, though they could be unaware of Machiavellian principles in politics. In this condensed phrasing, Original Sin, which must be the main reference, is phrased in a way that turns it from cause into effects—effects that these boys cannot even dream of, so free of harm/incapable of harm is their "innocence." It is not only that they were innocent, but they socialized innocence, "exchanged innocence for innocence," again an odd phrasing. Indeed, in that light the "stronger blood," although it might include the dynastic politics nowhere present in this play (though a capacity for it is shown), must refer to sexuality, a sexuality persistently connected with "sin" in the popular imagination, and giving a ground for the immediately ensuing banter about "temptation," here effectually defined as "sexual appeal of the prospective bride" and so, strictly speaking, no temptation at all. This too, so far, is part of the banter. Courtly balance entails a management and even an evocation of all this froth of sexual undercurrent—here extended, as a contrary-to-fact, into memories of childhood and courtship. And Leontes' loss of balance hinges on his overinterpreting this froth as the substance of interactive demonstration.

Time distorts this very syntax, packing it into the absolute construction of these last five words, "The imposition cleared / Hereditary ours." But this theology takes a very long backward look, indeed, to the Fall of Man. So in the materializing death threat to Polixenes, there will be a passing reference to the betrayal of Judas, in Polixenes denial of the adultery, "O then my best blood turn / To an infected jelly, and my name / Be yok'd with his that did betray the Best!" (1.2.417–19).

In turning away for his aside, Leontes slacks his attention, loses his grip on the deep sociabilities and their tempos. He turns, for a kind of consolation, to his son Mamillius, and he shows his stress by breaking what is surely a taboo in the Renaissance as well as now for all the "adulthood" of Renaissance children[10] when he takes Mamillius cryptically into his confidence about Hermione's adultery. Though Mamillius is later able to banter with the ladies of the court about his own future sexuality, he here does not understand. The effect of this failed conversation across the generations is to begin that severance of son from parents which will eventuate in his psychosomatic failing and death.

It is to the bewildered Mamillius that Leontes delivers his cryptic definition of the profound principle of human reaction that he is here misapplying as well as misevoking, breaking the rhythm of felt interchange:

> Affection! thy intention stabs the centre.
> Thou dost make possible things not so held,
> Communicat'st with dreams—how can this be?—
> With what's unreal thou coactive art
> And fellow'st nothing. Then 'tis very credent
> Thou may'st conjoin with something; and thou dost—
> And that beyond commission; and I find it,
> And that to the infection of my brains
> And hard'ning of my brows.
>
> (1.2.138–46)

This puzzles not only Mamillius, we may assume, but even the listening Polixenes, "What means Sicilia?" Hermione interprets the whole statement in wifely fashion as a sign of her husband's emotional state rather than as an utterance calling for decoding: "He something seems unsettled." Indeed, his lack of settlement marks the very tempos of this speech, which interrupts itself with more enjambments than the prior ones while at the same time trailing off into paratactic additions and amplifications.

The formulation of Leontes, though admittedly difficult, is arguably no more so than the "twinn'd lambs" speech. That other statement, however difficult, is assimilated in a context whose alertness (quickness or compactness in time) and leisure (delectated slowness) both submit to the quick of interchange. Leontes' break in the discourse, which turns out to be guilty as it projects guilt, makes the thread of his thought difficult to pick up other than as the expression of a mood Hermione correctly reads.

Leontes' formulation also is correct, but misapplied. These principles do apply to Leontes himself, but this physician would not heal himself: the principle is perversely and falsely applied to the other.[11] And the principle of doubt he addresses is also correct, only it has been too quickly, and indeed previously, resolved.

The "centre" as Pafford remarks, "can mean the center of the universe,"[12] and the more so, perhaps, that it is capitalized in the Folio text. It unites the microcosm, then, in the macrocosm. And in its correct, general pre-Freudian principle of the primacy and accuracy of emotion, it is gender-free, even though applied to a woman and phrased in a Freudian structure of "stabbing the center" where the masculine action is phallic without any concreteness of reference to an actual phallus for the stabbing or to an actual vulva for the center. In its temporal dimension it is at once instantaneous—as a stab implies—and undetermined. This rule about "affection," or "strong feeling with a sexual component" (as the Jacobean term may be glossed) is always followed in this play (and also in life, according to Freud), as against the slow fumbling of the psychological-intellectual process here spoken of as trying to come to terms with the effect of this principle, the activation of a set of schematic defense mechanisms that are failing to work in the very moment of their intellectually correct formulation.

The dream reference involves not only a doubtful (but possibly prophetic) reality but also a realm where actions are suspended out of time while somewhat slow.[13] The dream of Antigonus, as he tells it in recollection (3.3.19–37) begins slow ("Sometimes her head on one side, some another . . . thrice bow'd before me") but speeds up at once ("And gasping to begin some speech, her eyes / Became two spouts"). Slowing down to deliver her message, the dream figure speeds off in shrieks.

In losing his grip on reality, Leontes loses his perception of time-management and characterizes Camillo, who is to display a remarkably prompt response to complicated imperatives, as "a hovering temporizer" (300–304), adducing the possibility of an immediate death for Hermione. Later, in the "spiritual" time his arbitrariness has invoked, he will be suspended for a whole generation, but first he is run through a series of instantaneous reversals. In the space of seventeen lines (3.2.140–156), he declares the oracle to be false, then hears the news of Mamillius's death, then repents at once, and then has his queen, as he thinks, die before him. As he slows into repentance, Paulina then declares the insufficiency of even a millenial purgatorial contrition:

> A thousand knees
> Ten thousand years together, naked, fasting
> Upon a barren mountain, and still winter
> In storm perpetual could not move the gods
> To look that way thou wert.
>
> (210–14)

Not just in the passages cited, the language of the play tends to conflate the natural and the supernatural rhythms in its reference. So with the term "grace," when Time, across the sixteen-year gap, is moved to declare that he both hurries and succeeds (the senses of "speed") to summarize Perdita's development: "and with speed so pace / To speak of Perdita, now grown in grace / Equal with wond'ring" (4.1.23–24). The word "grace" falls at the last of many enjambments in his speech, itself then comprising both a significant pause and a syncopation across the line ending. The meanings of this polysemous word fall across both natural and supernatural domains, and most of those in the NED can be detected to govern the sense here. Included would arguably be (1) pleasantness (with the sub-senses of appearance, willingness, doing honor—all qualities of Perdita); (2) attractiveness; (3) embellishment (as in a grace-note, which her very existence may be taken to be); (4) one of the Graces (an iconographic type which her role when she presides over the sheep-shearing assimilates to); (6) favor; (7) condition of being favored; (8) an instance of favor; (10) share of favor allotted by Providence; (11) unmerited favor of God: (13) benificent virtue or efficacy; (14) a delay allotted by favor, as a grace-period (this time-sense defines the sixteen years); (15) mercy, and even (19) thanksgiving. This rich repertoire lingers, and the word is applied to Florizel's "princely exercises" as Derek Traversi reminds us.[14]

At the same time the sense of grace gets beyond Florizel's hopeful but overconfident celebratory air.

The long, full pastoral of the sheepshearing has its temporal evenness undercut, so that it is *not* wholly a reversal of the interrupting difficulties of the previous act. It begins with the fear of Perdita, and the secret identities of this generation require constant management. This long, celebratory act culminates in a breakup and a flight, in which the ire of Polyxenes strangely matches the ire of Leontes, as though this were an attribute of kings.

There is a silent temporal recapitulation prepared for in the fostering presence of Cleomenes and Dion in act 5, scene 1; they had last been seen sixteen years before arriving from "Delphi" and then delivering the seemingly ominous oracle. In the next scene, as their measured benificence hints, its good side will be narrated in a general joy, "The Oracle is fulfilled" (5.2.21).

Indeed, there is a large presentational break, with a corresponding break in tempo from verse to prose, between these two scenes. The central scene of reconciliation and discovery that is almost always shown on stage is narrated by anonymous gentlemen, and strangely to none other than Autolycus. This defective, amoral consciousness is interposed between the audience and the reunion of the kings, the discovery of Perdita's identity, and the blessing of her marriage. The joy of these is shrunk by being set in a remembered, recent past and so removed from swelling dramatic participation.

The light air of unreality that attaches to a romance plot has a temporal effect. This distancing, which reinforces the initial distancing of action on stage, tends to put the events out of time, to modify, comment on, and even to orchestrate, relative times. It is in this sense that the air of unreality takes away, or at least modifies, the strain, and entirely removes the perversion inherent in Paulina's dominance over Leontes, which the last scene of the play notably exhibits, and exhibits more than any other. It does so at a moment still to be revealed, the restoration of the queen. Leontes enters this scene fortified by the joy of restoration in act 5, scene 1, and by the exercise of royal power in conducting Florizel toward a reconciliation with his father, the old friend he wronged sixteen years earlier and has not seen since. Scene 2 cannot avoid giving us this meeting of joyous reconciliation, and it does so; but in the daring representation of a distancing and mediation through the voices of narrators, the narrators being none other than Autolycus and three anonymous Gentlemen. And they, when their story is told, are joined by the Clown and the Shepherd, who recount the grace note of their own ennoblement—at which they head off, all of them "to see the queen's picture."

Paulina times this presentation, and time gets three modalities in the final lines of the play: first, the leisure that graces the paradisiacal aspect of this court, one where at the beginning of the play the kings are shown as in a round of constantly pleasurable visits all but wholly uninterrupted by the business that Polixenes says he must attend to. This is itself a glistering vision, for in the normal kingdoms as all of Shakespeare's other plays represent them, a king should not absent himself even a few days, let alone for months on end, from his throne. Second, there is the wide gap of time, the sixteen years and then some of the actual play. And finally, there is the alertness of prompt and propitious movement into which Leontes can once again enter, and command:

> Lead us from hence, where we may leisurely
> Each one demand, and answer to his part
> Perform'd in this wide gap of time, since first
> We were dissever'd: hastily lead away.

Metaphysical Poetry and
Measure for Measure

S hakespeare as a child of his time followed Renaissance practices not only in choice of theme and expression of idea, not only in his omnipresent rhetoric, but also in the structure of two plays. These are the "problem" plays, *Troilus and Cressida* and *Measure for Measure*, where the logico-rhetorical or metaphysical method is preeminent, as it is with Shakespeare only in some sonnets. It is not surprising that Shakespeare's poetic drama would at times tend to resemble in structure the poetry of Donne, whose major poetic activity was contemporaneous with his own.

Empson in his essay on the double plot demonstrates how the private theme of love interrelates with the public theme of war in the plot, language, and character of *Troilus and Cressida*. Empson's unusual critical talent consists simply in discovering the metaphysical element of any literary work, and it can be said that his discussion of *Troilus and Cressida* clarifies its "problem" nature and solves its problem.

Measure for Measure similarly in (complex, single) plot, language, and character, works with the logical interrelations of government, religion, sex, and death, subjects often combined speculatively in metaphysical poems.

The problem of sex is central. But the plot relates it at once to Catholic dogma, civil law, and death: fornication is a sin and in Shakespeare's Vienna a capital offense. The plot's interaction is initiated by Claudio's condemnation for getting his fiancée, Julietta, with child. His sister Isabella pleads for his pardon with the substitute duke, Angelo, who has condemned him, unwittingly tempting the seemingly virtuous puritan to trade a pardon for her virginity. It is arranged (by the real Duke disguised as a priest) for Angelo's rejected, though contracted, fiancée to substitute in this bargain under disguise of darkness. The disguises are successively revealed and appropriately judged by the real Duke in the last act. Measure is meted for measure.

The Duke unites in his person the themes of the play: he is the head of the government disguised as a priest, and in the end marries the chaste Isabella. He is an idealized ruler who, like Prospero, initiates all the action in the play, so generalized that no name is given him in the text (though he appears as Vincentio in the list of characters). Under the guise of a foreign mission, he entrusts the rule to Angelo and remains in Vienna as a disguised priest. His expressed reasons for this action are pride in his own virtue, and finally in his commercial-governmental ambitions. L. C. Knights in *Drama and Society in the Age of Jonson* points out that the relation described by Weber and Tawney between Protestantism and capitalism is exemplified both in the commercial careers of the Elizabethan and Jacobean eras and in their drama. Angelo is such a character. Like no one else in the play he is curiously both unaristocratic and unplebeian in temperament: a bourgeois. He is the hardest worker in the cabinet. He talks continually in metaphors of the counting house. He originally refused to carry out his marriage contract with Marianna because her dowry went down with a foundering ship. His puritan zeal and pride that refuses to take things as they come is brought to a head in the central sexual problem: he condemns Claudio to die where the Catholic Duke would simply ask him to marry at once, confess, and atone. Yet he will pardon Claudio in return for the mortal sin of Isabella's sacrificed virginity, and he finally orders Claudio's execution for fear of retaliation from the freed brother of the dishonored girl. His own rigorous conscience demands the death penalty for himself when his two crimes are revealed in the last act. The wise Duke realizes, as many critics of Shakespeare have failed to do, that Angelo's repentance is a true one and that he can finally be trusted to serve the state and remain a faithful husband to Marianna. After all, the crimes did not come off: compulsory intercourse turned out to be fulfillment of a marriage contract, and judicial murder, the execution of a bona fide criminal. The crimes (sins) were perpetrated in the first place because with delegated power the inner contradictions in his motives became quickly objectified. If his intent was black, his repentance is commensurately strong.

At the end of the play, the Duke's government is all-powerful but merciful, religious dogma is satisfied, death has been avoided, and sexual rampancy has been regularized to everyone's satisfaction with multiple marriages realized and prostitution forbidden—all through the plot's logical interworkings. The logical counterpoint and counterbalance of the plot is described in the title as well, and reflected in the almost allegorical destiny of the characters; this has led M. C. Bradbrook to relate *Measure for Measure* to the morality tradition.

Government, sex, religion, and death interrelate in the language as well as in plot and character. Shakespeare, following the tradition of Jonson and others, has given many of his characters significant names: Pompey, surreptitious emperor of bawdry, whom Lucio contrasts with the lawful "Caesar" of Vienna as the pimp is being haled off to prison; Master Froth, the light-headed idler about town; Elbow, the shoving constable; and not least Angelo, who calls himself a saint and an angel and is reputed to have superhuman virtue (an "angel" is an Elizabethan coin, and puns on the two meanings of the word occur often in the plays of the period). The ambiguity of Angelo's character is just such a pun: he is a seeming angel actually motivated by commercial interest.

The puns of the comic relief characters reveal the interplay among, and the debasement of, government, sex, religion, and death. Pompey tells Mistress Overdone that she need not fear for customers when Vienna's whorehouses are razed: "Good counsellors lack no clients." If law forbids sex, sex is itself like law. Elbow, whose self-extension of his constable's term expresses supposedly his civic responsibility but actually his obscene pride and curiosity in being an official superego, reveals this in his malapropisms (the Renaissance vice *cacozelia*):

> *Elbow.* First, an it like you, the house is a respected house; next, this is a respected fellow; and his mistress is a respected woman.
> *Pompey.* By this hand, sir, his wife is a more respected person than any of us all.
> *Elbow.* Varlet, thou liest; thou liest, wicked varlet; the time is yet to come that she was ever respected with man, woman, or child.
> *Pompey.* Sir, she was respected with him, before he married with her.
> *Escalus.* Which is the wiser here? Justice or iniquity? Is this true?
> *Elbow.* O thou caitiff! O thou varlet! O thou wicked Hannibal! I respected with her, before I was married to her! If ever I was respected with her, or she with me, let not your worship think me the poor Duke's officer. Prove this, thou wicked Hannibal, or I'll have mine action of battery on thee.
> *Escalus.* If he took you a box o' the ear, you might have your action of slander too.

Actually, the "respect" of Elbow, and of his wife, is really an obscene public thing, a debasement of true civic virtue. So Pompey, the destructive "Hannibal," is both that and the "cannibal" that unwittingly punning

Elbow had really meant to say. A pimp destroys and devours his customers. And "slander" is really "battery" against Elbow's constantly as-
saulted reputation.

Elbow's hypocritical self-righteousness is shown by his statement,
identical with hypocritical "prenzie" Angelo's implicit claim, that he and
his wife are too "respectable" to have ever—before or after marriage!—
indulged in sexual intercourse. His wife, as he says before, is "an honest
woman" whom he "detests before heaven and your honour." He "detests"
her bad reputation, as he "respects" her, which he had meant to say; and
he employs "respects" later in a further malapropism that doubles back on
her sexual reputation. His consistent failure to express his desired meaning
lays bare the contradictions in the true meaning of his actions, as when he
calls Pompey a "benefactor," meaning to say "malefactor." For though
Pompey the bawd is a malefactor to the state, he is a benefactor to Elbow
in that his existence as a patent bawd allows Elbow continually to indulge
the orgy of righteous indignation that is his chief joy in life. That a
"malefactor" to the state could actually be a "benefactor" to its constable
suggests something rotten in the constable's purpose. Actually he harbors
in his mind as in his speech an illicit commerce between religion, sex, and
government; all are reduced to smutty respectability in a false logic that is
superseded and deprived of its nourishment by the triumph of the Duke's
true logic toward the end of the play. Pompey is put in jail, and Mistress
Overdone ("nine husbands sir, Overdone by the last") is left without
livelihood as the condemnation on "houses of resort" is allowed to stand.
In act four Pompey is significantly apprenticed to a hangman. He finds
that many of his best customers are in jail for one crime or another, and in
discussing the "mystery" (in a religious sense) of the hangman's trade with
the Hangman Abhorson (abortion, abhor, whoreson), he puns on cutting
off a man's head in the double sense of execution and sexual satisfaction
(equivalent to the metaphysical pun "die").

In the rhetorical texture of the language, as in the puns, metaphysical
logic is dominant. When Angelo attempts to induce Isabella to "sell" her
virginity (2.4), he speaks of religious matters solely in financial metaphors.
Sister Miriam Joseph shows that the most famous speech in the play, the
Duke's long discourse on life and death to the condemned Claudio, breaks
down strictly into the three terms of an Aristotelian syllogism. Isabella
argues as a keen logician with Angelo. The Duke's speech at the beginning
of the play is characteristic of its exclusively rhetorical temper:

> *Duke.*   Of government the properties to unfold
> Would seem in me t'affect speech and discourse,
> Since I am put to know that your own science
> Exceeds, in that, the lists of all advice

> My strength can give you: then no more remains
> But that to your sufficiency, as your worth is able,
> And let them work. The nature of our people,
> Our city's institutions, and the terms
> For common justice, y'are as pregnant in
> As art and practice hath enriched any
> That we remember. There is our commission,
> From which we would not have you warp. Call hither,
> I say, bid come before us Angelo.
> What figure of us think you he will bear?
> For you must know we have with special soul
> Elected him our absence to supply.

Even the predominant images are taken from rhetoric. This for Shakespeare is curiously bare of "modern" tropes, like all the language in the play except the prose of the comic relief characters, and even they speak, on occasion, in metaphysical puns.

In both *Troilus and Cressida* and *Measure for Measure,* structure and texture are nearer the rhetorico-logical tradition of the Renaissance than in any other play of Shakespeare. Both are deficient in the immediately interrelating images that are characteristic of modern works and of which other plays afford us supreme examples: *Antony and Cleopatra, Lear, The Tempest, Hamlet.* Both have a curiously ironic tone, like the logic of metaphysical poems. In fact, logic and comedy, of which irony is one attitude, are different aspects of the same philosophical-aesthetic outlook. The most striking example of this is the total work (mathematical and comic) of Lewis Carroll.[1]

Only the problem plays display dominantly the rhetorico-logical technique. The recent vogue, following long obscurity, of the metaphysical poets is paralleled in the problem plays, whose structural and ideological difficulties have repelled all but modern critics. Johnson, Coleridge, Swinburne, and many others have found fault with *Measure for Measure.* Modern men of letters as different temperamentally as Eliot and E. A. Robinson have accorded it high admiration, and it has begun to attract the close critical attention it deserves.

SECTION THREE

Seven Pillars of Wisdom:

Turns and Counter-Turns

I n *Seven Pillars of Wisdom,* Lawrence masters the fusions and disjunctions between military campaign and diplomatic maneuver, between the self-realizations of an informed stranger and the observations of an inquiring observer, between the confector of meanings and the reporter of a specific action, the Desert Campaign. Coming in to supplement, and to overarch, these fusions and disjunctions is some sort of religious feeling. Religious feeling is at the same time marginal to his book and one of the subjects of his observation, as well as the mode that gives it its initial definition.

"Wisdom hath builded a house: she hath hewn out her seven pillars." This quotation from Proverbs (9:1) is turned into an evocative phrase for the title of a book that T. E. Lawrence compared to *Moby Dick* and *The Brothers Karamazov,* and Nietzsche's *Zarathustra.*[1] The title, then, may be taken to announce, somewhat obliquely, a "Titanic" book. And he did, at this peak of perception and expression, arduously carry off one that may be characterized as such. As Jeffrey Meyers puts it—and the encomium will stand testing—"It . . . shares Proust's perceptive self-scrutiny, Mann's intellectual profundity, and Joyce's virtuoso prose styles."[2]

However, *Seven Pillars of Wisdom* as a title is somewhat disjunct from the contents it labels, in both tone and reference. And so in its high-flown resonance as well as in its biblical source, the title brings the book, its impulse, and all its compoundings of vision, within the orbit of a large religiosity that in chapter three Lawrence wishes to claim the desert peculiarly sponsors. He characteristically both limits that religiosity ("The desert dweller attained a sure trust and a powerful trust, but of how limited a field!" [41])[3] and declares it to be an ideal of which he himself, and the English generally, fall short ("The desert spirit escaped through our coarse texture" [42]). The title itself means to suggest a religiosity, but what religiosity? It stands as a declaration, biblical, millennial, and indecipherable, as against one of Lawrence's endless speculations and qualifications about his book, in which he claims a completeness for the image: "'Wisdom hath set up her seven Pillars'—meaning a complete edifice of knowledge."[4]

The further inclusion of the title as a phrase in the intimate dedicatory poem personalizes the "seven pillars" and at the same time turns the defining phrase toward the high goal of the "Freedom" that Lawrence invokes. He is addressing the young Arab friend who died before Lawrence carried through the long action he is describing; and at the same time he mentions "Death," "love," "the inviolate house," "fit monument," "I shattered it, unfinished," and a "marred shadow." "I loved you, so I drew these tides of men into my hands / and wrote my will across the sky in stars / To earn you Freedom, the seven pillared worthy house." But the man was already dead, and the book departs astringently in its actual text from the personal motive declared here. These instabilities among terms are matched in the history of Lawrence's use of this title; he had originally applied it to a book about seven cities. For him the title was large enough, it may be said, to apply to anything, unlike *The Mint*, which signifies one process in particular: the stamping of raw men into obedient soldiers.

Seven Pillars of Wisdom presents fusions of high intensity to overshadow these instabilities. The achievement, indeed, finally locates and expands these instabilities in this autobiographical apologia, which attains the temper and vision of the best contemporary historians. Under the most arduous conditions, this commander found time not only for keen analysis: he applies the keen analysis to the shifting intricacies of several interdependent command structures without either betraying his loyalty to all or surrendering his loyalty to any. And he finds the narrative thread, the historiographic means, to delineate the revelatory particulars of this balancing act in a way not unworthy of Gibbon, whom he invokes at the outset (7). He invokes Gibbon, to be sure, as a reader, and not as in any sense an emulator, and the restricted scope of what Lawrence narrates would make the analogy a weak one. In any case, a more exact analogue would not be just a historian but a commander who is a commanding historian. One would have to go back to the *Commentaries* of Julius Caesar, perhaps, to find a comparably trenchant historical account by a comparably gifted commander.[5] This modern commander, though, does not aspire to command. He distances himself introspectively, and at the same time agonizes over the constant failure of a work that he subtitles "A Triumph."

Taking first the historiographic dimension of the work, already in his second chapter Lawrence presents a historicized geopolitics, a bracing dose of historiographic analysis that is reminiscent of the geographical introduction to Henry Adams's *History of the United States*. This stretch of writing is as perspicuous as Michelet's introduction to the *Histoire de France,* and considerably more compact. Each phase he then discusses is dense with defined actions, and crosscut with reflections on them equally dense. Lawrence's book headings concern Feisal's first push north, the Medina campaign, the expedition against Akaba, the sorties using Akaba as a base, the failure to cut the Yarmuk Valley railway bridge, the lull of the winter campaign when Lawrence joined Allenby in Palestine, the failure of the combined assault on Maan, the autumn offensive toward Deraa, and the liberation of Damascus.

Lawrence's historical overview leads out of, and lends tone to, his still more supple version of the already muscular prose of Doughty. His historiographic register empowers him to carry off complex judgements of others at varying length, sometimes quite succinct ones, as "an odd pair in one chariot—Murray all brains and claws, nervous, elastic, changeable; Lyndon Bell so solidly built out of layers of professional opinion, glued together after Government testing and approval, and later trimmed and polished to standard pitch" (320). Lawrence, himself, indeed, at one tangent of his many characterizations of the *Seven Pillars,* describes it firmly as historiography: "I was brought up as a professional historian, which means the worship of original documents. To my astonishment, after peace came I found I was myself the sole person who knew what had happened in Arabia during the war: and the only literate person in the Arab Army. So it became a professional duty to record what happened."[6] In this letter, written while asking advice of Shaw about a draft of the work, he verges on calling it the raw materials of history rather than the act of historiography that his request for literary advice logically implies, and of course abundantly justifies. His analytic acuteness is folded into the narrative that it punctuates, elevates, and coordinates:

> Hussein, as politician, as prince, as moslem, as modernist, and as nationalist, was forced to listen to their appeal. He sent Feysul, his third son, to Damascus, to discuss their projects as his representative, and to make a report. He sent Ali, his eldest son to Medina, with orders to raise quietly, on any excuse he pleased, troops from villagers and tribesmen of the Hejaz, and

to hold them ready for action if Feisal called. Abdulla, his politic second son, was to sound the British by letter, to learn what would be their attitude towards a possible Arab revolt against Turkey. . . .

Feysul's position was hazardous in the extreme. He was at the mercy of the members of the secret society, whose president he had been before the war. He had to live as the guest of Jemal Pasha, in Damascus, rubbing up his military knowledge; for his brother Ali was raising the troops in Hejaz on the pretext that he and Feisal would lead them against the Suez Canal to help the Turks. So Feisal, as a good Ottoman and officer in the Turkish service, had to live at headquarters, and endure acquiescingly the insults and indignities heaped upon his race by the bully Jemal in his cups. (50–52)

And these intricacies have themselves been introduced by intricate analyses:

The old Ottoman Governments regarded this clan of manticratic peers with a mixture of reverence and distrust. Since they were too strong to be destroyed, the Sultan salved his dignity by solemnly confirming their Emir in place. This empty approval acquired dignity by lapse of time, until the new holder began to feel that it added a final seal to his election. At last the Turks found that they needed the Hejaz under their unquestioned sway as part of the stage furniture for their new pan-Islamic notion. The fortuitous opening of the Suez Canal enabled them to garrison the Holy Cities. They projected the Hejaz Railway, and increased Turkish influence among the tribes by money, intrigue, and armed expeditions. (49)

Passages like these have the ring not only of A. J. P. Taylor, Namier, or de Tocqueville. They almost match the trenchancy of Thucydides and Tacitus, though at the same time they are assimilated to a heroic and wavering attempt to forge a personal identity and then express it. Such running analyses function strategically and diplomatically at the level of the astonishingly perceptive "Twenty-Seven Articles."[7] Diplomatic-strategic astuteness is, so to speak, a key pillar in Lawrence's wisdom; throughout his narrative he draws constantly on this Realpolitik, as though its system were simultaneously in constant process of evolution and already fully formed as a deep structure in his mind—again, very much the effect of Thucydides. Though he was mainly managing the Arabs, he approaches his various British authorities, and even the French, with a Realpolitik of quite comparable complexity, as is evident through-out and especially evident in chapter sixteen. This awareness plays through his text as a strong historian's irony, which on the reduced scale of this long campaign will take personal form, about Lawrence himself, but also about others:

The revolt had begun haphazard, on their father's explicit orders, and the old man, too independent to take his sons into his full confidence, had not worked out with them any arrangements for prolonging it. So the reply was only a little food. Later some Japanese rifles, most of them broken, were received. Such barrels as were still whole were so foul that the too-eager Arabs burst them on the first trial. No money was sent up at all: to take its place Feisal filled a decent chest with stones, had it locked and corded carefully, guarded on each daily march by his own slaves, and introduced meticulously into his tent each night. By such theatricals the brothers tried to hold a melting force. (94)

At the outset Lawrence, with exaggerated but typically British modesty, speaks not of "Titanic" books but of a "personal narrative pieced out of memory" (6). He says at the same time, though, that he had notes. Thus in the apparent contradiction, he obscures the particular historiographic purpose of his writing, as he also does in the counter-Tacitean declaration of his Preface, "It does not pretend to be impartial. I was fighting for my hand, upon my own midden" (6). This could be taken as a further modest description of the restricted and firsthand nature of the episode he recounts, though the pieces fit so fully into the large-scale war of which it was a part that it has an even more historiographic answerability to questions than does, say, *Ten Days That Shook the World*. John Reed was merely an enthusiastic reporter of what, in the context of World War One, is also an episode, though one of far greater importance in other contexts—as the expedition to Damascus may also be taken to be in the light of later Near Eastern developments. Another analogue would be Xenophon's *Anabasis*—if Xenophon had been a party to Cyrus's policy decisions and a Thucydidean analyst of them rather than a mercenary officer in the position of distant observer-adventurer.[8] But all historiography is arguably synecdochic.[9] By a kind of accident, Lawrence found himself with a narrative task that was a synecdoche ready-made, the *multum-in-parvo* of a single, much-reflecting part of the global war.

Throughout this narrative a sense of largeness and variable intricacy is imparted by the very length of Lawrence's account, by the bristling detail, by the low but dangerous pressure of awareness under threat, and by the particular character of each particular phase of the long, irregular, relentless movement toward Damascus. In the more relaxed passages of his narrative flow, Lawrence punctuates his text with descriptions of the terrain and the weather, with a particularity that helps pull his text toward the documentary. At the same time, the descriptions pull them toward the dramatic, since these physical conditions function to inhibit or to further—often we are suspended without knowing which—the immediate military goal, and also the long-range one:

> His prudent talk whiled away the slow passage of abominable desolation.

The Fejr Bedouin, whose property it was, called our plain El Houl because it was desolate; and today we rode in it without seeing signs of life; no tracks of gazelle, no lizards, no burrowing of rats, not even any birds. We, ourselves, felt tiny in it, and our urgent progress across its immensity was a stillness or immobility of futile effort. The only sounds were the hollow echoes, like the shutting down of pavements over vaulted places, of rotten stone slab on stone slab when they tilted under our camels' feet; and the low but piercing rustle of the sand, as it crept slowly westward before the hot wind along the worn sandstone, under the harder overhanging caps which gave each reef its eroded, rind-like shape.

It was a breathless wind, with the furnace taste sometimes known in Egypt when a khamsin came; and, as the day went on and the sun rose in the sky it grew stronger, more filled with the dust of the Nefudh, the great sand desert of Northern Arabia, close by us over there, but invisible through the haze. (246–47)

Doughty's style is here being stretched, purged somewhat of its afflatus, and dynamized with the account of a constantly purposive action, where even waiting is a strategy.[10]

Here, typically, is Doughty himself, who roots his own movement through the heat only in observation and expostulation:

We journeyed on the morrow with the same high country about us, beset with bergs of basaltic traps and granite [the steppe rises continually from el Kasîm to el Tàyif]. We came early to the brackish pits *er-Rukka;* and drew and replenished our girbies: this thick well-water was full of old wafted droppings of the nomads' cattle; but who will not drink in the desert, the water of the desert, must perish. Here is a four-square clay kella, with high walls and corner towers, built by those of er-Russ for shelter when they come hither to dig gun-stations,—wherewith the soil is always infected about old water stations. We drank and rested out an hour, but with little refreshment: for the simûm—the hot land wind—was blowing, as the breath of an oven; which is so light and emptied of oxygen that it cannot fill the chest or freshen the blood; and there comes upon man and cattle a faintness of heart.—I felt some relief in breathing through a wetted sponge.[11]

Doughty also keeps a control over his powerful impulse to biblicize, and one barely catches a trace of it in this passage.[12] He arrests himself at the moment, from moment to moment, and here, as generally, he does not get into his text what he did not have in the purpose of his own remarkable ventures, the onward thrust that Lawrence gets into even a confrontation with a hot, breathless desert air. Even in his random (but always implicitly strategy-related) encounters with the landscape, Lawrence is mobile for pure observation: "The blades (single, straight and very slender) shot up between the stones. If a man bent over from his saddle and looked downward he would see no new colour in the ground; but, by looking forward, and getting a distant slope at a flat angle with his eye, he could feel a lively mist of pale green here and there over the surface of slate-blue and brown-red rock" (140).

Lawrence's text is less randomized on the surface and therefore more symptomatic in the depth than Doughty's. Doughty takes the terrain for natural observation, not for military strategy, emphasizing the past for the most part, and not just the present, though as Edward Said demonstrates, the Western Orientalizers do tend to conflate past and present in a timelessness.[13]

As Lawrence says in introducing Doughty (Doughty, 1, xxiv) "the great picture-book of nomad life became a military textbook." Doughty himself explicitly declares (viii) that the Nabatean inscriptions he was pursuing for antiquarian, really, rather than historiographic, interests, were "hardly of less interest" than the extinct volcanoes on the same horizon. Geography and history stand on a par as part of the same complex, and this confrontation in the 1870s is asserted to have a timeless authority by Lawrence, under whose aegis it was reprinted and for which he wrote an introduction.

In this introduction Lawrence says (xv) that "Doughty's completeness is devastating" (xvi); "the sheer endurance of his effort is wonderful"; "none of us triumphed over our bodies as Doughty did" (xvii); "He broke a road for his religion" (!).

Here (xviii) Lawrence delineates two kinds of Englishman in the Orient, those who imitate the native and those who "assert their aloofness." Lawrence repeats this typology in *Seven Pillars:*

> The Englishmen in the Middle East divided into two classes. Class one, subtle and insinuating, caught the characteristics of the people about him, their speech, their conventions of thought, almost their manner. He directed men secretly, guiding them as he would. In such frictionless habit of influence his own nature lay hid, unnoticed.
>
> Class two, the John Bull of the books, became the more rampantly English the longer he was away from England. He invented an Old Country for himself, a home of all remembered virtues, so splendid in the distance that, on return, he often found reality a sad falling off and withdrew his muddle-headed self into fractious advocacy of the good old times. Abroad, through his armoured certainty, he was a rounded sample of our traits. He showed the complete Englishman. There was friction in his track, and his direction was less smooth than that of the intellectual type; yet his stout example cut wider swathe. (346–47)

Lawrence combines and transcends both his kinds of Englishman, putting the slave-master dialectic into a sort of sublated endless regress. He describes the second as "the cleaner class." Yet he speaks, shockingly, of Doughty's "picture of the Semites sitting to the eyes in a cloaca, but with their brows touching Heaven," a picture which he judges "sums up in full measure their strength and weakness, and the strange contradictions of their thought which quicken our curiosity at our first meeting with them."[14]

Now the Chinese monks of the third century went deeply into another culture, that of Buddhist India, while remaining rooted in their own; but their purposes were religious, and for a religion already flourishing in China. Lawrence had a religious element in his purposes too; but it was torqued with political and personal cross-purposes, to the vanishing point. Other analogues, Western ones, are hard to find, and they tend to be less complex, involving the purposes either of detached research on the one hand (like the magisterial historian of philosophy and religion, Henry Corbin) or complete absorption on the other (like the Moslem convert René Guenon). The war allows Lawrence to remain encapsulated in a complete Britishness, to which he returns—and also to stay literary. But paradoxically also the war allowed him to suspend his relation to Britain "on detached service," so that the tensions could reach full development, and then the literary expression to which he declared a primary allegiance we cannot confidently confine it to.

Lawrence's psychic substructure is so complex as to remove him somewhat from the totalizing strictures of Foucault and the Said who follows Foucault's cues. Pride and shame, defrauding authority and remaining in subjection to it, through all the psychoanalytic substructure of his illegitimacy, get redeployed in his reaction to the Bey's rape, his failure to mention his pleasure under searing sincerity (here is only the pride in the naming of shame). This in turn symmetrically reflects his relation both to the British authorities and to the Arab, both of whom he is at once serving and bilking, each symmetrical set necessary to the other. Enclosure into England breaks the series.

Attention to arduous rewriting draws him into strange verbal conflations, accompanied by the psychologically symptomatic loss of his completed manuscript, which he left in a railway waiting room. His personal physical prowess, his mastery of strategy, his religiosity, an impacted sexuality, through the writer's detachment and crepitating literary insight, enter the narrative for fusions, and get pulled into the stylistic tensions of *Seven Pillars*. The objectivity of *The Mint* breaks this complex mold.

Lawrence's own endless regress complicates his flat characterization of the Arabs, "They know only truth and untruth, belief and unbelief, without our hesitating retinue of finer shades" (138). This quotation can itself be put into endless regress, if his hesitancy is set against the boldness of his move from the British staff in Egypt to the Arabs. Doughty and Lawrence both have "a private mythology," says Said (237), who rightly emphasizes that Lawrence's impulse was "to stimulate the Orient into movement, to impose an essentially Western shape on that movement . . . to contain the new and aroused Orient in a personal vision" (241). Lawrence imposes meaning (242–45); he "equates himself fully with the struggle" (243); he is an "imperial agent" (196). And all these counterstatements set a harsh schema for his actions. At the same time, however, there is, as it were, a Said at work within Lawrence declaring all of this, and simultaneously making Arab claims against the West, which he simultaneously falls short of and transcends. "There seemed no straight walking for us leaders in this crooked lane of conduct," Lawrence says, "ring within ring of unknown, shamefaced motives cancelling or double-charging their precedents" (551–52).

Lawrence was impressed by the ring of Conrad's rhythms; his own imitate that halting, carefully composed robustness, though they have a ring that is peculiarly his own:

> Some of the evil of my tale may have been inherent in our circumstances. For years we lived anyhow with one another in the naked desert, under the indifferent heaven. By day the hot sun fermented us; and we were dizzied by the beating wind. At night we were stained by dew, and shamed into pettiness by the innumerable silences of stars. We were a self-centered army without parade or gesture, devoted to freedom, the second of man's creeds, a purpose so ravenous that it devoured all our strength, a hope so transcendent that our earlier ambitions faded in its glare. (29)

Here, as he begins, Lawrence moves at once into his labyrinth of purpose and remembered suffering and then throws over it the veil of a transcendent hope shedding a glare that causes ambitions to fade. A rational resolution to this titanic psychological process cannot be effectuated: why would not hope have caused the ambitions to strengthen; why would that which causes ambitions to fade be called a transcendent hope? Presumably because of a merging into collectivity that Lawrence at the same time tells us was neither possible for him nor desirable for him, except as he could carry it off histrionically, but also with the amazing actuality of military success. But then he *does* merge into a "we" that is by no means editorial: "As time went by our need to fight for the ideal increased to an unquestioning possession, riding with spur and rein over our doubts. Willy-nilly it became a faith. We had sold ourselves into its slavery. . . . By our own act we were drained of morality, of volition, of responsibility, like dead leaves in the wind."

We cannot subscribe—he does not really subscribe—to the automatic subjection he claims to have invoked. If that were so, the rest of his

reflections would be nullified, and all the conscious diplomatic manipulation he carries off so dazzlingly would have been not only impossible but
unthinkable.

II

On the very limit itself of the novel's generic disposition to let its
creator live an excessive parable are the writings of this *aventurier* whose
life Malraux finds so archetypical.[15] The ambiguity of his life (did he act,
ultimately, to write or write to record action?) reflects exactly that of his
work. Is *The Mint* the equivalent of a novel? And what is the nature of the
relation between historiography and personal experience in *Seven Pillars of
Wisdom*? Is it a historical novel à la Henry Miller and Malraux, or a piece of
history? This question is radically ambiguous because in Lawrence we find
the point at which history and fiction meet. That they do so in his writing
is significant because Lawrence's life is an anguished parable of ideological
conditions archetypical of the fictive mind and of what writes fiction, the
modern temper.

T. E. Lawrence, more sophisticated than Henry Miller and Thomas
Wolfe, realizes, like Goethe in *Dichtung und Wahrheit,* the necessarily
artificial, because selective, character of autobiography. Yet Valéry's mal-
aise attacks him: ("If I say Duchess F went up the stairs in a fiction, and I
mean Duchess G, I am already lying.") He is comfortable only in the
narration of fact, feeling at the same time, like all the romantic autobiogra-
phers from Rousseau on, that the sequence of his life has extraordinary
meaning.

Whereas Rimbaud left splendid artifices realized as unmagical behind
him in his past and probably thought of his rejection as a talisman of
superiority both to the writers left in Paris and to the blacks with whom he
traded, Lawrence thought of his inability to produce splendid artifices as a
humbling limitation on all his action while at the same time offering an
account of his break into action as a "Titanic" book. In the unity of his acts
and his writings, for all his lack of the wilder romantic errors (literature as
magic-artifice or gospel-reality), he exhibits in a pure, almost desperate,
form, the sundering tensions of fictive ideas. This is the irony of the
triumph of *Seven Pillars,* the agony of his minting.

As an autobiographer Lawrence agonizes between "I cannot write it
because in literature such things have not ever been, and cannot be. To
record the acts of Hut 12 would produce . . . not a work of art but a
document,"[16] and, "The irony was in my loving objects before life or
ideas. . . . It was a hard task for me to straddle feeling and action; I had

one craving all my life—for the power of self-expression in some imaginative form—but had been too diffuse ever to acquire a technique. At last accident, with perverted humour, in casting me as a man of action, had given me a place in the Arab Revolt, a theme ready and epic to a direct eye and hand, thus offering me an outlet in literature, the technique-less art. Whereupon I became excited only over mechanism. Memory gave me no clue to the heroic" (549). The modesty of the second statement is curious if compared with his painstaking composition of *Seven Pillars,* and if he believes the first statement, written from the Air Force, why did he write *The Mint?* Lawrence tries to assert and deny at the same time the genius order and his membership in it. Which did he believe? Both ambivalently and neither. In his imagination he held partial belief, just as in his action he held partial involvement.

The state of partial belief in idea, or partial involvement in action, vacillates between the reality of a common humanity and the illusion of the difference of the genius order. Among alien people partial involvement is impossible; a craving for such superiority, perhaps, helped to draw young Lawrence first to the ideal past of Crusader castles, then to inspecting them *in situ,* then to further archeology in the Near East and travel there, then to military assignments, then climactically into direct contact with the alien Arab Revolt (which he was able to join, he says, by deliberately antagonizing his colleagues in Egypt so that they would be anxious for him to leave), then as an emissary to Versailles who gave up all action as humanly relative when he found that his pure purposes were compromised by the wills of others, then briefly as a projected publisher of fine editions, then as an author who refused the human limitations of fame and the necessity of money, then as a private in the Air Force, committing "mind-suicide," holding himself there "till the burnt child no longer feels the fire,"[17] seeking, like a god, freedom from the past, which one might imagine could have furnished his novelistic material. Finally there was scrupulous anonymity, peace in what he called a secular equivalent to monasticism, in the society of the disillusioned and the precision of working with photographs, machine tools, speedboats, and motorcycles.

"I did not believe finally in the Arab Movement," he says, and the reason is repeatedly given. He feels, and is, superior to the Arabs, even in his primitive admiration of their "intuition which left our centrifugal minds gasping." "They knew only truth and untruth, belief and unbelief, without our hesitating retinue of finer shades" (38). And he himself delineates many fine shades in his accounts of Arab diplomatic manipulations. Is his categorical statement meant as praise or blame? Both at once, it may be said, in the ambiguity of a partial belief that made him feel always like an actor among the Arabs, "my sham leadership a crime," "the godless fraud inspiring an alien nationality," "the event for me sorrowful and the phrase meaningless."

So he felt about the Air Force. "Do you ever feel like a unicorn strayed among sheep?" he asked after examining his motives in a letter. "Angels, I think, we imagine. Beasts, I think, we are. And I like the beasts for their kindliness and honesty, without really managing to make myself quite like them."[18] In the famous chapter 100 of *Seven Pillars,* he probes his own motives through the comparison of himself with the sacrificed Savior. Lawrence was both immolating his active and intellectual powers to his pride, and, unlike most romantics, scrutinizing his own fallacies. In the power of that scrutiny, beyond even Rimbaud's (though Lawrence is the lesser writer), his excellence resides. He has the honesty of a saint in admitting his diabolical fallacies, and in this virtual confession, we have what verges on autobiographical fiction.

The metaphorical correlatives of his illusion—the evanescent appearances of reality—we find in the frequent mirage or mirage-like images of *Seven Pillars:* "The irrational tenth was like the kingfisher flashing across the pool, and in it lay the test of generals" (193); "Things at their heads stood matt against the pearl-grey horizon, and at their feet melted softly into the ground. Our shadows had no edge: we doubted if that faint stain upon the soil below was cast by us or not" (451); "The ground was vivid with new grass; and the sunlight; which slanted across us, pale like straw, mellowed the fluttering wind" (512); "Feisal was on the hill-top, on the very edge, black against the sun, whose light threw a queer haze about his slender figure, and suffused his head with gold, through the floss-silk of his head-cloth" (519); "The road was bestial with locusts, though from a distance they looked beautiful, silvering the air with the shimmer of their wings"; and, "But when at last we anchored in the outer harbour, off the white town hung between the blazing sky and its reflection in the mirage which swept and rolled over the wide lagoon, then the heat of Arabia came out like a drawn sword and struck us speechless" (65).

He interprets the sword for us in a letter: "The sword was odd. The Arab Movement was one: Feisal another (his name means a flashing sword); then there is the excluded notion, Garden of Eden touch; and the division meaning, like the sword in the bed of mixed sleeping, from the *Morte d'Arthur* . . . and the sword also means clean-ness [hyphen Lawrence's] and death."[19] And the quotation is blazoned on the cover of the book. In an unpublished letter to Ezra Pound, Lawrence gave as his reasons for going to London in April 1920 that he had moved there "for peace and cleanliness." This is at very least idiosyncratic, since many would find Oxford in some ways cleaner than London (283). And to Charlotte Shaw he writes, "Consider wandering among the decent ghosts hereafter crying 'Unclean, Unclean!'"[20] In his first chapter, after his eulogy about the "clean bodies" in Arab homosexuality, Lawrence adduces the term "clean" again in a context of self-doubt about both types of Englishman, shifting abruptly back and forth from the first person to the third: "in neither case does he do . . . a thing so clean as to be his own" (31)— where cleanness is associated with the attainment of identity in action. "I was . . . become like Mohammed's coffin," he says, completing the circuit that is both joined and interrupted in the phrase "clean-ness and death."

The sword was odd indeed that could identify clean-ness and death. This identity is realized also in those Blackmur shows us, as between subsistence and the stuff of life, leisure and death. Blackmur has well qualified Lawrence's literary achievement: ". . . the weakness is basic only; and in the worlds of the mind what is basic is not necessarily conclusive, what totters at the bottom does not always fall; the towers of imagination fling up, like Lawrence's active pains and joys, out of quicksand and stand firm in light and air. It may be there is a type of imagination, of which Lawrence would be an exemplar, incapable equally of the bottom reality and the top ideal, yet tortured by both, which exhibits its strength solely in the actual confronting world—the flux—and is confounded only in those terminals which, so to speak, it could never reach." "In Lawrence the intention everywhere counts, which is to say is questionable, uncomposed."[21] That is, in my terms, his being at once a novelist and not a novelist is both his weakness and his strength.

Lawrence's failure of action is the breach between his purpose and his act due to the shifting of the purpose itself: reality's process was so evasive that one could not recognize its appearances. The corresponding breach in his writing is the failure to integrate, to "compose," as Blackmur says, which causes him to verge on the enumerative and the anecdotal. Blackmur notes that he did not quite ever create a character, "not even his own." And he envied David Garnett most for his ability to write novels.

Why else than because he himself felt this breach did he hyphenate the word "clean-ness"? A breach exists between two sides. These two sides in *Seven Pillars* and *The Mint* are, to begin with, the closely observed natural detail and the moral or historicizing generalization, both almost obsessively characteristic of Lawrence's writing, as of fictional statement. They always combine or become interchangeable in achieved fiction. Lawrence keeps them separate, preserving the unfiction of his fictional material. Detail rarely becomes analogy, moralization never points toward plot.[22] The natural detail unfolds to become the vast and changeable desert and its settlements. The moral observations, in all their complexity, feed into the strategic-historical narrative that transcends them.

Observed natural detail and moral generalization almost pull asunder, too, in the novels of Hemingway and Céline. The succession of nearly repetitive events in *Seven Pillars* has no parallel more close than the structure of Hemingway's early novels. Yet Hemingway's observed natural detail integrates better than Lawrence's; and his moral perspective always enters his work as a structural element, whereas it confuses Lawrence's artistic attitude. Hemingway's certitude is aesthetically superior, if morally inferior, to Lawrence's vacillation. Céline gives a cue to the depth of Lawrence's negativism, and also, through the shrillness of his novels, to the dimensions that are permitted it.

The minting never takes place in *The Mint;* it never rises to fiction; though Lawrence's style has smoothed off since *Seven Pillars,* the degeneration of his choice implicit in the self-generating progress of his confusion was mirrored in his autobiographical writing as a solipsistic concern with anecdotes and individual landscapes. The moral observation operates as powerfully as ever, but in a vacuum; he ironically notes that corporateness is the only spiritual quality of a military unit, and yet he fails to express the growth of that corporateness which was his book's stated purpose, as the title announces it. The duality between body (observed natural detail) and spirit (moral generalization) was felt as an obsession rather than unified in writing.

III

As Lawrence retreats after *Seven Pillars* from the pressures upon him, the turns and counter-turns he has mastered at his peak escape from his control. The style itself in *Seven Pillars* crepitates under those pressures, where Lawrence the writer balances the intensifications that called on Lawrence the agent for heroic balancing acts at the intersecting points of pressure. His situation, in all its contradictions, could easily have induced some sort of despair, a retreat into failure and silence. That he speaks of despair and berates himself is another question entirely; Saint Anthony in the desert is not a Judas. On the one hand, his conviction that he had deceived the Arabs "far outweighed the reality."[23] On the other hand, "This dual purpose was inescapable . . . having been built into his situation from the outset."[24] His role is not just double, actually, but at least triple—a British officer under orders to conduct a mission, orders he has himself intrigued out of his superiors; an adviser-enthusiast (the way the Arabs defined him, according to Mack, 54); and at the same time an absolute leader who arrogated authority to himself for decision after the taking of Damascus. Or, in the summary of Jeffrey Meyers, he was "commander, liaison and adviser."[25] Under, or over, all these was the dreamer who agonized about his varied roles in a sort of transfiguration of Christian penance—or (finally) of conventional British modesty. Here, as often, exhibitionism has its roots in concealment, but the counter-turns of one against the other in *Seven Pillars* bring him to a transcendence of both as each role is turned to fortify the other. But these realizations, already present by July 1916 in the "Twenty-Seven Articles," had not yet found their way into his written expression, where awareness of others has not yet been tempered into dialectical counter-turns with awareness of self. His earlier state papers on the Middle East, as Mack says, are "cynical, coldly written documents" (144). The figure he will become, and be able to write in *Seven Pillars* about recalling, labors under a sort of Coriolanus complex; but Lawrence manages the complex so that it inures him to command rather than to a self-defeating solitary prowess. There, in the achieved vision, he is, so to speak, at once Coriolanus and Menenius.

Seven Pillars is the "complete temple" against which his further strenuous gestures are measured, even his keen diplomatic work. There, right down to the small details of style, the counter-turns are pulled into expression as delineated forces. He tends to characterize those he encounters after the fashion of his own perception of contradictions. Those moral-judgmental capsule portraits may mount as many as three or four contrasting adjectives, which are then subordinated, in idea and in phrasal organization, to merge into, and grow out of, the insoluble complications of the public contestation he is bringing them all to serve. In that public contestation only Lawrence holds all the cards: the Arabs do not know of the Sykes-Picot Treaty, a prior secret written agreement between the British and the French about their spheres of influence in the Near East that compromises what the Arabs are doing. Neither the British nor the French know of Lawrence's hope, and contrivances, toward the Arab independence he in fact did partially bring off later at the Versailles Conference. They do not know that specifically Lawrence is hoping to subvert the Sykes-Picot Treaty, which would make him a "traitor" as well as a heroic patriot.[26]

Beside the subtler factors of the allies he is managing, the Turks are simply an enemy Lawrence can best by carefully devised guerilla tactics. What he hopes to gain by his constantly adjusted manipulations against all parties (British, Arabs, French, Turks) is kept steadily in view, but in such a complicated way that the final taking of Damascus seems like relief as well as like "triumph." The subtitle remains declarative, but also ironic, because the very complications, especially (he does not say) without Lawrence to manage them, foreshadow the result, that the victory will not be able to carry against the folly, cross-purposes, cultural limitations, and degeneration of such circumstances. The guile of the narrative presents them as

having the power eternally to supervene over such extraordinary events as
the capture of Damascus. The countercurrents will nullify this triumph;
the narrative implies they must do so.[27] The will that held them together is
the will that after the falling apart writes about their hope and prowess of
holding together. Lawrence's control, and his detachment, and also his
neo-medieval idealism, are figured in the Malory he carried with him as his
reading of choice on the campaign: "In my saddle-bags was a *Morte
d'Arthur*. It relieved my disgust. The men had only physical resources; and
in the confined misery their tempers roughened. Their oddnesses, which
ordinary time packed with a saving film of distance, now jostled me an-
grily; while a grazed wound in my hip had frozen, and irritated me with
painful throbbing. Day by day, the tension among us grew, as our state
became more sordid, more animal" (485–86). Now it is the men who are
blind, Lawrence a contemplator of the heroic as well as a nostalgic reviver
of his medieval studies, pulling the whole range of his ideals and perceptions together so as to measure men, and to distance himself from them.
The turns and counter-turns of this political and psychological wisdom
attain far wider arcs than the mere prudence of the letters, which they also
help generate.[28]

And also to separate from. The letters draw away from the heroic, and
Seven Pillars stands at the distance of a willfully archaized period of this
writer's life, which otherwise will never yield to the retrospective interpretation of this Rousseau who will not see his way clear, this Marcel who will
not recapitulate. Our tribute to Lawrence consists in our imitating him in
the posture we take toward his work, simultaneously admiring the extraordinary pitch of action and the condensed realization of literary expression
while deploring the unaccommodated and unassimilated strains that bear
on what he did and wrote. But then even the *Seven Pillars* overshadows as
well as foreshadows its aftermath:

> The everlasting battle stripped from us care of our own lives or of others'.
> We had ropes about our necks, and on our heads prices which showed that the
> enemy intended hideous tortures for us if we were caught. Each day some of
> us passed; and the living knew themselves just sentient puppets on God's
> stage: indeed, our taskmaster was merciless, merciless, so long as our bruised
> feet could stagger forward on the road. The weak envied those tired enough to
> die; for success looked so remote, and failure a near and certain, if sharp,
> release from toil. We lived always in the stretch or sag of nerves, either on the
> crest or in the trough of waves of feeling. This impotency was bitter to us, and
> made us live only for the seen horizon, reckless what spite was inflicted or
> endured, since physical sensation showed itself meanly transient. Gusts of
> cruelty, perversions, lusts ran lightly over the surface without troubling us; for
> the moral laws which had seemed to hedge about these silly accidents must be

yet fainter words. We had learned that there were pangs too sharp, griefs too deep, ecstasies too high for our finite selves to register. When emotion reached this pitch the mind choked; and memory went white till the circumstances were humdrum once more. (29–30)

Memory has indeed gone white, so as to blank out the nuances we are empowered to know through the rest of his account. And yet, like many writers, he has found a way to make words express what is here spoken of not only as inexpressible but as irrecoverable. To say so is, as it were, a kind of amulet against something like a Proustian immersion. In this respect, as in so many others, it is only by mounting the turns of his contradictions and coiling them into counter-turns that Lawrence attains his peak of expression. And the same can be said for the drift—or, more appropriately, the current—of this passage, setting the note at the beginning, for a license in *Seven Pillars* to let what seems like digression show itself as the surface manifestation of a control so strenuous that it abjures the goal of ordinary consistency (to which *The Mint* is kept in strict subservience). In the longer passage from which this is an excerpt, he moves from evil to physical hardships, to overall characterization of his army, to the relation of body to soul, to God, to the criteria for strength, to the psychological and physical effects of testing that strength—and then to the defense of casual homosexuality, the most digressive, but also (and for that reason) the most revealing-concealing part of this run, and so properly climactic. One could subject this passage, and perhaps any in *Seven Pillars,* to an elaborate structuring of the relationships among its rhythms, its transitions, and its subjects. Here, astonishingly, Lawrence begins at a pitch that promises what he performs, a sustained self-portrait in action that is at the same time a historiographic demonstration and a study of "the assertion and denial of the romantic will," to borrow the terms of Thomas J. O'Donnell.[29] The constant editorializing thrust of adjectives and verbs dramatizes the mental and verbal agility of yoking such contradictions. Consequently, one's own terms for characterizing the self-transcendences verbalized here themselves tend to yoke contradictions: "idealistic and didactic," "hierarchic and democratic," "exposes and disguises."[30]

And again, in the endless backing and filling of the self-definitions with which he punctuates the book, one recurrent note is the plea that he misrepresents (the plea, of course, constituting part of the representation, and rhetorically doing a turn on the figure of preterition):

Of course our rewards and pleasures were as suddenly sweeping as our troubles; but, to me in particular, they bulked less large. Bedouin ways were hard even for those brought up to them, and for strangers terrible: a death in life. When the march or labour ended I had no energy to record sensation, nor while it lasted any leisure to see the spiritual loveliness which sometimes came upon us by the way. In my notes, the cruel rather than the beautiful found place. We no doubt enjoyed more the rare moments of peace and forgetfulness; but I remember more the agony, the terrors, and the mistakes. Our life is not summed up in what I have written (there are things not to be repeated in cold blood for very shame); but what I have written was in and of our life. Pray God that men reading the story will not, for love of the glamour of strangeness, go out to prostitute themselves and their talents in serving another race. (31)

But all this is not quite true: there are many "beautiful" descriptions, nubbly and succinct but sharp and powerful, that are carried off in *Seven Pillars of Wisdom*. And his very conception of a "Titanic" book would imply that the beautiful and the cruel are not exclusive categories.

> Before them [some of the "better men of the tribe"] we began to combat in words this crude prudence of the Serahin, which seemed all the more shameful to us after our long sojourn in the clarifying wilderness.
>
> We put it to them, not abstractedly, but concretely, for their case, how life in mass was sensual only, to be lived and loved in its extremity. There could be no rest-houses for revolt, no dividend of joy paid out. Its spirit was accretive, to endure as far as the senses would endure, and to use each such advance as base for further adventure, deeper privation, sharper pain. Sense could not reach back or forward. A felt emotion was a conquered emotion, an experience gone dead, which we buried by expressing it. (412)

Were these remarkable philosophical expositions made to his men in so many words? It is possible; and if so, it is a record of philosophical depths and levels of what amounts to despair, beyond not only *The Mint* but any account of awareness by men within the ranks, in fiction or history. In another connection:

> The irony was in my loving objects before life or ideas; the incongruity in my answering the infectious call of action, which laid weight on the diversity of things. It was a hard task for me to straddle feeling and action. I had one craving all my life—for the power of self-expression in some imaginative form—but had been too diffuse ever to acquire a technique. At last accident, with perverted humour, in casting me as a man of action had given me place in the Arab Revolt, a theme ready and epic to a direct eye and hand, thus offering me an outlet in literature, the technique-less art. Whereupon I became excited only over mechanism. The epic mode was alien to me, as to my generation. Memory gave me no clue to the heroic, so that I could not feel such men as Auda in myself. He seemed fantastic as the hills of Rumm, old as Mallory. (549)

And now, suddenly, the commanders of these Arabs are equal to Ma[l]lory in their action.[31] Life and ideas, indeed, abound here, as Lawrence must know. What are these "objects" that he put before them, unless by this he means the "objectives" of his campaign, rendered with a word that could confuse them for inert objects that are the opposites of what he opposes to them, life and ideas?

The numerous probes toward defining just what he was doing in *Seven Pillars* illustrate the gamut of Lawrence's psychological assurances and hesitations. Yet, as in all his work thereafter, they remain somewhat random. Those same responses and formulations inform *Seven Pillars* itself, where he has obdurately mastered and expressed their turns and counter-turns.

In the summary of chapter 103, embedded in his usual turns of self-deprecation, Lawrence declares himself "cured . . . of crude ambition," confessing to ambition of an extremity associated with future emperors: "I had meant to be a general and knighted, when thirty" (462). By then he was much more than that, but the extraordinary intention here revealed gives the measure of an aspiration that combines the toploftiness, the omnipotence fantasies of adolescence with the consciousness of unusual powers, the program of a Caesar or a Napoleon. For, if he had confined himself to that supreme ambition in the active life supremely realized, and if he had held to it, where could he not have gone? Surely beyond just a British administrative post in the Near East. He had already surpassed his sponsor Winston Churchill or any of his other contemporaries in their careers up to that age. His acumen equaled theirs; he had shown that he surpassed them in will and in intelligence. And yet in addition to all that, he wanted to write a Titanic book as well. The literary purpose expressed the integrations he had carried off. And also it compromised them to the point where he dissolved them. In Lawrence we have, at the highest level, the type of a vitiated early achievement, a modern type—of which *Seven Pillars* is not so much the record as the precondition. Isolation in his Arabian command could keep the Napoleonic action and the Dostoevskian contemplation in balance and fusion. Reintegration into England was bound to set them at odds, if for no other reason than that both the purpose to write and the time it would take would have had to conflict with any further active political purpose. He aspired to no higher posts, but if he had, he could not have carried out the final act of that tremendous phase, the concentrated withdrawal which results in the forging of *Seven Pillars*.

We may imagine that something in the treacherousness of an early environment that required vigilance to maintain middle-class respectability for the illegitimate family in which Lawrence was a child bred in him a keenness of vigilance that was sapped by a keenness of self-doubt. Vigilance and self-doubt reinforce each other, fortified by supreme intelligence, in the Arab campaign. But the hero and survivor of that campaign finds them conflicting with each other once he is loose in England, without hostile forces of various kinds around him and silence bearing in upon him. The silence of writing will allow him to express the conflicts, but not to come back for a further round of resolutions. This super-Rimbaud recounts the conditions of his own self-exile. Lawrence of Arabia disappears into the agonies that had made him what he was, and unmade him into what he became, the crotchety, proud, residually keen-thoughted self-denigrator and -destroyer. *Seven Pillars* gives the dimension of the making, and the terrible terms of the unmaking too.

Dialectic, Irony, and Myth in *Plato's* Phaedrus

The truth value Plato would have assigned to the whole utterance that constitutes a Platonic dialogue cannot be ascertained by adjudicating the etymology of *aletheia*.[1] Heidegger, who proposes a philosophy based not on enchainment of argument but on a hermeneutic "laying bare" (*Unverborgenheit*) of the human situation, reads the word, and the work of Plato, as corresponding to his enterprise. Yet there is much in Plato's discourse that will sustain reading *aletheia* as just a fair synonym for English *truth* or German *Wahrheit*. The intricacy of Plato's thought with respect to enchained propositions, and his responsibility to some canons of logic, have been ascertained through attentive deduction in the tradition of modern interpretation running, say, from Natorp to Vlastos. Yet Plato does not always resolve his questions; he often, and characteristically, leaves them open. In doing so he can easily be assimilated to a third modern tradition, that of the later Wittgenstein, in which philosophy is conceived as a technique for bringing thought beyond getting bogged down in pseudo-questions and preliminary questions to a brink of questioning.[2]

Plato can be accounted pretty much the originator of "hermeneutic" philosophy. He is a strong developer of philosophy based on propositions and the philosophy of radical questioning. Except for Heraclitus, most of his predecessors, from the evidence we have, occupied themselves exclusively with expounding and amplifying—and it would seem only rarely, even refining—a comprehensive cosmological or social system.

The Eleatics, Parmenides and Zeno, did enchain propositions. Zeno, too, was a radical questioner. Yet though Plato, in his dialogues, accords respectful attention particularly to the Eleatics, he is of course much more than a post-Eleatic. Furthermore, except in late works like the *Laws,* the dramatic method of the dialogues, and the myths they often contain, are not just a clever presentational strategy and a method of graphic illustration. The drama and the myth are inextricably interwoven with the hermeneutic function, the arguments, and the questioning of a given dialogue.[3] Writers who center their consideration of Plato on the enchainment of propositions or on his hermeneutics are not unaware of his dramatic method, and they do not ignore the myths. But they effectually bracket them by subsuming drama under "irony" and by translating the myths, if they treat them at all. In so doing they effectually deny their force, and their indissoluble connection, with propositions and questions.

To begin with, Stenzel has shown that "*doxa* and *diairesis* . . . are two logical operations in dissoluble union; each method depends on the assistance of the other." *Doxa* often roughly comprises the hermeneutic function (*doxa,* 237e, etc.) and *diairesis,* the reasoning division into categories (a main locus in the *Phaedrus,* 266b), is a function of testing logical propositions. Further, a central topic of the *Phaedrus,* the meaning of *eros,* is bound up with the gods, and with myth, as Gerhard Krüger has shown.[4] "Surely at this point," Socrates says near the end of the *Phaedrus,* "let it be that matters about *logoi* have been played through for us proportionately" (278b). The very "play"[5] cannot be confined to any utterances less than the whole dialogue, though the immediate reference is to a discussion about *logoi* in the writing and speech.

Socrates, in the *Phaedrus,* goes on further to qualify by suggesting a future logical test (*elenchos,* 278c) to the writings of Lysias or anyone else, and among the writers put on a par for future testing, Homer, the writers of odes, and Solon. His doing so introduces within this one dialogue three different, and irreconcilable, views about poetry—one that places it higher than other utterances (245a),[6] another here that puts it on a par, and a third (259c–d; 264e) that somewhat denigrates it, in terms different from the censure on poetry in the *Republic* and the *Laws.* The first and second views, indeed, can be found in this one passage, since Phaedrus is to go tell Lysias that he and Socrates got these *logoi* empowering them to question and judge "in the vale of the nymphs and the Muses"—where they "went down" (278c). Again, the irony that hovers over the reference to the nymphs and the Muses does not vacate the relation of the religious and mythical domains to Socrates' propositions, embedded, we may say, always in much different material, rather than enchained, as modern philosophers would organize them. Moreover, the linking of their utterances to the fact of their betaking themselves to a particular spot frames them and further qualifies them, by a dramatic context.

Generally, to take Plato's view of discourse, poetic and other, beyond a single dialogue would further complicate, contradict, extend, and qualify this important segment of his thinking. But in many respects he contradicts and qualifies himself, as in his views on poetry, and the more so the more important the topic is to him. This irreconcilability is especially the case in his thinking about the ideas. And in fact, the *Parmenides* faces that irreconcilability in well-nigh Wittgensteinian fashion—while still being modified by the dramatic condition that the dialogue is reported from a remote past, the youth of Socrates, and at fourth hand.

Nor can Plato's contradictions and irreconcilabilities merely be chalked up to "development", since often as not they occur in dialogues that very possibly were written fairly close together. This would be the case between the *Phaedrus* and the *Symposium,* if the *Phaedrus* did not resist firm placement in a sequence. One would be tempted, indeed, to characterize as reckless the work of the enchainers of propositions in the Natorp-Vlastos tradition who do not confine themselves to a single dialogue, still less to a single passage, in testing one statement against another—were it not for the fact that the enterprise of enchaining propositions integrally defines one inescapable focus of Plato's discourse. Moreover, the questions he raised are still alive, whereas the dialogue quickly became a moribund literary form, and Socratic irony would seem to be possible only within that form. So that our own concerns distance us from the form, but in Plato's case thereby also from the meanings, of his dialogues.

For one thing, we do not share whatever was Plato's credence in the Greek gods. He gave them some form of credence, however,[7] and even the myths that do not supplement them or use them as figures partake of that credence. In trying to account for the unified utterance of a whole dialogue of Plato, we have to try to be anthropologists, literary critics, and responsible philosophers all at once, at the risk of putting asunder what it was his unique achievement to put in perilous equipoise together.

The myths of the Platonic dialogues do not remain stable, nor do other features of organization within them. The Prometheus in the *Protagoras* and the Isles of the Blest in the *Gorgias* come at different high points of each dialogue. But in the *Republic* the sequence of the Line and the Cave, and then the Myth of Er, are more complex. Some of the speeches in the *Symposium* offer myths and others do not. Their coordination puts the myths and the plain discourses into a sort of equivalence, but at the same time the seven accounts of Eros stand in a hierarchy. Dialectic enters the *Phaedrus* fairly late, and its myths vary in length, in complexity, and in relation to the topic at hand, without any firm hierarchies beyond Socrates' stated preferences.

Moreover the progression of presentation, and the final bearing, of the individual dialogues vary considerably. Leaving aside the early, simple, elenchic, and aporetic ones and the late expositions like the *Timaeus* and the *Laws,* they do not all conform to the "ladder of certainty" type, the principle of organization followed by the *Republic,* and differently by the *Symposium.* In the *Protagoras* Socrates reverses his position on the central question with his interlocutor, symmetrically; in the *Gorgias* he does the same asymmetrically. There are also the *Apology* and the *Phaedo,* the *Crito* and the *Euthyphro,* which subordinate the doctrines they include to the offering of an exemplum, Socrates, as the great philosopher under mortal duress. There is the *Euthydemus,* which is organized so as to take back at the end what it had seemed to be developing. The principle enlisted here differs both from the intricate evolution of *aporiai* in the *Parmenides* and the development of modified doubt in the *Cratylus.* Nor are these types, even in the beginning of a typology that I am sketching, mutually exclusive.

The *Phaedrus* in some respects pretends to develop a ladder of certainty that it does not establish, except in some ways, for its main topics, *eros* and rhetoric. It also strongly illustrates the connection between the personality—as distinct from the capacity—of Socrates and what is said. It also in some respects takes much back at the end by concluding on the faintly ironic praise of Isocrates (278a–279b), who is to outdo Lysias. The connection is left quite open, for example, among the kinds of good madness; and nothing explicit is made of the fact that the other three besides love-madness—the madness of prophecy, of ritual, and of poetry—all involve verbal expression. Full closure is not effectuated for the connection between the best rhetoric and the best love,[8] though in this instance, to be sure, the connection is easily inferred.

The *Phaedrus* also produces *aporiai* without exactly emphasizing them, while at the same time it skillfully dodges a full resolution of the modified doubts it raises.

In addition to its bearing on the questions that it raises and the functions of the myths it broaches, a dialogue may vary as to the circumstances under which it takes place, the persistence and depth of doctrinal disagreement it engenders among its participants, the relative semantic loading of the participants themselves (Gorgias and Aristophanes are "heavier" than Phaedrus), and the number of topics it interconnects. The *Phaedrus* is highly specific as to its physical setting by the Ilissus. The participants mention the temperature, the distance from Athens, the neighboring shrines, and the very species of trees shading them. At one point they even speak of dipping their feet in the water (229a). At the same time the *Phaedrus* restricts itself to two participants, though what could well be an actual speech of a third "heavy" person, Lysias, is quoted verbatim and is always in view. It discusses only two main topics, rhetoric and love, though these prove to entail notions of large import for Plato elsewhere—poetry, the gods, good and evil, *sophrosuné,* the ideas, and the transmigration of souls. And it presents *aporiai* for all these topics. None of these conditions lacks implications for the propositions brought forth in the *Phaedrus.*

II

Eros is the subject under discussion, and the discussion is conditioned by being offered not in the form of an elenchic discourse between Socrates and Phaedrus but rather in the form of a speech that Socrates fashions to compete with the prior speech of Lysias. It is aimed, then, ambiguously at the form of Lysias's speech, to which Socrates refers, and at the content.

So far as the content is concerned, Socrates begins with a story about a lover of youth, in whose mouth he then places a speech. Within the speech Socrates has the lover himself begin with the very same thesis (*tout'auto,* 237b) that Lysias has propounded—though it is soon qualified. The speaker is made to begin, in rudimentary Socratic fashion, at square one. The beginning he enjoins (*archē,* 237c) asks for a definition of *eros,* and produces one without elenchic intermediation: "It is apparent to all that eros is a desire (*epithumia*), and even non-lovers desire things that are beautiful (*ton kalon*)". He then quickly expands to "two primary and leading characteristics" (*idea archonte kai agonte,* 237d) that are to be found in lover and non-lover alike, an innate desire (*epithumia,* again, soon defined as *hybris*) for pleasures and an acquired judgment (*doxa,* soon defined as *sophrosuné*), that aims at the best. Socrates' imagined lover allows that the lover himself can pretend disinterest. And this possibility, as applied back to either Socrates or Lysias himself, leaves open the question as to whether either or both have erotic designs on Phaedrus as a defining impetus for their speeches. Indeed, both Socrates and Lysias offer speeches that can be treated as generalized specimen addresses to a beloved. The designs of either speaker are in any case muted, but they cannot be discounted, since Socrates' imagined speaker himself raises such a possibility (237b, 256e). To apply such possibilities to Socrates' own utterances would at once bring the delicacy of a combined indirection and frankness into play—and "play," once again, is a term he uses to define his discourse (278b). Such delicacy easily shades into irony, but it would belong to a larger range of effects, a range that would include irony but not be confined just to irony. Lysias's speech is notable for lacking just such effects. It is rigid in tone, while Socrates' conversation provides a constant demonstration of psychological and rhetorical flexibility. Lysias's earnestness carries the implied claim that he at every point has moved from square one. In the contrast Socrates is besting Lysias philosophically, rhetorically, and poetically. Is he also proving himself the better lover?[9]

All that Socrates says, as doctrine, does not really contradict the principle of continence or chastity in Lysias's speech, since he finally recommends a sublimation that rarely, but emphatically, permits physical fulfillment.[10] Instead of just contradicting that speech, or testing it dialectically, Socrates amplifies it by other considerations while he is outdoing it in rhetorical variation and subtlety. Along with offering a large theory of psychology to implement his discourse, Socrates puts into words an example of a fuller and more acute psychology by marshaling his "nuanced" presentation through "irony," myth, and drama, rather than just by straight contradiction or disproof.[11]

Though widespread in Greece at the time, homosexuality stood under some legal interdict, and under the kind of family opprobrium that both Lysias's and Socrates' speaker graphically depict (231c).[12] It was a topic on which, except for Sappho, literature other than comic was usually silent up till then, in spite of the myths about it, and in spite of Sophocles' and Pindar's traditional proclivities in that direction. Plato can be said to transmute some air of opprobrium or encapsulation around homosexuality. The *Phaedrus* makes it the main basis for defining love, where the *Symposium* does not confine itself just to homosexuality. Plato's insistence on the ideal of near chastity is not just negative; love is the highest of his four forms of divine madness (*mania*). "The lover" (*ho erōn*) is called "a lover (*erastēs*) of things beautiful," and "every human soul by nature has beheld things as they are (*ta onta*)" (249e). The last expression can be taken as also reflexive; among *ta onta* would be the nature of love, in the gradual exaltation brought to comprise philosophy, the immortality of the soul, and the idea of the beautiful. Socrates exhibits, and dramatically exemplifies, a corresponding participation in these ideals, and a demonstration of himself as an *erastēs*, by the inspired trenchancy of his definitions, by the clarity of his charioteer myth, and by the exuberant effusions he employs when addressing Phaedrus.[13] Eros, to begin with, is revered as a god (243), and the speakers' mutual exchanges are characterized as close to dithyrambs (238d).

III

Poetry leavens the discourse of Socrates, helping it surpass the discourse of Lysias; just so does inspired poetry, and Socrates invokes inspiration (237a), surpass uninspired poetry. Still, Socrates' speech remains rhetorical, a contest speech. It competes with the speech of Lysias not only to the end of philosophical exposition for preferable ideas but also as a demonstration of superior rhetoric. It is offered as the sort of oral performance that in some ways surpasses a written one, though ironically it will have been written down in the *Phaedrus* of Plato, where we read it rather than hear it. Part of its rhetoric is to invert the conditions of Lysias, as it expands and qualifies the assertions of Lysias about love. As Lysias's speech is a real one written for oral delivery later, Plato's speech, attributed to Socrates, is an imaginary one, taken down, as it were, in writing after having first been delivered orally.

Socrates' switch from a version of Lysias's praise of the non-lover to a positive praise of love is mediated by abjuring his "error" (*hamartēma*, 242d) against the "god." "The customary sign" (his daimonion?) nudges him, and he compares his action of reversal to the verses Stesichorus wrote to expiate his denigration of Helen (243a–b). All of this rhetorical complex modifies the doctrine to be expounded by irony, by lightness, and by a version of piety toward the gods quite removed from straight devotion. At this rhetorical turn Socrates performs one of the two functions of logical discrimination he later classifies; he is subsuming his discourse, all under one heading of inspiration, poetry and prophecy (*eimi mantis*, I am a prophet, 242c). The *Phaedrus* in general exhibits, but intermittently, at controlled rhetorical positions, a penchant for classification. As a counterpart to this fusion of discourse-types, Socrates toward the end of the dialogue urges the desirability of distinguishing types of auditors (271–73), in a context where rhetoric has at last become explicitly the topic under exclusive discussion, and where a share in truth (*alētheias metechein*, 272d) and similitudes of truth (*homoioteta tou alethous*, 273d) are at issue.

Lysias's speech stands as a constant counterexample, to be pointed at explicitly or to be contrasted implicitly by what outdoes it. On the one hand, its completion of technique implies a lack of adaptive technique: it is as finished as a piece of joinery (234e). On the other hand, it has no proper order and could begin anywhere (253–54). These seemingly opposed defects are aspects of the same lack. It is not just that Lysias is tendentious. We may say that Plato, as opposed to his represented character Socrates, is comparably tendentious in the irreducibly rhetorical cast of his own discourse. The tendentiousness of Lysias assumes that its object has fixed attributes and can thus be rounded out like joinery and completed. Plato's differing practice has to mean that he values the contrary of these qualities. Lysias's very last word, "ask" (*erota,* 234e), advertises an open-mindedness about further questions, but it actually implies a closure, whether actual (if all questions turn out to have been adduced) or possible (if it turns out that there are some left). "I consider for my part that what has been said is sufficient," he says; "But if you desire further and consider something has been left out, ask." This one-dimensional notion of completeness, in which something might be "left out" or "omitted" helps underscore, by contrast, the discourse of Plato—and that of Socrates, which it contains— open-ended on all sides because its rhetoric is *not* confined by a single relation to the truth that remains at the same time its constant objective.

Socrates says that this speech has filled him like a bucket (235e), touching satirically on the quantitative assumption in Lysias's presentation.[14] He begins his qualifications with a reference to the old *sophoi* who are not sophists or even philosophers but poets like Sappho and Anacreon. Their discourse will soon be adduced as offering the inspiration to which he will aspire (235c). Quite late, when Socrates takes up his characteristic definition-by-questioning (263), he has begun by continuing his assessment of Lysias's form. And the method applies also to Lysias's content. Lysias began where he should end (264d); Eros should have been defined at the outset (263d).

IV

Lysias too is himself fixed in place as he is imagined to deliver his speech. There is no interplay between him and his auditors, the sort of interplay that gives life to the Platonic dialogue. Particles—which Lysias's speech employs sparingly—touch in these delicate qualifications, and a fine air of self-deprecation, often not measurable or sometimes even traceable, turns Socrates' statements reflexively back on the speaker. In something like courtship he must show himself somewhat bold while at the same time being somewhat modest.

Socrates certainly shows not only the irony of understatement, traditionally the root meaning of the term, but what might be called the irony of hyperbole, and notably in this dialogue. Nor are hyperbole and modesty necessarily at odds. Hyperbole is the extra effort of the man here dramatized as modest, just as modesty is the come-on that sharply frames his philosophical assuredness.

Possibly Socrates is courting Phaedrus—they are, after all, reposing on a river bank in the country, as Plato emphasizes (230b). This possibility shadows every statement Socrates makes with a qualification of its assumed impartiality—a faint infinite regress that would turn him into a case that could be subsumed under his version of Lysias's point, the lover tendentiously acting as the non-lover. Whether or not this is so, there is a momentary playfulness, even at such points of definition as the summary of an earlier speech (265), which suggests delectation as well as philosophical definition. Or it would do so were it not for the fusion of delectation and definition in Plato's discourse, itself to be understood as an instance of his stated principle that love entails philosophy and vice versa (256a).

When he speaks of "Sappho the lovely (*kalē*) and Anacreon the wise" (*sophos*), Socrates speaks of himself as "hearing" them (235c), and therefore in a sort of silent and admiring subordinate position. Their discourse is stated to be superior to the prose he has just been discussing—and at the same time, by implication, to the prose he has so far been uttering. Moreover, the term *sophos* applied to Anacreon picks up and ironically redeploys the other uses of the word with which it partly overlaps. Anacreon is a *sophos* in the old sense: *Sophos* is a Pindaric word for poet.[15] Anacreon, though a mere twitterer about pleasure, is still wiser than the sophists, to whom the name may be applied. His devotion to love in the very act makes him wiser in some respects even than the philosopher, to whom the term could also be applied. Yet, by the principle applied to Lysias, it is not enough just to celebrate love; the true *sophos* must define it.

And this is not all. Being paired with Sappho the beautiful, Anacreon the wise can only admire what she actually embodies, unless wisdom attains to beauty—which poetry also does. So the adjectives could also be reversed. The terms apply to the poetry and not to the persons here; the poetry of Sappho is beautiful. Is there an ironic suggestion that the beauty of her verse makes her not only Anacreon's equal but his superior? If so, it is only a touch. Socrates moves past it quickly.

When he mounts his very first myth, however, before even the introduction of Lysias, it is framed by no less than five ironic qualifications. Questions about physical location quickly yield Socrates' much-modified reply to Phaedrus's direct question about belief. I underline the terms of qualification:

> *Phaedrus.* I hardly noticed it [the altar of Boreas]. But tell me, by Zeus, Socrates, do you *believe* this mythologeme[16] to be true?
>
> *Socrates.* But if I *disbelieved* as the *wise* do I would not be out of place if I should *speculate*[17] and then *say* a gust of Boreas had pushed her while she was playing with Pharmakeia down from the neighboring rocks and that she *be said* thus to have met her end *being* seized by Boreas—or else from the Areopagus. For there is this account, too, that she was seized from there and not from here. (229c–d).

This myth, from the common stock, teems with foreshadowings of conditions contrary to the loves that will shortly be under discussion. At issue here is a heterosexual affair involving a god and a mortal woman, or nymph, not a homosexual one involving men. Its consummation is doubtful and in the past, not in a hoped-for future. And it was brought about, if at all, by force and not by persuasion. The myth, thus heavily shot with ironies in its relation to the theme of the dialogue and through the qualifications of its telling, was brought up lightly, as a feature of the landscape (229b). When Socrates has passed beyond it they return to the landscape; having led out from the waters, they pause to admire a tree (230a).

Before they do so, however, Socrates—who will be involved in rich mythologizing for the rest of the dialogue—ironically forswears attention to myths. To try to attain greater certainty about this myth would soon involve one in others, he says. A man thereupon would have to "set straight" a species or form or idea (eidos) of Pegasuses, of Hippocentaurs, of the Chimera, of Gorgons and a host of other prodigies. He declares that he himself—who is here at great leisure—does not have the "leisure" to do so. And what prevents him is that he cannot yet follow the adage of the Delphic oracle, "Know thyself." It would be laughable, he says, to examine other matters before knowing that. And he does not yet know—he here dovetails his own identity with the very mythical terms he is abjuring— whether he "happens to be some 'wild beast' more multiplex and swollen than the Typhon or a tamer and simpler creature, partaking of some divine and unpuffed (*atyphou*, 'non-Typhon') destiny" (230a). Now we hear nothing more directly in this dialogue about the famous Socratic and Delphic self-knowledge. Indirectly the psychologizing about love, and the mythologizing, fill out such a general picture—thereby ironically contradicting the assertion here that mythology is a distraction having nothing to do with self-knowledge.

V

Here the introduction of a fragment of a myth, and then the bare names of mythical creatures, at once activate several systems of ironic qualification. And further, as the richness of mythologizing in the *Phaedrus* particularly demonstrates, no one of the several myths that this dialogue raises has a similar dramatic impetus, a similar ontological set, or a comparable complexity, with respect to any other myth in the dialogue. Such a variety of myths in itself can be taken at once as an ironic demonstration of the instability in myth and also as an indication of the delicate insight, tinged with untrustworthiness, that inheres in this supreme lin-

guistic resource of Plato's. That is, the myth is ironic in function while at
the same time hyperbolic in expression.

So later (264–65) Socrates introduces his principles of classification,
when he explicitly says he has been playing. He does so in a context where
he assigns the good madnesses to separate gods, and when he distinguishes between the "not wholly unbelievable account" (*logos*) and the
"mythic hymn." He then offers the two principles (*eidoin*) of association
under one heading and of subcategorization. These Stenzel calls "the
plainest statement of the method of abstraction from particulars that can
be found anywhere in Plato."[18]

The myth itself is earnest and playful at the same time. And some
myths would seem to be more playful than others; in this way too they
differ from one another. The most earnest would seem to be the longest,
the myth of the charioteer who drives the winged horses of the soul, one
white and one black. The final myth, that of Thoth, strikes me as a little
less earnest, though nearly as long. It is hard to produce evidence for this
view; yet the sun and charioteer are honorific, whereas Thoth is exotic,
and there is much byplay with particles at the introduction of this myth.
The seed-plants of Adonis would be more earnest than Thoth, less so than
the charioteer. Most playful of all is the myth of the playful and endlessly
chirruping grasshoppers. Actual grasshoppers sing in the grass, linking the
mythical ones to ones that can be simply seen. They function as simple
analogues for discourse or music, an aspect of their love. That grasshoppers somehow live for the pleasure of the day perhaps recalls Aesop (mentioned by name in the *Phaedo,* 60c). The grasshoppers have been brought
up in the discourse about discourse as an example of discourse. This
recursiveness and simplicity are mutually reinforcing.

The myth of the charioteer is adduced as a demonstration (*apodeixis,*
245c) and after a preliminary demonstration of the immortality of the
soul. This myth does not map a homology of resemblances, even though
names could be given to the charioteer and his two horses. On the one
hand his task is quite simple: to move them ahead and on a celestial path.
But in another way the difficulties arising from the mismatched team lead
to millennial cycles of transmigrations. In accounting for these Socrates
himself shifts ground, and the wings become those not of horses but of the
soul. The details of sprouting new wings (250) in turn provide another
myth, which opens up another angle on love and the celestial strivings.
The final return to the horses (254) engenders a graphic physical description of the black one, which does then have allegorical applications, but
partial ones, and only to one undesirable psychological state. Before that
the unfolding transmutations of the myth have produced a typology of
souls defined, in still another modality (252), by their attendance to, and

dominance by, some particular god, Zeus or Ares or Apollo or Hera. This
assignment in turn redirects the typology of the eleven-gods-plus-Hestia,
which had been brought in as a contrast to the striving human charioteers
(246c–247b). As for credibility, "it is possible to believe it and also possible not to" (252c).

The complicated Thoth myth offers an account of origins, along with
a typology of the intellectual functions enabled by writing. It comes up to
fill in the insufficiency of an account of rhetorical expression. While the
distinction between technical skill (*technē*) and its lack (*atechnē*) has been
sufficiently established (274b) that between seemliness (or decorum, or
that which is fitting—or handsomeness) and unseemliness (*eupre-
peia/aprepeia*) has not. The myth of Thoth, unlike the others, in avoiding
its introductory topic, has little to say about *euprepeia*. It is as though the
solution of how writing will work carries with it a solution to other
problems related to expression.

The last myth, that of the seeds in the garden of Adonis, serves more
as a metaphorical parable than a myth. It arises, and is addressed to, the
problem of making what one learns permanent. Since it fuses memory and
expression, the intellectual and the moral, as well as a technique of care,
what it includes in its reference is more complex than its elements. Hence
this small myth may be said to recapitulate the large myth of Thoth as the
grasshoppers myth partially recapitulates the charioteer. But all these
myths differ among themselves so much in function, status, origin, structure, and tone, that such correspondences as these would only provisionally apply.

VI

The parable of the seeds is brought in to clarify a refinement not
possible through the myth of Thoth. Qualifying and supplementary, it
provides a measure to discriminate among kinds of writing. What is written down, including speeches for delivery (*logoi*) like those of Lysias, do
permit recall. But they will not answer an auditor (274–75): they lack the
suppleness of the "writing" engraved on the living memory, the "knowledge (*epistēmē*) that is written on the soul of a learner" (276a).

Such orally revived "writing" has the advantage of being remembered
and at the same time of allowing for dialectic—for the decision "toward
whom it is necessary to speak and to be silent." Of such a "living" piece of
writing, the actual physical writing is, properly considered (*dikaiōs*), just an
image (*eidōlon*). "Since the power of *logos* happens to be soul-leading (*psy-*

chagogia), it will be necessary for the would-be rhetorician to know how many forms the soul has" (271c–d).

The argument brings dialectic to the fore as a resolution of speech modes, but a discrimination is still needed between that which is merely an amusement, like an eight-day garden of Adonis, and that which is serious (*spoudē*, 276b) like the seeds a husbandman tends for eight months.[19] The eight-day garden is to the husbandman's seeds as play to earnest. But the dialectic quickly takes over the distinction as well, since Plato recommends not the solemnity of Lysias but an admixture of play in a higher seriousness. The "serious" man (*spoudē* is repeated, 276c) will not write his words on water. Having treasured them in "the garden of letters," he will spend his days "playing" (*paizein*) with them. At an earlier extreme of play, the grasshoppers are fancied as produced by the Muses (259c).

The dialectic in itself is not enough, however. Socrates has earlier indicated that even the skill (*technē*) of "the Eleatic Palamedes" (Zeno) can be used to convince hearers that "the same things are like and unlike, one and many, abiding and fleeting" (261d). This definition supersedes itself also by a playful touch: in calling Zeno by the name of the legendary discoverer of the alphabet and many other things, Socrates assimilates him to a parallel of the later myth of Thoth. In being called a Palamedes, Zeno is treated to the irony of hyperbole. At the same time higher uses are attributed to him than the paradox-mongering of court controversy (*antilogikē*) for which it is here said his technique can be used. The mere rhetor is defined by a plain contrast between the horse and the ass (260), itself adduced as an example of false and superficial classification.

When Socrates is conducting his surely playful etymology connecting the prophetic (*mantikē*) with inspired madness (*manikē*), he is engaging in a dialectic that leads him shortly to a whole repertoire of intellectual functions—investigation (*zētēsis*), mind (*nous*), conception (*oiēsis*), inquiry (*historia*) and thought (*dianoia*). Yet all these are playfully, and dialectically, caught up in a discussion of how bird-signs may be interpreted. In the charioteer myth a pure thought (*dianoia*) and knowledge (*epistēmē*) nourishes the good horse so that he can see justice (*dikaiosunē*), prudence (*sophrosunē*)—and, once again, knowledge (247). These are the horses of the gods, whereas human soul "scarcely catch sight of things as they are (*ta onta*)."

The very beginning of Socrates' first speech is caught up in drama and dialectic, as well as irony. Phaedrus's swearing by the plane tree, and his declaration that he will never say another speech, lay a "necessity" (*anankasō/anankē*) on the "unwilling" Socrates (236d–e). He professes that shame will induce him to gallop through his discourse, and he invokes the

Muses at once (as Lysias will not have done). "I shall speak under a veil," he says, and the word *enkalupsamenos* points ambiguously both to the drama of hiding one's face and the indirect speech of the veiled stories and myths he will begin forthwith. Drama and indirectness perpetuate the dialectic on another plane, extending it, and keeping it playful.

VII

Much has been said about the transition from oral to written expression in Greece, and Havelock has impressively demonstrated how intimately such conditions are bound up into Plato's outlook and expression.[20] However, these main conditions are not exempt from dialectic—or for that matter from contradiction. Much in Plato substantiates Havelock's contention that Plato was striving for a preponderance of the written over the oral. Yet in the passages surrounding the seeds parable he gives primacy to the oral—an oral that at the same time is defined as a kind of writing in the head, as indeed Derrida has insisted.

Plato's very vocabulary in this dialogue seems aimed at combining the oral and the written into dialectical complications. Elsewhere, as Havelock has persuasively shown, Plato associates poetry with oral transmission. Here in one instance he applies the less common sense of *poiētēs*, "writer," not only to prose but to the uninspired written prose of Lysias (236d), which he contrasts throughout with inspired writing, oral effusion, and verse. The other nine uses of *poiētēs* and its adjective in the dialogue all refer either to lyrical poetry or to dramatic poetry, or at least to highly imaginative writing inspired by the Muses and by the divine madness (especially 245a). Socrates' own discourse pretends to this higher form of writing, as against Lysias's, though it is a kind of prose that in dialogue form carries some of the character of theatrical discourse as well as of the divine inspiration he repeatedly invokes. Furthermore, the term *syngraphein* ("compose in writing") and its cognates, habitually applied to prose writers, and usually by prose writers, from Herodotus on, occur sixteen times in the *Phaedrus,* where Plato unusually applies them not just to prose—though he sometimes does that (as for example 272b, 258a, 258c). Rather he uses *syngraphein* terms in the sense of "writing in general" or even applies them in cases where only poetry is in question. And at the point of their highest frequency (257–58), they are called into dialectical use, meaning "writing in general" but at the same time applied back recursively to Lysias. And since the *Phaedrus* itself is a written presentation of an imagined oral conversation, it both incorporates and contradicts its own final recommendation of informed oral discourse as the highest form.

Even if this recommendation is taken as aiming at Plato's unwritten doctrine, it retains its qualifying dialectical force within the statement of this particular dialogue itself.

The very act of reading is dramatized at one explicit point (230d); and the reading-recitation of Phaedrus himself, the speech of Lysias, is prepared for dramatically at the outset of the dialogue. The procedure vaguely resembles the way the client of such a *logographos* would read a memorized speech in the law courts. Oral and written are combined in the later designation of Lysias' text as having been "delivered orally from a book" (243c).

VIII

One can apply back to Plato's dialogues generally two complementary notions developed in the *Cratylus* (385–86): Plato's version of Protagoras's notion that the truth is individual to every man, and Euthydemus's notion that all men are equally right. Both of these follow from the differentiation of persons through self-consciousness, and the community of language, which Socrates forces upon his auditors, implies a concord to be envisioned, if never reached, through various kinds of testing. In the *Phaedrus* Lysias is out of reach, but the dialogue concludes, as always semi-ironically, with the praise of a young Isocrates. Thus Plato has Socrates act as though he were falling back to the rhetoricians, but in a form that will include potential philosophers, since Isocrates ran a rival school. The very semantic spread of the word *sophoi* in the *Phaedrus* carries with it such a possible tolerance. The word "to agree" (*homologein*) and its derivates occur eight times in the *Phaedrus*.

Socrates' critique of Lysias's dialogue as lacking order refers us back to the order of his own discourse, which slides in and out of myth and permits all sorts of qualifications and interruptions. And then there is the overarching order of the *Phaedrus* itself, with a return to the initial topics, physically symbolized in the return to Athens at the end of the dialogue. Socrates and Phaedrus go out from the city at the beginning and return to it at the end. "Let's go" (*iōmen*) is its very last word. The dialogue is almost wholly circular in beginning with Lysias but almost ending with the encomium of Isocrates. At the very end poetry, myth, and love are delicately touched on by the concluding Prayer to Pan, which seals it as a kind of triptych.[21] A conclusion has been reached about the nature of rhetoric, and another about the nature of love, but the connections between them have only been sketched by comparison. Nor do these topics have the obvious relation to one another that, for example, rhetoric and virtue do in the *Gorgias* or proper classification and proper government do in the *Republic.*

It is, however, Phaedrus who first mentions "Isocrates the fair" (*ton kalon,* 278e). Does this mean that he is ironically shown not to have fully assimilated Socrates' teaching? Socrates takes the praise up and agrees with him. Does this mean he is somewhat tired, or somewhat infatuated, or both? Again, here at the end the dramatic relations, and positions, all sorts of interplay, perfuse the notions presented.

The term *eidos,* form or idea, a large one in Plato, runs casually through this dialogue, as I have shown above, sometimes as a place-marker for categorizations, sometimes in a weak sense that cannot be pressed. The dramatic presentation, the irony, and the very dialectic, permit it to remain fluid while other notions are set complexly into place. Plato's form in the *Phaedrus,* as sometimes differently elsewhere, serves also not only to keep questions open but to let them participate in various degrees of being open, from the faintly ambiguous hint to full closure.

Equanimity and Danger:

The Distribution of Questions and Style of Confrontation in the Four Dialogues around Socrates' Trial

I n the four dialogues around his trial, Socrates is not only a leader of discussion. He is also an exemplum, and a historical exemplum. Uniquely, these dialogues center on his capital exposure, a circumstance that should be taken as orienting and in a sense subordinating all these discussions, and also as orienting each of them toward the others.[1] Consequently an interaction is set up between positions canvassed or taken and the person of the central figure. The duress under which Socrates reviews ideas makes him something other than a disinterested inquirer.

This situation, common to the four dialogues around his trial, groups them together, nor would the prevailing careful assessment of plausibilities about dating much dissociate them one from another—nor can the topics themselves be used in any firm way as indicating points in a development. So, for example, the fact that the *Phaedo* does not dwell on politics, which Hackforth mentions, is not just to be taken "developmentally" in a way that allows us to put its individual emphasis down as "earlier" than the *Republic* (for that reason).[2] Nor would the *Phaedo*'s nearly total concentration on one pressing question, the immortality of the soul—at an unusual length—derive just from its having been written later. Its associability to the other three is independent of when it may have been written, especially since Plato may be conceived as holding onto all the dialogues, and even of adding touches to them, throughout his lifetime.

For all four dialogues, though Socrates speaks in the *Apology* (31e) of having avoided politics during his life, the situation in view is a highly political one, and cannot be divorced from other manifestations of Plato's historical consciousness, either the more short-range one of the types of government and their causal sequence in the *Republic,* or the more long-range ones in the *Timaeus* and the *Critias,* which overlap in topic with the arguments about the soul and the Pythagoreanism of the *Phaedo.* In this dialogue one can say that Plato is most political when he is least political. A beginning of a long-range view is given with the reference to a legendary religious custom still being observed as the dialogue opens.

It is germane for our purposes, if not for Plato's, that nobody would now find Socrates' arguments about the immortality of the soul convincing, not even a believer in the immortality of the soul. So that even the sharp discrimination of what his doctrines are here (and elsewhere)—the prolonged questioning that has preoccupied most modern commentators—must be subordinated, for our purposes, to ascertaining what the thrust of the dialogue is as it has been constructed in context. Our own interest, finally, is historical, not systematic, and the discrimination of particular doctrines serves that historical interest. As it happens, and even in the most elaborate and almost surely the latest of the four, the *Phaedo,* one account of its structure, at least, would make the doctrines a subset of the whole presentation, the siting of Socrates' preoccupations on the threshold of death. The elaborate exordium about Apollo and the ship to and from Delos can be intricately coded not only to anticipate but also to situate those later arguments.[3] The same constraint applies to Socrates' preoccupations before the dialogue as they are told in it, where he has been drawing on Aesop, honoring Apollo, following an injunction in a dream, writing poetry and/or music, and at least potentially equating this activity with philosophy—"philosophy is the highest music" (61a). This series of situation-equations and propositions can itself be taken to govern all the other propositions, and notably the philosophical deductions, to which the dialogue rises. The philosophical deductions, however, as the qualifications surrounding these presentations imply, must at the same time be accorded pride of place within the dialogue; they are the highest music. But they are still music, the same in kind though higher in degree, in a way that perhaps goes beyond Pythagoras, for whom the music that was highest, and most mathematical, would still be audible or at least available for composition. And probably for Pythagoras and the Pythagoreans (since music, perhaps often in association with poetry, would be the defining expression), poetry qua poetry would not be in the picture at all, as it is for Plato here, and for Socrates.

There is another poet brought in as an inquirer about the poetry of

Socrates and a measure for it, Evenus. He is also a Sophist, one spoken of in the *Apology* as commanding a large fee (20c), and so his name belongs on the list of thinkers in this dialogue, a list of so many philosophers that one could almost construct a map of the philosophical landscape in 399 B.C. by extending their names into the doctrines associated with them and their various masters.[4] This would be all the more the case if these names were supplemented with those of others who held notions germane to the doctrines, Socrates goes on to expound. The doctrines of wholeness, of opposites, of mind, of coming to be and passing away, of the permanence of the invisible, of number theory, are topics, if not exactly of the same stripe, that were discussed by Parmenides (65b, 78d, 83b), Empedocles (71c, 96b), Heraclitus (on exchange, 69b; on waking and sleeping, 71c; on harmony, 93–95), Anaximander (109a), Anaxagoras (97c–98d), Philolaus (61d), and perhaps Zeno (96e), as well as by Pythagoras and his followers.

As Socrates says, "My life seems to me not to be sufficient in length for the logos" (108d). This puts the dialectic and the exemplum on the same line, incommensurably. Simmias lightly contradicts, "But these things do suffice." The dialogue as a whole offers evidence for both views, which means that the logos neither disappears before the life nor can be assigned prominence over it.

II

Of these four dialogues, the *Phaedo* alone, though conditioned by the external circumstances, does not, for the best of reasons, address them other than incidentally or analogously. Because Socrates faces death it recounts his answers to questions about what happens to the soul after death, whereas typically the occasion for a Platonic dialogue is somewhat fortuitous and the topic is presented as coming up freely, somewhat randomly chosen by the discussants. The dialogue immediately preceding in dramatic circumstance, the *Crito,* discusses the ethical question that bears upon an immediate possibility of choice: shall Socrates accept the means to escape offered by his supporters?[5] This situation, in turn, is different from that in the preceding circumstance (though like it in determining what is discussed), the trial in the *Apology,* where Socrates is a defendant and not an inquirer, standing before an audience that has a life-and-death power over him. The first of this series in dramatic time, the *Euthyphro,* also deals with judicial circumstances, but obliquely and ironically; there is a silent irony that Socrates is on the eve of being convicted as he engages in his discussion with Euthyphro, an irony that overrides and conditions all the specific, more usual ironies, of the interchanges that in this case are closest of all four dialogues to the usual elenchic situation. And questions about morality and the gods are confined to this dialogue of the four (*Euthyphro*, 8). The other three, whatever else they ask, take the gods for granted.

Euthyphro, as a blind unjust accuser within the family, and as an unreflective professional with respect to the gods, is inversely symmetrical to Socrates, and his circularity around "the holy" contrasts with the exemplification of ordinary justice in Socrates' devotion to the gods, not just in the family sphere but publicly, as it is shown especially in the *Apology*, but in the *Crito* and the *Phaedo* as well. It is ominous that, just before Socrates' trial, Euthyphro, a representative if exaggerated custodian of religious values, is so unresponsive to the *elenchos* in his sanctimoniousness. He provides a social base for the attitude of the judges, sealing off the possibility of dialogue by his automatic response.

In the *Euthyphro* Socrates is engaged in conversation with someone who by contrast with Socrates advertises his self-satisfaction. Euthyphro ignores the very large distress that Socrates allows to pass by, even though the possibility of dire conviction hangs over the dialogue for him and us. Thus does he demonstrate a capacity he once again demonstrates in the *Phaedo*, and more resoundingly, of being able to carry on the *elenchos* in the face of death. The *elenchos*, in this context, proves the selflessness of Socrates' devotion to moulding good citizens, even in so casual and unpromising an encounter as this one with Euthyphro—an encounter that is unpromising because Euthyphro armors himself in a blind devotion to the very gods Socrates will be condemned for supposedly contemning by the very fact of entering an *elenchos*. The living situation, and the best way to teach the connections among knowledge, virtue, the holy, the public life, the private life, and the soul to other citizens, are all embodied in the image of the central figure, in each case properly angled for the question he both bears upon and discusses. Yet this Socrates stands already under the shadow of a future trial that qualifies his utterances.

Euthyphro from the beginning (3b–c) is careful not to get into open debate, but the *elenchos* proceeds relentlessly. As a soothsayer Euthyphro is the opposite of Socrates—more speculative about the gods, and at the same time more conventional. In his attitude toward himself, and also in his posture toward others, he is self-centered and self-protective and self-righteous, perverting family values by his heedlessness to them, indiscriminate in his complicated case.

The comparison between the two is emphasized at the outset by Euthyphro's assumption that Socrates, like himself, has come to the King's Porch not as a defendant but as a plaintiff, and he sees his own prophetic powers as analogous to the *daimonion* of Socrates. Yet they are on opposite sides not only of the court but of an attitude towards the gods. Euthyphro is "piously" bringing a charge against his own father of manslaughter by neglect for leaving a murderer to die bound in a ditch.[6] He sees this rigidity and self-importance as a proper "holiness," where Socrates, confronting constantly both in the charge and in this dialogue what holiness truly means, is called an innovator, a "poet about the gods" (3b). And later (6c) Euthyphro says that poets make up stories about gods, which echoes the charge that Socrates has reported. Where Socrates is accused of corrupting the next generation—which he stresses in the metaphor about young plants in his initial description—Euthyphro is actually violating the family pieties about the prior generation. Socrates tries to take the pride of Euthyphro as a handle in getting him to "defend" Socrates, but the interlocutor misses this cue, as he misses every other, in a way that is ominous for how the Athenians judging Socrates will assess his arguments. They will turn out, just like Euthyphro, to substitute blind censoriousness for true piety. Over the irony, then, that this super-hypocrite walks free while Socrates will be condemned, there plays the further irony that his situation is a reverse mirror of Socrates'. Toward the end Socrates continues the identification, though ironically; it is Euthyphro, he says, not Daedalus's "descendant" Socrates, who has been manipulating the argument like the famous mobile statues of Daedalus, with the result that they have come right round in a circle. And this reversion is the more ominous that in this instance the *elenchos* lacks its usual function of sharpening the mind of the interlocutor, which is felt to happen even in dialogues where no progress has been made.

Again uniquely, the speakers stand before two single, specific, public events: Euthyphro's arraignment of his father and Socrates' preparation for his defense. These two trials do not just add qualification to the encounter, as does the festival of Bendis before the discussion of the *Republic*. The two trials center and orient the bearing of the discussion. Euthyphro's casual assumption of priestly solidarity gives him the function of a Job's comforter here. Socrates' cross-questioning about holiness is aimed at giving Euthyphro pause, at inducing him to doubt about the arraignment. But Euthyphro's failure to consider, or even raise, this possibility, hints at a corollary obtuseness in the judges of Socrates, and leaves the theological discussion hanging in the air as it touches on the forms and on the mystery of how holiness cannot be defined as that which is pleasing to the gods. The advanced notion that holiness cannot be conceived of as either prior to the gods' pleasure or posterior to it escapes Euthyphro entirely and is left as an austere, Pyrrhic conclusion for the Socrates who heroically continues producing definitions under these conditions.

Euthyphro says he has never made a prediction that did not come true (3c), but then predicts Socrates will carry his case (3e)! Socrates himself in the *Apology* (39e) will make the more accurate prediction, based not on vague good will but on an exact sense of his situation.

As for the questions in the *Euthyphro* about the relation between fear and reverence—these definitions can be brought to bear on the other three dialogues. They would help define a tone of equanimity maintained in the face of danger. They are evaded here by Euthyphro, to whom the *elenchos*, ominously, ends by doing no good. Is the holy just? (11e). This large question cannot get off the ground under these conditions. The real difficulty of the questions about the holy, and the further incapacity of Euthyphro to understand the difficulty (let alone participate in solving it), has a further corollary in the difficulty of defining what its opposite, impiety, might be, in the charge against Socrates. Indeed, this question is so elusive that in his defense he wisely refrains from any such rarefied definitions, and instead confines himself to pleading piety along the conventional lines whose contours we can measure from the philosophical superiority of the discussion in the *Euthyphro* to that in the *Apology*.

III

The *Apology* is not a dialogue; or rather, it shows a defendant on a charge that could be (and has turned out to be) mortal, conducting his defense under conditions that empty dialogue of its exploratory force. The pressure of concentrating circumstance in this work is so great as to subvert the possibility of Socrates' constant method. And Meletus easily frustrates his one attempt to get one going in the court. The *Apology* begins with ominous abruptness by quoting Socrates' answer to charges that are not yet given. In other dialogues the speakers all proceed under the risk of returning to square one of the question or questions asked, and they do so more or less willingly, even Euthyphro. But even if they do return to square one, they are enriched by some momentary clarification, and also by having experienced the possibility of clarification. They have, minimally, been trained for the *elenchos*, and such training is presented as the road for proceeding to "know thyself"—largely a knowledge of starting with the clarification that you so far do not know. The *Apology* has Socrates assert the self-definition of "know thyself" while withdrawing, under pressure, the means of its realization.

In what could well be Socrates' actual recorded words, or an edited version of them,[7] it is assumed that square one is the best that can be hoped for; if Socrates were to be returned to his normal life, he would not be intellectually enriched, only spared. And even if his judges had gone so far to accede to his reasonable but contextually absurd proposal that his punishment be to be fed for life at public expense (36d–37a), they, for their part, would still not have been enlightened. They would simply have performed the just decision that Socrates' acquiescence in it shows is their normative function (though in this instance unjust). Of course, he is neither spared nor honored but first voted guilty and then condemned to death. This condition leads back to his being a normative exemplum, since "many other good men have been caught" in the emotional undertow that governs the process of the trial, which carries the ironical name of a "justice" (28b). There is, he says, "no danger of the rule breaking in my case." It will "stand." And so Socrates stands fast in the law though caught in the emotional undertow that governs the law, a living *elenchos*.

Still, Socrates does lay bare paradox after paradox in the charge against him. If it were true, effectually, it would not be true. This argument holds both with regard to the gods and with regard to teaching the youth. At the same time, he "will construct arguments in my usual way" (27b), and this permits him easily to extract the admission from his accuser that to believe in divine activities is to believe in divine beings. Not then to be acquitted does reveal that "what will catch me, if it does, is not Meletus or Anytus but the slander and envy of the multitude" (28b). Socrates is right in this counter-accusation. His correct, but fatally incapable, assessment that such slander underlies the accusations has led him from the beginning (18d, where "slander and envy" is first introduced) to build his speech on the circumstance of old and new slander. Many times through the whole of his speech, he invokes the noun and verb for slander—based on a root (*dia-ballo*) that emphasizes the displacement of the allegation from its object. This begins the paradox that he is proved right in his assessment by the conviction that declares him wrong; to show the old accusers wrong will not stay the new accusers.

The *Apology* (33c) refers in passing to the entertainment value of conducting an *elenchos* and the possibility of distraction. Entertainment and distraction are just the increments that cannot accrue to the discourse here, though even on the threshold of death they are not wholly absent from the *Phaedo,* with its kindly, pious, celebratory politeness, a tone for very good reasons not to be found so strongly in dialogues of less dire circumstance. In the *Apology* Socrates stands constrained to carry out an *elenchos* combined with a speech, whereas in the *Gorgias,* the *Protagoras,* and elsewhere, as well as in the *Phaedo* (among this group), he presents a dignitary delivering a set speech against which he contrasts an *elenchos.* Protagoras, after delivering a speech in the *Protagoras,* initially refuses the *elenchos* on the grounds that "if I had let my opponent declare the method of my presentation, I would not be famous in Greece" (335a). Now this is just what the court circumstances force Socrates to do. He is constrained to make the speech that is foreign to his nature and shown in Plato's dialogues as intrinsically constraining for anybody, whatever the person might think.

Belief in the god keeps him from being willing to offer the condition of desisting from philosophy if he is guilty of not believing in god (29d–30). Here Socrates takes the unusual circumstance that is not a pair of philosophical assertions but a pair of legal charges. "There is nothing greater in the city than my service to the god" (30a). He also combines both parts of the charge and turns them upon each other and around. His last word is of the god he has been condemned for not believing in or innovating about. Throughout he has assumed that the court is governed by emotional prejudice, and there is a tradition of making an emotional appeal to it that he will not avail himself of (35c). He holds up a model of how the court should act by standing on argument rather than emotional appeal. Therefore the very circumstances he invokes in his trial rebuke the judges and bear witness to best judgment.

The Arginusae case, to which he refers and in which he would not cooperate in helping arrest for execution the admirals supposedly implicated in that defeat (32c), is in a sense an earlier version of factors that will stymie the trial.[8]

Socrates addresses not inquirers but judges, and the reply comes not in words but in the votes: of guilty, then of death. In the cross-examination of Meletus, he acts as a defendant and not just as a philosopher; it is not a voluntary act he is performing here. Still, he invokes the *elenchos,* and on a subject about which he has long been seasoned, how to educate the youth. The replies of Meletus, however, are cruelly curt, almost insulting; and they are far from being truly responsive, to say nothing of their constituting arguments. Refutation, under these constraints, provides neither enlightenment nor exoneration. It irritates and enrages, tipping the jury, presumably, further toward the first conviction (281 to 220), because his next proposals and defenses tip them still further toward the death penalty (360 to 141).

"The unexamined life is not worth living" (38c), and Socrates makes this statement in his initial response to the act of conviction, serenely continuing to examine his own life under this maximum duress, filling out this exemplum in the imagined context, before his sentencing, of how he should live if they let him. Both what he has chosen to say and the conditions under which he says it base his defense on the exemplum of himself.

IV

The *Crito* begins with a reference to the return of the ship of Delos, which will signal Socrates' execution, as does the *Phaedo,* and it also opens from an account of a dream, the vision of a woman in white who tells him he will be going to the other world by quoting a line of Homer. This framework picks up the notion expanded at the end of the *Apology* when the desirability of the other world is characterized by the dead man's access to the poets and heroes of the past (40d–41c). This possibility sets the scene and the tone for Socrates' confrontation, uniquely in this dialogue, of an actual and extremely momentous choice, whether or not to accept the proposal that he escape with the help of the friends who have sent Crito on the errand of finding this out. He casts his refusal in the form of a truncated dialogue, deferred at the end by a long imagined speech put in the mouth of "the laws," who expound a sort of categorical imperative that for them to exist they must be obeyed precisely when they are to a man's disadvantage. In the *Apology* Socrates makes the distinction between uncertain justice and the justice of the judges of the afterworld, "Minos and Rhadamanthus and Aeacus and Triptolemos" (41a). Here the principle of a higher justice is entailed by piety toward the city that has reared him, embodied in its laws. Duty to city is of the same kind as duty to father, but greater (50d). And the term touched on for piety, *sebesthai* (51b), exactly reverses the charge of impiety, *asebeia,* on which he had been condemned.

Here, under radically transformed circumstances, the path of the *Euthyphro* continues to be followed, "the just" once more recombining with "the holy" (51c). Socrates has been hurt by men and not by the laws (54b); and if he were to move to another city, he would not be himself because the ground on which he exercises his characteristic activity would be taken from him by his act of inconsistency toward the laws, and toward the principle, often repeated here and elsewhere in his work, that suffering harm is preferable to doing it (53a–54b). As always in these four dialogues, he is an exemplum. What counts is "not living but living well . . . beautifully and justly" (48b). This entails dying to be consistent with himself (46). The many do what they happen to do, whether sensible or senseless (44d). If he builds on opinions, he will build on sensible ones (47a); and this emphasis on the opinions of the wise, too, refers the activity of discourse to the personal example, as the personal example is also measured by its activity, of which this dialogue is itself a succinct example, as well as an exploration of a moral question and the record of an actual decision.

V

The *Apology* ends in a coda over whether there is an afterlife, in an aporia: "To die is one of two things: either the dead man will be as nothing, having no perception of anything; or according to report there will be some change and transfer for the soul of place from here to another place" (40c). "I am to die, you are to live; which of these comes to the best result is unclear to anyone except the god" (42). The principle of Socrates' wisdom as one who knows he does not know is asserted here to the very end; the doubt he asserts under the fresh death sentence proves him to be true to himself.

Obviously the *Phaedo* proclaims a far greater certitude on this question. It "contradicts" the aporia of the *Apology;* and on the alternative about the afterlife, the preponderant view of Plato himself if we are to judge from the *Republic,* the *Gorgias,* and elsewhere, it offers a far more elaborate account and rationale, but one that is situational with respect to the final hope of Socrates. The *Phaedo* is to be integrated into the range of responses in this final phase, if also into the development of his ideas. Yet it should be remembered that the situation is in the text, whereas the development is conjectural and is based on the questionable assumption of consistent evolution.

Death frames all four of these dialogues, but the *Phaedo* most impendingly. Pitched dramatically at the moment of death, the *Phaedo,* at the same time, is the most speculative philosophically, the longest and the most intricately reasoned. The *Phaedo* (70d) implies that transmigration may or may not be true. So do other passages in the dialogue, and notably the large shift from the proofs of the first half to the hypotheses of the latter half.

One guide to the complexity of the *Phaedo,* and also to its singlemindedness, and even to its resultant sketchiness on many topics germane to its discussion, is the initial situation. Its frame is set long after the actual event and very far away from it, unlike the other three, which are set at the (itself distant) time in Athens. Phaedo is at a distant place and a later time, looking back as he tells his Pythagorean host about a discussion Socrates had with two other Pythagoreans just before his execution. The initial complexity of this situation matches and projects the arguments about the immortality of the soul, which are in turn implied by, or at least consonant with, the assumptions of the other three dialogues. Those assumptions are preliminary to the dialogue, however, because it moves to the full argument of long-range notions that can be taken in turn as preliminary to them, involving the god mentioned at the very end of the *Apology* and constantly adduced in the *Crito*. The *Phaedo* gives both a range of what a soul can attain through philosophy—the *theion genos*—and what a clear view a soul either freed from the body or uncontaminated by it might attain.

Especially in so complex a dialogue as the *Phaedo,* too great a focus on the clarities of Plato's sometimes close-marshalled reasoning in specific nodal points of ongoing definition—the mode of Vlastos—may result in a stated opposition between rational and irrational elements in Plato (Hackforth, 101, citing Dodds). Yet as just the phrase *theios logos* (85d4) implies,[9] Plato conceived of the divine not as irrational, Dodds' subject, but as rational. Putting a passing use of this phrase in the mouth of a Pythagorean might be taken to imply that some questions would have to be left begging, however great a claim the speaker might lay to rationality. Simmias, in speaking of his own aporia, imagines that it is "difficult or impossible to know clearly" about the topics under discussion. The *elenchos* and other means they employ are like "sailing through life dangerously on a raft, unless one could make one's way through more safely and less dangerously upon a firmer support, some *theios logos.*" Here, in the mode of the same metaphor that Socrates uses later on for the "second sailing" of hypothesis, the *theios* is beyond, and inclusive, and endorsing of reasons. Moreover, "know thyself" has its origins in the oracle of Apollo, though it is also a defining apothegm for the goal of the *elenchos*. Plato has Socrates propound one repertoire of possibilities for the afterlife in what, seen minimally, are two proof-modes of demonstration and hypothesis.

The opening question exactly frames the interaction between the situation of the condemned Socrates and his topic of discourse, "What did the man say before his death and how did he die?" (57a). The trial is then mentioned, and passed over, not as irrelevant, but as not needing summary. What gave this group the possibility of holding the discussion was first the permission of the rulers; it is stated that they did not forbid Socrates' friends access to him. And, most protractedly, the enabling condition is the delay of the embassy to Delos sent in memory of the "seven pairs" (of youths and maidens) that Theseus saved from sacrifice, "the Athenians say," on the last annual embassy to Crete. Since the embassy is in honor of Apollo, in whose service Socrates has spoken of spending his life (*Apology,* 23c), and whom he will shortly honor by composing poetry, the "unnecessary" story of these circumstances invites an inquiry as to the analogues between the embassy to Delos and the execution of Socrates. The embassy commemorates an execution forestalled by a leader who saved groups of youths and so the state; at the same time the state has decreed the execution of Socrates on the false charges of corrupting the youths (whom he continues to be in the act of "saving") and of failing to honor gods, when it is especially this god, Apollo, whom he continues to honor. A residual sacrifice is commemorated without being carried through, while at the same time an execution is being decreed that, in a modern context, looks like a sort of sacrifice.[10] For Crete, Athens substitutes Delos; since Athens is in the position of unjustly demanding the death of Socrates, it has put itself in the position of Crete, and not even of all of Crete, since the good side of Cretan organization serves Plato frequently as a model of good government.

The situation cannot be changed, but it can be modified by the delay brought about by chance (*tuchē*). And the chance is actually a double one: that the beginning of the embassy should happen to fall the day after the condemnation of Socrates, and that the winds should delay the round-trip voyage of the ship. (Socrates cannot make any trip out of Athens, and he has refused a one-way trip in the *Crito*.)

Before the summary of the long discussion is given, the mood is described; Socrates is "happy" or "blest in being happy." Consequently he evokes no pity. And the first answer to the initial question, "How did he die?" (the expression is repeated, 58e4), describes his mode, a mixture of pleasure and pain that is spoken of as "unusual." The possibility of such an unusual mixture makes it analogous in its fullness to the later attunement of elements, the "harmonia" in the soul. The unusualness associates Socrates to those of heroic virtue who enjoy the higher salvation in the *Gorgias* and the *Republic*. The mood is spoken of as modifying the accustomed "pleasure" of philosophical discussion—an assertion that shades the mood into the flow of the discussion while at the same time subjecting the discussion to the mood—a philosophy that will soon be characterized, but only provisionally, as "the highest music."

Remarking on his leg pains, Socrates comments on the "seeming opposites," the minimal variants of physical pleasure and pain that he calls the "sweet" and the "troublesome,"[11] describes them as "attached to one head," and projects a fable of Aesop that does not exist about them; if Aesop had written such a fable, it would tell about how the god had tried to separate them but could not, and so he attached them. Aesop, too, is analogous in some ways to the Socrates who is then declared to have set Aesop's fables to verse (and perhaps also to music), after first writing a hymn to Apollo.[12] The Delphians, citizens of that other city sacred to Apollo, falsely accused Aesop of the crime of sacrilege, as Socrates has been accused of impiety; they then, citing an oracle, absolved of guilt anyone who would kill Aesop, as one man finally did (Herodotus 2.134).

The poems are written to discharge a sacred obligation enjoined upon Socrates by a repeated dream "to make this music" (60e). The whole activity is further explicitly connected to the fact that "the festival of the god prevented me from dying" (61a), so that he could then make "that which people call music."[13] He claims that to obey this injunction is "safer," thus linking the act of poeticizing to the presumptive redemption of the philosopher acting as poet, making "mythoi but not logoi,"[14] since he is not a "mythologikos." (61b). Evenus, to whom he is imagining this reply, in his personal situation presents the same two constituents, philosopher and poet, in a slightly different mix, since he is a sophist and an established elegist. Yet there will be a slight revision when Socrates says (61e) that it is fitting to mythologize about the beyond—a declaration that turns "philosophy is the highest music" once more back on itself. All the intricacies of these connections are matched by the ambiguity, noted by Hackforth, in the logos about suicide. Suicide is more simply forbidden by the Philolaus who had been the master of Simmias and Cebes when alive. A further answer is given by the adduced analogy to "the logos spoken about them in the acts about which it cannot be spoken" (alternatively, "the mysteries").

The question about suicide, to begin with, is a sort of counter-case to the *Crito,* since there Socrates opts for what could be called a passive suicide. But more precisely here he simply welcomes death (63b) because he will be in the presence of (1) gods who are (2) wise and (3) good, an attribution repeated later (80d–81). At a later point, 99a can be taken as a summary of the *Crito* from the angle of causality.[15]

The injunction not to commit suicide is backed, first of all, by the argument that the gods are good masters (62a), and Socrates asserts that in this connection he will give a better apology than he did to his judges— a reference that places this dialogue in connection with the *Apology,* and as superior to it. All this discussion about what the philosopher will do when facing death is prior to the question of what death is. The very preparation for death will lead him to have knowledge (65e)—the philosophical attitude, rather than the pursuit of philosophical questions. The ensuing *phronesis*—far more powerful here than the "practical intelligence" later ascribed to the term[16]—will put him in a position of overcoming the desires, fears, loves, and phantasms of the body (65a), and as a purified spirit to comprise virtue itself in such virtues as courage, prudence, and justice (68), here offered as a simple list guaranteed in their true (as opposed to false) manifestations by "purity," where the whole of the *Republic* is concerned with ascertaining what *dikaiosune* may be, and large portions of other dialogues devote considerable elenchic energy to the others—to courage (*Laches*), to *sophrosyne* (*Gorgias, Protagoras*), not to speak of the large, intricate question of *arete* itself.

Here these virtues are easily comprised in an attitude rather than an *elenchos,* and they are sketchily listed as the result of a purification attained through attitude, and through a mood of the "hope" Socrates speaks of. "Fair is the contest, and the hope great" (114c). Perhaps echoing the reference to hope at 70a, the very intonation pattern of this sentence almost seems to assimilate to the term's Christian sense, but in any case it radiates a confidence, of equanimity and something more than equanimity, that must be accounted a rich base for the message of this dialogue. The concept of "purification" keeps recurring here, having first been introduced casually and, as it were, routinely, in the account of what the embassy to Apollo does for the city. This purification, bringing the death-like philosopher who is almost free of the body to his *phronesis,* allows for a principle of "exchange" beyond the simple trade of pleasure for pleasure, pain for pain, fear for fear, and so on (69a). And all of these attainments come about through the detachment from the body, rather than from the proper philosophical definitions that, in this presentation, it precedes. The philosopher, or rather, "those who have philosophized rightly" are effectually compared to Bacchants; it is not clear that there is not some commutative spillover, since being a Bacchant may also purify, notably for the few successful Bacchants among the many who aspire to that state (69d). In fact, this whole passage condenses the intellectual, the religious, and the spiritual affirmations of Socrates, since the *phronesis,* which is alone the "right coin" allowing for "exchange" (of "pleasure for pleasure, grief for grief," and so on), is incommensurate with that which it "buys and sells," and that incommensurability, taken logically, presents insoluble puzzles as a calculus of pleasures is at once invoked and transcended. The overriding term "intelligence," applied to elements of exchange, recalls the Heraclitean formula in which fire is an overriding term that governs the exchange of gold for goods and goods for gold (B90). And there is a further Heraclitean echo in the full reference at the end of this passage to Heraclitus's connection of Hades and Dionysus (B15), and perhaps also to the mud (B5) that Plato here has Socrates say the uninitiated will lie in (69c6) when they come to Hades. These Heraclitean echoes, of course, are themselves in turn fused into the Pythagorean echoes, themselves indistinguishable here from the more regular references to initiations into the mysteries.

   In this dialogue as in others, one can largely derive Plato's differences of emphasis, refinements of definition, and even implied contradictions about anamnesis, the immortality of the soul, the moral constituents of the soul, and even the Forms, as readily from the structure of the dialogue in question as from a "development" in Plato. And these four dialogues insist on their structure, and even on their connection to each other, by their dependence on Socrates' actual trial. Of course, the context-specificity of the dialogue does not contradict the notion of a development from dialogue to dialogue, but keeping that context-specificity in view has the advantage of focusing on the whole utterance, rather than on the runs of reasoning within it, however brilliantly worked through and centering for the dialogue itself these may be presented as being.

The kinship of the soul with the Forms is most fully stated here in Plato's work, and it is oddly appended to the doctrine of recollection, called a frequent subject for Socrates (72e), and now applied to much more than the mathematics of the *Meno*—to equals, to similar objects, to the forms, and even to the possibility of recognizing defectiveness in the match of an individual with the form. The optimism of the dialogue culminates here too, embracing anamnesis not only as a proof of immortality, if combined with the distinction of opposites, but as an organ enabling participation in the highest kinds of realization, in "the beautiful, the good, the just, and the holy" (79). It easily assimilates to the philosophy that is the means to break out of the threat of a bad transmigration (82d), a question more pressing here than the need to prove transmigration itself, which is taken for granted, even if not with full certitude.

There is in fact a play of certitudes through this dialogue, and the shift into a "second sailing," the *deuteros plous* of hypothesis, is only one among many, though especially emphasized by modern commentators attracted by the subtlety of the ensuing definitions about how one does build from hypothesis in Plato's fullest statement of the subject. Since Socrates undertakes the second sailing in the first place because of the impossibility of allowing Anaxagoras's causes, which even Anaxagoras seems to misapply by looking for physical causes instead of the presence of his "Mind," the second sailing is preferable in the immediate context for its applicability, though at the same time inferior as to certainty. But kinds of certainty are qualified constantly throughout the dialogue. The superlative assertion "philosophy is the greatest music" is not refuted, but it is contextually qualified as an inference mistakenly applied by Socrates to the injunction of the dream figure. His self-correcting change to "setting" fables of Aesop is also a false trail for him because he is neither poet nor "mythologos"; and the ensuing distinction between mythoi and logoi cannot be disentangled from the stated subjective limitations of Socrates or from the undispelled force of either if it were taken separately. In the passage about the "right coin" of *phronesis* to govern exchanges, *phronesis* is the result of a purification, and one that can most fully come when the soul is wholly released from the body. This is stated at the conclusion of the passage; he will know with full certainty when he gets there (69e). It is a contingency for the future as well as a possible realization for the philosopher in the present, who, in still another qualification, risks the state of being a hater of reasonings, a "misologos," if he allows mere reason to take over (84d). This confrontation of uncertainty comes at the end of a demonstration that had begun by asserting the completeness of a proof arrived at by combining the doctrine of anamnesis with the doctrine of the generation of opposites (77a). Again, without preamble a simple story, a mythos, depicts at some length (107–14) the physical and spiritual characteristics of this world and the next in a conclusion that is itself qualified as an approximation under doubt (114d). In the light of all these qualifications, and many minor ones, the *deuteros plous* of substituting propositions for sense experience (99d) is just a high point of shift in a constantly shifting presentation, one governed, as always, by the circumstance that the speaker stands imminently on the threshold of death. These are "last words."

Yet on the other hand, as in "philosophy is the highest music," there is a tone of assertion here that dominates the dialogue throughout. It rises to implied assertions in addition to the obscure foreshortening in the leap from "cause" to "hypothesis." The *theios logos,* discussed above, is a possible firmer support, but one not likely to be available, though at the same time its superior logos is here at least envisioned. And even in moments of qualification the affirmation comes through. Socrates characterizes his discourse as one of ongoing joy, a swan song (85a). There is a persistent superlative cast to the language, even more pronouncedly than usual in Plato. So, for example, the positive terms in it give a eulogistic cast to the prevailing cautionary sentence, "Simmias, I think, disbelieves and fears that the soul, though more godly and beautiful than the body, may nevertheless finally perish, since it is in the condition of attunement" (91c–d). This is true of "more godly and more beautiful," in their tone signature. It can even be said that a strong sense of "the Form of harmony" shadows the weak, main sense in the phrase "the condition of attunement." The phrase *harmonias eidei* even though given in a summary of why Cebes thinks the soul may perish, carries a very strong undercurrent by bringing the terms of two systems into intersection. The first system comprises Plato's version of Greek harmonics in music, developed positively elsewhere, though here negatively. In 89a Phaedo's reference back to the strength and beneficence of Socrates's *logoi* is itself stronger than the suggestion in *harmonias eidei.* And that phrase itself in this context must be heard as preserving, under the sense of a passive attunement, a faint suggestion of the more general sense of harmonia—proportion, balance, and the like—in a dialogue where it is combined with the honorific term for the Forms that have here already been invoked (though not under that name) and will soon be named and subjected to prolonged and intense discussion. The Forms themselves stand firm as a measure for memory and a guarantee of the possible purity and permanence of the soul. Putting the two together as *harmonias eidei* grazes both systems, and it does so by way of beginning to frame a more comprehensive system in which this combination is embedded, while caught in a denial. All this is by way of advancing (and refuting) the notion that the soul is to the body as the tuning of a musical instrument. Harmony is further linked playfully to myth in the later reference to Harmonia and Cadmus (95a), a mythic residue left as a sort of affirmation in the equanimous spirit of the (prevailingly negative) summary; and it is never clear to what "Cadmus" may be taken to refer—a failure of application that is not at all bothersome in context, since both the naming of the myth and the adduction of a wholly new topic testifies to the serene inventiveness of the philosopher under stress.

The notions of the soul in its relation to the body are themselves, in turn, and specifically here, connected to the relation between knowledge and virtue, as these two will define the disposition of the soul after death. Virtue even "without philosophy and mind" can still bring salvation to a man who uses it, even unreflectively, in "general and political life."

Throughout these four dialogues, in abundant implied refutation of the charge of impiety against Socrates, the godly remains steadily in view. And at least four notions of the godly bear upon, modify, and possibly transcend the philosophical demonstrations: (1) the millennial embassy to Delos, and all its possible analogies to Socrates; (2) the Pythagorean ideas insofar as these are religious as distinct from philosophical; (3) the *theios logos* to which Socrates refers, as a supersession of the philosophical discussions; and (4) the simple, popular gesture at the end of Socrates' last words, "I owe a cock to Asclepius."

None of these four notions overlaps exactly with the large piety into which the Socrates of the *Apology* swells as he receives the death sentence. And the view of the afterlife then, a wise conversation of spirits in the realm of Hades, matches not one of the possibilities of salvation and restriction that are laid out in the *Phaedo* (leaving accounts in other dialogues aside)—not even the long discussions about the realm of Hades that amplify the possibilities of the afterlife without suggesting that happy conversation would be included among them. Nor is any of these five notions of religiosity coterminous with the elaborate *elenchos* about the holy in the *Euthyphro*, where Socrates is engaged in conversation with someone who ignores the very large distress he himself allows to pass by, thus proving the selflessness of a devotion to framing good citizens and men with a respect for the very gods he was condemned for contemning.

In the *Phaedo* the whole discussion about logical procedures with hypothesis is, among other things, metalinguistic in constituting a description of the *elenchos*. This fullest of Plato's accounts of hypothesis here has the character of an introspection about already existing method rather than a search for a new one, and it is not clear that the *deuteros plous* is really a second best.[17] Coming before death, it simultaneously gives up on arguing the tentativeness out of inquiry, settles for that tentativeness, and declares a nobility to inhere in the tentativeness that the auditors are seen—at a great distance of time and place—to share. The immortality of the soul is thus enacted in a discussion about it by a man unjustly condemned to death, glancing indirectly off the gods, if with many strands of assent, that in some ways go beyond Sophocles, Aeschylus (108a), and the possibly misologistic Euripides, and in other ways do not. Since Plato contents himself with their explorations, fails to extend them, and stays indirect while being syncretic about the gods, he is intellectually more exploratory but at the same time more archaic than they (as Homer is more archaic than his time) and more advanced (as Homer also is).

"It is not easy to show, nor is time sufficient in the present circumstance" (114c). This is a pair of reasons that are themselves conditions of, and also constraints upon, discourse—and both vague. Does "not easily" mean "it could be done with difficulty," or is it litotes for it cannot be done? A middle term puts it in an athletic-eschatological metaphor, "Fair is the contest, and the hope great." This seems to match with radiant equanimity the "fair danger," the *kalos kindunos*, it would be to believe. Which is not at all the same thing as saying it would be false to do so. All this amounts to a further level of qualification from the *deuteros plous*. But the match between the soul-disposition in the concluding myth and that offered earlier in the *Phaedo* might be taken to extend the qualification backward, equanimity encompassing all dangers, including that of logical gaps and even possible errors, bringing to a large coda, at once questioning and optimistic, Plato's act of connecting this great range of topics to four points around the trial and death of Socrates. Thus is implicitly asserted a relation between the questions raised and an actual life—or between ideas and history. That, too, is a connection Plato addressed complexly, so much so that to assess that connection would involve an even longer discussion.

Notes

Projections of Measure: The Continued Synergies of Pound and Williams

1. See John Thompson, Jr., *The Founding of English Meter* (New York: Routledge & K. Paul, 1961). Blake's seven-beat line is often incorrectly called a fourteener. See William Kumbier, "Blake's Epic Meter," *Studies in Romanticism* 17 (1978): 163–92.

2. See Albert Cook, "Milton's Abstract Music," in Arthur Barker, ed. *Milton* (New York: Oxford University Press, 1965), pp. 398–415 = *University of Toronto Quarterly* 29 (1959–60): 370–85. Adapted, with amplifications, in Albert Cook, *The Classic Line* (Bloomington: Indiana University Press, 1966).

3. See Albert Cook, *Thresholds: Studies in the Romantic Experience* (Madison: University of Wisconsin Press, 1985). For Blake, "Blake: The Exaltation of Fluidity," especially pp. 53–61.

4. For Whitman, see Albert Cook, *Prisms: Studies in Modern Literature* (Bloomington: Indiana University Press, 1967), p. 89. For Dickinson, "Emily Dickinson's White Exploits," in *Thresholds,* especially pp. 187–88.

5. Pound does not entirely escape the strictures of Blackmur here: "Syllable and stress are not enough to make a metric into style, although they are quite enough to make a doggerel." R. P. Blackmur, "Lord Tennyson's Scissors: 1912–1950," in *Form and Value in Modern Poetry* (New York: Anchor, 1957), pp. 369–88. Doggerel is the limit threat for any poetic music, standing ready to seal off utterances in phonetic irrelevance.

6. A recent doctoral thesis at the State University of New York at Buffalo by

Charles Martin has demonstrated astutely how rich Pound's access to Catullus is generally, and how the attention persists in Pound's tradition, notably in the work of Zukofsky and others, including Martin himself, who has translated Catullus. In this continuing tradition, so has Bernadette Mayer, who in her own work notably employs a long line that is, so to speak, more Poundian than it is Whitmanian. And, in our complex situation, Martin's own attention to Pound and Zukofsky in his own poetry is audible only in the alert and supple modulation of his regular pentameter lines (*Steal the Bacon* [Baltimore: Johns Hopkins University Press, 1987]).

7. For a fuller analysis of Pound's meter, see *Prisms,* especially chapter 3, "Rhythm," pp. 74–98.

8. Charles O. Hartman, *Free Verse* (Princeton, N.J.: Princeton University Press, 1980), pp. 32, 36.

9. Robert Creeley, "A Note on Ezra Pound," in Louis Zukofsky, *"All: The Collected Short Poems 1923–1958,"* as reprinted in Donald M. Allen and Warren Tallman, editors, *The Poetics of the New American Poetry* (New York: Grove Press, 1973), pp. 247–54.

10. Hartman, p. 52.

11. In *Prisms* I have discussed (89) the principle of what I there call the "syllabic margin," which could be redefined as a control rule for isochrony: "'no more than this number of syllables in a line and no fewer than that.' This important rule, which might be called the rule of the syllabic margin, has not been formulated by metricians. And yet it is to be found very widely exemplified in free verse, most notably in Whitman, who operates under the rule of the syllabic margin when he can be shown to operate under no other rule."

12. *Prisms,* chap. 3, "Rhythm."

13. See Albert Cook, *The Classic Line: A Study of Epic Poetry* (Bloomington: Indiana University Press, 1967), pp. 144–76, for an analysis of Propertius's metrical precision, in coordination with the normality of his "refined style."

14. *Prisms,* chap. 3.

15. William Carlos Williams, "The Work of Gertrude Stein," in Allen and Tallman, pp. 130–39.

16. Jerry McGuire, "The Discourse of the Two Cheeks: Robert Frost's Concept of 'Colloquiality,'" in *American Poetry* 2 (Spring 1985), pp. 34–50.

17. Harvey Gross, *Sound and Form in Modern Poetry* (Ann Arbor: University of Michigan Press), pp. 116–18.

18. Hartman, p. 68.

19. *Prisms,* chap. 3, "Rhythm."

20. Ezra Pound, "In Retrospect," *Literary Essays* (London: Faber and Faber, 1954 [1918]), pp. 3–13.

21. Robert Creeley, "Interview with Linda Wagner," in Allen and Tallman, p. 283.

22. Robert Creeley, *For Love* (New York: Scribner & Sons, 1962), p. 45.

23. Olson's original, profound, and comprehensive formulations are not my subject here, though, of course, they move at the center of, and center, the body of

his poetry. Their energy of possible interaction with the best in the whole tradition of philosophy, anthropology, and poetic thinking from Novalis and Blake to the present is well exemplified in John Clarke's *From Feathers to Iron* (Berkeley: Tombouktou, 1987).

24. Charles Olson, *The Distances* (New York, Grove, 1960), p. 61.

25. Charles Olson, *Selected Writings* (New York: New Directions, 1966), pp. 162–63.

26. George Butterick, ed., *The Maximus Poems* (Berkeley: University of California Press, 1983), pp. 6, 7.

27. For a discussion of how this works in Apollinaire, see Albert Cook, "The Windows of Apollinaire," in *Figural Choice in Poetry and Art,* (Hanover, N.H.: University Press of New England, 1985), pp. 64–85.

28. "Quantity in Verse, and Shakespeare's Late Plays," in *Selected Writings,* p. 32.

29. See Elder Olson, *General Prosody: Rhythmic, Metric, Harmonics* (Chicago: University of Chicago Libraries, 1938). This treatise in its general principles anticipates or parallels much of the best modern discussion of measure, though its specific analyses do not do full justice to the principles. "Prosodic structure may be generally distinguished as of two kinds: rhythmic and harmonic. Both of these are sensibly proportional relations of speech-sounds *qua* speech-sounds, but they differ in that the proportions are of a different character and in that, as a consequence, the relata of those proportions are differently determinate. The term *proportion* here has the meaning of an equivalence of relation among speech-sounds considered as speech-sounds. The addition of the word *sensible* is intended to differentiate relations which are perceptible by sense (here, of course, the auditory sense) from those which are known only by an act of understanding" (p. 2). "Prosodic structures may be differentiated according to whether they are proportions having as relata speech-sounds taken as limited in some way by number or as to whether they are proportions of likeness and difference in abstraction from any quantitative determination; in other words, according to whether they are *quantitative* or *qualitative*. Quantitative proportions will here be termed *rhythm;* qualitative, *harmonic figuration*" (p. 3). Elder Olson's statements about letter and syllable are suggestive of Charles Olson's later statements about syllable and line. And, as he says in approaching his examples, "the (prosodically unequivocal) relations so exhibited are then tested upon the parts which are equivocal" (p. 100)—Elder Olson has here begun to provide a system for a poem that surpasses his analyses and so enters the territory of the measures that mobilize our attention:

> Red river, red river
> Slow flow heat is silence
> No will is still as a river
> Still. Will heat move
> Only through the mocking-bird
> Heard once? Still hills
> Wait. Gates wait. Purple trees,

White trees, wait, wait,
Delay, decay. Living, living,
Never moving. Ever moving
Iron thoughts came with me
And go with me:
Red river, river, river.

T. S. Eliot, "Virginia," *Selected Poems 1909–1935* (New York: Harcourt-Brace, 1936), p. 172.

30. Charles Reznikoff, *Testimony, The United States 1885–1890, Recitative* (New York: New Directions, 1975), p. 23.

31. Lorine Niedecker, *The Granite Pail* (San Francisco: North Point, 1985), p. 44.

32. Louis Zukofsky, *A* (Berkeley: University of California Press, 1978), A23, p. 538.

33. Hugh Kenner, *The Pound Era* (Berkeley: University of California Press, 1975). This was a printing direction for Harriet Monroe, which resulted in breaking the two-line poem into five phrasal clusters. Both Pound and Olson, along with many others of modernist spiritedness, felt that the typewriter let them into such possibilities of breaking up the line. The possibility is already there, polyphonically, so to speak, in Mallarmé's "Coup de Dès." The typographic means is, of course, logically incidental, though situationally it was evidently not so.

34. Louis Zukofsky, "Pussy Willow," *80 Flowers* (Lunenburg, Vt.: 1978), p. 8.

35. Dylan Thomas, "A Refusal to Mourn the Death, by Fire, of a Child in London," *Collected Poems* (New York: New Directions, 1953), p. 112.

36. Robert Creeley, "Was," *Words* (New York: Scribner's, 1967), p. 119.

37. Robert Creeley, *Later* (New York: New Directions, 1979), p. 32.

38. Robert Creeley, *The Charm* (San Francisco: Four Seasons, 1969), p. 18.

39. Robert Kelley, *The Mill of Particulars* (Los Angeles: Black Sparrow, 1973), p. 25.

40. Charles Doria, *The Game of Europe* (Chicago: Swallow Press, 1983), p. 124.

41. Gary Snyder, "Through," *Left out in the Rain* (San Francisco: North Point, 1986), p. 156.

42. The details are from Paul Mariani, *William Carlos Williams* (New York: McGraw Hill, 1981), pp. 2–15.

43. Hartman points out that middle Williams's use of "save" as a preposition is British, not American.

44. There are those who think of this option as a guarantee against metrical flaccidity and poetic superfluity, as though any such choice could work that way. At the same time, not only in J. V. Cunningham and Richard Wilbur of earlier generations, or John Hollander, L. E. Sissman, David Galler, and Edgar Bowers, but (choosing randomly) in such as Robert Mezey and William Logan as well as Charles Martin, the old forms show themselves as viable as the more open ones— which themselves are no guarantee against flaccidity and superfluity!

45. Denise Levertov, "Central Park, Winter, After Sunset," *Here and Now* (San Francisco: City Lights, 1957), p. 19.

46. Ezra Pound, "Poems of Alfred Venison," *Personae* (New York: New Directions, n.d. [1949, poem from *The New Age,* 1930s]).

47. Edward Dorn, "A Theory of Truth," *The North Atlantic Turbine* (London: Fulcrum, 1967), p. 19.

Some Thoughts on How to Discuss Epic Poetry

1. Vladimir Propp, *Russkii geroicheskii epos* (Leningrad: Izdatelstvo Leningradskovo Universiteta, 1955), p. 5.

2. Marshall McLuhan, *The Gutenberg Galaxy* (Toronto: University of Toronto Press, 1962); *Understanding Media* (New York: McGraw-Hill, 1964). Eric Havelock, *Preface to Plato* (Cambridge: Harvard University Press, 1963). Walter J. Ong, S. J., *The Presence of the Word* (New Haven, Conn.: Yale University Press, 1967).

3. Martin P. Nillson, *A History of Greek Religion* (New York: Norton, 1952).

4. Charles Segal, "The Myth Was Saved," *Hermes,* 106, Band 2 (1978): 320.

5. Michael Nagler, *Spontaneity and Tradition* (Berkeley: University of California Press, 1974). Berkeley Peabody, *The Winged Word* (Albany: State University of New York Press, 1973). Gregory Nagy, *Comparative Studies in Greek and Indic Meter* (Cambridge: Harvard University Press, 1974). Norman Austin, *Archery at the Dark of the Moon* (Berkeley: University of California Press, 1975).

6. Benjamin A. Stolz and Richard Shannon, eds., *Oral Literature and the Formula,* (Ann Arbor: University of Michigan Press, 1976).

7. Joseph H. Duggan, *The Song of Roland: Formulaic Style and Poetic Craft* (Berkeley: University of California Press, 1973).

8. Stolz and Shannon, op cit., with citations of Russo's earlier work.

9. Denys Page, "Archilochus and the Oral Tradition," in *Archiloque,* Entretiens Hardt, 10 (Geneva: Hardt, 1963): 181–222. Dover's argument is the Occam's razor of the question: "If, whenever we find a word or phrase common to epic and Archilochus, we are to say that it is an epic formula, we leave the Ionians dumb" (p. 164).

10. H. M. and N. K. Chadwick, *The Growth of Literature* (Cambridge: Cambridge University Press, 1932–1940), 1: 28–48. Later (1:404 ff.) they add a sixth category, "descriptive poetry."

11. Albert Lord, *The Singer of Tales* (Cambridge: Harvard University Press, 1960). Ruth Finnegan, *Oral Literature in Africa* (Oxford: Clarendon Press, 1970); and *Oral Poetry* (Cambridge: Cambridge University Press, 1976).

12. Stith Thompson, *Motif Index of Folk Literature* (Bloomington: Indiana University Press, 1958).

13. Lord Raglan, *The Hero* (London: Methuen, 1936).

14. Georges Dumézil, *Mythe et Epopée* (Paris: Gallimard, 1968).

15. Emil Staiger, *Grundbegriffe der Poetik* (Zurich: Atlantis, 1965).

16. Walter Muschg, *Tragische Literaturgeschichte* (Bern: Francke, 1957).

17. Thomas Greene, *The Descent from Heaven* (New Haven, Conn.: Yale University Press, 1963).

18. Peter Dronke (*Medieval Latin and the Rise of European Love Lyric* [Oxford: Clarendon Press, 1968, 1:25]), in the course of a vast and finely perceptive discussion that includes the troubadours and Minnesänger, speaks of *Tristan* as one of the greatest Western love romances.

19. Piero Pucci, *Hesiod and the Language of Poetry* (Baltimore: Johns Hopkins University Press, 1977).

20. Charles Doria, "The Orphic Sacred Stories: Religion and Mystery Cults," *Denver Quarterly*, Spring, 1978, pp. 69–86.

Prophecy and the Preconditions of Poetry

1. For a diagram of these, see Cedric Whitman, *Homer and the Homeric Tradition* (Cambridge: Harvard University Press, 1958). Further discussion can be found in Albert Cook, *The Classic Line*, pp. 49–137.

2. For a general critique of the limits to Lévi-Strauss's schematizations of myth, see Albert Cook, *Myth and Language* (Bloomington: Indiana University Press, 1980).

3. Robert Alter, *The Art of Hebrew Poetry* (New York: Basic Books, 1985), pp. 8–10. Benjamin Hrushovski, "Hebrew Prosody," *Encyclopedia Judaica* 13. 1200–1202.

4. The Authorized Version has read the commoner verb *nahar*, but a less common one, "to shine," is preferred by modern commentators. The earlier reading, however, has the merit of coordinating more emphatically with the rest of the passage. If one of these verbs is taken for a metaphor of the other (a third, but remote possibility), then it would raise the whole question of metaphor in Hebrew prophecy, a question I discuss in *The Reach of Poetry*, a book in progress.

5. John L. McKenzie, *Second Isaiah, The Anchor Bible* (New York, Doubleday, 1968), p. 175.

6. "Behold, he prophesied among the prophets, then the people said . . . Is Saul also among the prophets?" (1 Samuel 10.11).

7. There the description of the shield speaks of the figures on it as singing and dancing, breaking the frame of ekphrasis: "In their midst a boy on a sharp-sounding lyre / Harped tenderly and sung the lovely Linus song / With a subtle voice, and, stamping along together / With tune and shout they followed, skipping with their feet" (18. 569–72).

8. For a discussion of these complex conditions, see Bruno Gentile, *Poetry and Its Public in Ancient Greece* (Baltimore: Johns Hopkins University Press, 1988).

9. Erving Goffman, *Forms of Talk* (Philadelphia: University of Pennsylvania Press, 1981), esp. pp. 128–50.

10. Dennis Tedlock, *The Spoken Word and the Work of Interpretation* (Philadelphia: University of Pennsylvania Press, 1983). "The measuring out of long runs of lines with equal numbers of syllables, moras, or feet does not occur in audible texts from cultures whose verbal arts are not under the direct influence of literary traditions" (p. 8). "There is a fusion of intimacies when the speaker calls attention to the fact that the stage set of a scene in the story was the same as the present set of its telling" (p. 11). "As much as half the time spent in delivering spontaneous discourse is devoted to silence, and 'pausing is as much a part of the act of speaking as the vocal utterance of words itself'" (p. 48, quoting Frieda Goldman-Eisler, "Discussion and Further Comments," in Eric H. Lenneberg, ed., *New Directions in the Study of Language* [Cambridge: MIT Press, 1964, pp. 109–30]). "It should be noted that all the phonological features we have just discussed—pause junctures, intonational markers, stresses, and vowel quantities—lie at the borders of proper phonology. Each one can be and often is treated as suprasegmental rather than segmental, prosodic rather than phonemic" (p. 204).

11. The *Mystic Theology* of (pseudo-) Dionysius the Areopagite, commented by John Scotus Erigena, as cited by Luigi Tonelli, *Dante e la Poesia dell'ineffabile* (Florence: G. Barbèra, 1934, p. 47).

12. Albert Cook, *The Classic Line*, pp. 141–76.

13. Sculley Bradley and Harold W. Blodgett, eds., *Leaves of Grass: A Critical Edition* (New York: Norton, 1973), p. 4. Other citations are to this edition.

14. "Preface to 'As a Strong Bird,'" 1872, p. 745.

15. "Starting from Paumanok," sections 2, 10; pp. 16–17, 21–22.

16. See Lee M. Hollander, *The Skalds* (Princeton: Princeton University Press, 1945), 55–101.

17. Hollander offers examples passim, and there is an elaborate analytic discussion of kennings in part 2 of Snorri Sturluson's *Prose Edda*, available in a translation by Arthur Brodeur, New York, 1929. In the range of recent discussions of this intricate topic might be mentioned Jorge Luis Borges, "Las kenningar," in *Historia de la eternidad* (Madrid: Alianza, 1951; rpt. 1971), pp. 45–70; E. M. Meletinskii, *"Edda" i rannie formi eposa* (Moscow: Nauka, 1968); and Samuel R. Levin, *Metaphoric Worlds* (New Haven: Yale University Press, 1988).

The Syllabic Module

1. Prose poetry, a limiting case, contains not "no meter" but the zero case of meter. "No meter" makes a stretch of language simply prose, whereas the label "poetry" on a stretch of prose-language announces itself as a case of zero meter, the full convergence of design with the instances.

2. The module of *Midway* is a syllabic line of three syllables:

    (a) *three* syllables
    (b) two (a) *six*
    (c) (a) plus one / *four*
    (d) (a) plus (c) / *seven*
    (e) two (c) / *eight*

(f) (a) minus one / *two,* occurs at "halts."

(g) four (a) / two (b) / three (c) six (f) / *twelve.*

3. *Due Dates* module:

    (1) a) 4 syllables

    (b) a ' $\frac{1}{2}$ a = b

    (c) 2 a = 8

    (2) change allowed only by steps of 2 syllables ($\frac{1}{2}$ a)

4. ONE-WAY MYSTERY has an elaborate set of rules:

8, the base module, is not used for single lines.

Pairs of lines in the sequence 3, 5, 7, 9 syllables, with 5 and 7 the norm, and the outer limit allowed only as a boundary.

From the following pairs:

    (x) 3 plus 5 equals 8   2x equals y

    (y) 7 plus 9 equals 16

These "imbalanced" pairs (in balance with each other) are complemented by the following "balanced" ones (out of balance with the others and each other):

    (w) 5 plus 5 equals 10

    (v) 7 plus 7 equals 14

    (z) 5 plus 7 equals 12

The four (or more)-line "stanzas" will be built of from 24 to 48 syllables, with a minimum differential in units of x (or 8), the base module.

1. The stanza is permitted to repeat a given pair directly only once, except (y).

2. One stanza must "cap" another; repetition allowed only once.

3. The transition from a low-syllable to a high-syllable stanza must preponderate over that from high to low.

4. The whole must conclude with a stanza of 48 syllables.

The Modified Modernism of Anna Akhmatova

I am grateful to my colleagues Victor Terras and Sam Driver for reviewing these versions, helping me to avoid error and improve style.

1. A much larger selection of Akhmatova's poems in my translation, together with a much shorter form of this essay, will appear in *The Burden of Sufferance: Women Poets of Russia,* ed. Pamela Perkins and Albert Cook (New York: Garland, 1992).

2. Dostoevsky's retreat, original of the village in *The Brothers Karamazov.*

3. Dostoevsky.

Some Observations on Shakespeare and the Incommensurability of Interpretive Strategies

I am grateful to my colleague Robert Scholes for suggestions both specific and general on shaping this essay.

1. The approach is most often used syncretically, though it is adopted at an exclusive intentional angle by Keir Elam, *Shakespeare's Universe of Discourse* (Cambridge: Cambridge University Press, 1984).

2. The same may be said for such a virtualizing approach as that of the speech-conditions described by Erving Goffman (*Forms of Talk* [Philadelphia: University of Pennsylvania Press, 1983]). Goffman's finely discriminating elaborations of the abundant features in the phonetic and contextual richness of a live utterance throw into strong relief the fact that some of these features are necessarily left out in a written work. See chapter 3. Such features as Goffman's would have to be artificially adduced—or reintroduced—for the live performance of a written text. These very facts put all such constituents, those that come through in writing or formal dramatic distancing and those that do not, on a par of instrumentality.

3. Stanley Fish, *Is There a Text in This Class?* (Cambridge: Harvard University Press, 1980), pp. 200–220. We could notice, incidentally, that Fish's relativism, seen without hierarchy, lays claim to the sort of rigor Lacan's perceptual and transactional schemes do, but it is more prescriptive and less thoroughgoing because it must operate at the level of the "first-order" constituents it analyzes. It would not allow the Marxian because it would, if consistent, relativize categories that such a dialectical reading would treat as absolute. And it would not allow the Lacanian for the same reason; such readings would all be "imaginary" in a Lacanian set; they would never attain to the symbolic.

Another mix is offered by the powerful reading of Stanley Cavell, which could easily be reconciled to Fish's, or treated as an extension of it ("*Coriolanus* and Interpretations of Politics ['Who does the wolf love?']" in *Themes out of School* [San Francisco: North Point, 1984], pp. 60–96). For Cavell the "politics" of his title is a first-order phenomenon that quickly partializes into pro-plebian or pro-patrician ("A political reading is apt to become fairly predictable once you know whose side the reader is taking," p. 63). He refers these questions to a second-order structuring that for him derives heavily from the psychoanalytical but is not confined to it, as it deploys love and war, feeding and hunger, "The paradox and reciprocity of hungering may be found registered in the question 'Who does the wolf love?'" (p. 69). This schema could be taken as including Fish's speech-acts, and as opening, through the "lamb" opposed to the "wolf," into quasi-Christian qualifications built into the dramatic structure, "I see Coriolanus not so much as imitating Christ as competing with him" (p. 75). But such a "competition" would involve an assimilation of Christlike gestures, not an erasure of them, on the part of the playwright. The strength and plausibility of Cavell's reading, I would argue, derives from his initial, almost stated, assumption that an attention to what is going on in the play must involve our perception of its fusion of the codes that we overfix when we select just one to carry the interpretative line.

4. Robert Scholes, *Textual Power* (New Haven, Conn.: Yale University Press, 1985), p. 152.

5. Such a claim of immunity from adaptation is signally the case with René Girard, who offers impressive illustrative detail and dialectical connections in society of the circular unconscious motives tending inescapably to trigger some form of sacrifice so as to differentiate identities. Girard is further convinced that his denial of the possibility of relativizing his observations will carry weight if he merely asserts that the circle is closed and total. Such a totally preemptive assertion can be found in Girard's work passim, but see especially René Girard, *Des Choses cachées depuis la fondation du monde* (Paris: Grasset, 1978), pp. 40–55. But in a system where both the presence and the absence (as an evasion) of its mechanism are taken as evidence, there can be no proof or disproof, only hermeneutic observation, which is open to supplementation. Girard's own horror before such implied differentiations, we may conjecture somewhat in the spirit of his own strictures, leads him to ironic rejections as well as to overassertions, as notably in the specific pages cited here. So one must keep Girard's readings of *Midsummer Night's Dream* and *The Merchant of Venice* open to other sets of possibility without at all invalidating the depth and persuasiveness of his delineation of unconscious anthropological constituents in these plays.

6. Jonathan Goldberg, *James I and the Politics of Literature* (Baltimore: Johns Hopkins University Press, 1983), pp. 186–92.

7. "Theatricality is ultimately inescapable" (p. 192). This is either an incipiently tautologous truism or an overemphasis verging on falsification.

8. Freud is meta-interpreted as a psychology paralleled with an economics and a linguistics in *Les Mots et les choses*. On this question generally, see Albert Cook, *History/Writing* (Cambridge: Cambridge University Press, 1988), pp. 174–205.

9. For qualifications of Foucault's "royalist" and perspectival reading of this painting, see Albert Cook, "A Wilderness of Mirrors," *Kenyon Review*, Summer, 1986, pp. 90–111. (This constitutes a chapter in *Dimensions of the Sign in Art*, Hanover, N.H.: University Press of New England, 1989).

10. *The Political Unconscious*, p. 47. So, for example, to go into the past, it would be quite easy to subsume Marx to a Hegel whom we would allow presumable Hegelians to revise as much as the modern Marxians revise Marx (though, of course, Marx claims to correct and supersede Hegel). It would even be possible to subsume Marx's whole system to Blake's—and much more difficult to do the reverse.

11. Leonard Tennenhouse, "The Counterfeit Order of *The Merchant of Venice*," in Murray Schwartz and Coppélia Kahn, eds., *Representing Shakespeare* (Baltimore: Johns Hopkins University Press, 1980), pp. 54–69.

12. Terence Eagleton, *Shakespeare and Society* (New York: Schocken, 1967), pp. 98–129.

13. Walter Cohen, *Drama of a Nation* (Ithaca, N.Y.: Cornell University Press, 1985), pp. 195–211; 327–45. Of course, Marxian and Marxist readings may vary in emphasis, and other angles on the different mercantile roles in *The*

Merchant of Venice are provided by Michael Nerlich, *Ideology of Adventure* (Minneapolis: University of Minnesota Press, 1987), pp. 138–82.

14. So—strangely to us—the rebels in *Richard II* and in *Henry IV, Part 2* are capitulatory to the point of what might seem self-abasing subservience. But in the society itself, the expectedness, and so the regularity of such capitulations, is well documented from royal treason trials of the time by Lacey Baldwin Smith, "English Treason Trials and Confessions in the Sixteenth Century," in David L. Stevenson, ed., *The Elizabethan Age* (New York: Fawcett, 1966), pp. 58–91 (= *Journal of the History of Ideas,* October, 1954, XV, 471–498).

15. Robert Weimann, *Shakespeare und die Tradition des Volkstheaters* (Berlin: Henschelverlag, 1975); *Shakespeare and the Popular Tradition in the Theater* (Baltimore: The Johns Hopkins University Press, 1978). Weimann, for example (German edition, 309–310) oversimplifies Falstaff under the folk clown motif.

16. See the discussion in Cook, *Shakespeare's Enactment,* pp. 16–18, and passim.

17. Leon Trotsky effectually claims otherwise, "Marxism does not maintain at all that ethnographic traits have an independent character. On the contrary, it emphasizes the all-determining significance of natural and economic conditions in the formation of folklore." ("The Limitations of Formalism," *The Modern Tradition: Backgrounds of Modern Literature,* edited by Richard Ellmann and Charles Feidelson, Jr., New York: Oxford University Press, 1965, 344; from "The Formalist School" and "Revolution and Social Art," *Literature and Revolution* [1924], translated from the Russian by Rose Strunsky, New York, 1925.

18. C. L. Barber, *Shakespeare's Festive Comedy* (Princeton, N.J.: Princeton University Press, 1959), pp. 69–70.

19. For such fusions of apocalypse with pastoral in Shakespeare's work generally, see Thomas McFarland, *Shakespeare's Pastoral Comedy* (Chapel Hill: University of North Carolina Press, 1972).

20. *Shakespeare's Enactment,* pp. 176–82.

21. Enid Welsford, *The Fool* (New York: Doubleday, 1935; rpt. 1961).

22. As Fredric Jameson subtly demonstrates, if one sets Lacan's "imaginary" and "symbolic" (as well as occasionally the real) into dialectical combination (rather than simply ordering the other two under the symbolic), this dialectical work may itself provide a kind of opening for further, necessarily qualifying, discourse about Lacan ("Imaginary and Symbolic in Lacan: Marxism, Psychoanalytic Criticism, and the Problem of the Subject," *Yale French Studies,* 55/56 (1977): 338–95): "We must understand the Lacanian notion of the Symbolic Order as an attempt to create mediations between libidinal analysis and the linguistic categories, to provide, in other words, a transcoding scheme which allows us to speak of both within a common conceptual framework" (p. 359); "correct the imbalance of our own presentation, and of the very notion of a 'transition' from Imaginary to Symbolic, by demonstrating that the acquisition of the Symbolic is rather the precondition for a full mastery of the Imaginary as well" (p. 360). "'Kant avec Sade' transforms the very project of a moral philosophy into an insoluble intellectual paradox by rotating it in such a way that the implicit gap in it between subject

and law catches the light . . . a similar use of the distinction between Imaginary and Symbolic . . . in the realm of aesthetic theory and literary criticism . . . (offers) psychoanalytic method a more fruitful vocation" (p. 371). . . . The 'Seminar on the "Purloined Letter"' cannot possibly constitute a model for [a Lacanian literary] criticism, since on the contrary the literary work is in it a mere pretext for a dazzling illustration of a non-literary thesis" (p. 375).

23. Apposite here is Ricoeur's statement, which is equally cautionary and enabling: "But the impact of cultural phenomena to the psychoanalytic 'theory' is not a direct one; in order to integrate this new material into interpretation, psychoanalysis has to make extensive use of *genetic* explanation. The reason for this is clear: the repressed, as we have said, has no history ('the unconscious is timeless'); what does is the repressing agency; it is history: the individual's history from infancy to adulthood; and mankind's history from prehistory to history." Paul Ricoeur, *Freud and Philosophy: An Essay in Interpretation* (New Haven, Conn.: Yale University Press, 1980), p. 179.

24. Fineman's particular syncretic approach is brought to bear with particular force on Shakespeare's Sonnets in *Shakespeare's Perjur'd Eye: The Invention of Poetic Subjectivity in the Sonnets* (Berkeley: University of California Press, 1985). I here quote from Joel Fineman, "Fratricide and Cuckoldry: Shakespeare's Doubles," in *Representing Shakespeare,* pp. 70–109. Here, as in other instances, I am, of course, dealing with exempla rather than with the whole vast field of psychoanalytic discussion about Shakespeare from Norman Holland to the present, and before him back to Ernest Jones and Freud himself.

25. Or references to the symbolic order through such constituents as the "Other." So Lacan's discussion of *Hamlet,* which took place before actual or prospective psychiatric professionals, quite properly uses the play as an illustration of his system in action (Jacques Lacan, "Desire and the Interpretation of Desire in *Hamlet,*" *Yale French Studies* 55/56 [1977]: 11–52). Only tangentially does Lacan interpret the play in this essay, and then almost exclusively in the light of Hamlet's relation to Ophelia, which a more comprehensive, drama-oriented interpretation would subordinate to his overall purposes and reaction to the death of his father. To put it differently, if one stayed with Lacan's reading, one would be caught either with the thesis that Hamlet, given the structure of his desire, would have put Ophelia off in any case (and so even if his uncle had not murdered his father to marry his mother); or else that the political-familial considerations that intrude on that relationship are wholly measured by it. However, one could in turn bracket such questions if one also brackets Lacan's implicit claim to totality and simply takes his reflections as penetrating schematizations of the interactions between just Hamlet and Ophelia.

26. E. D. Hirsch, *Validity in Interpretation* (New Haven, Conn.: Yale University Press, 1967).

27. Hans-Georg Gadamer, *Philosophical Hermeneutics* (Berkeley: University of California Press, 1976), p. 11.

28. Hans Georg Gadamer, *Wahrheit und Methode* (Tübingen: Mohr, 1975), p. 232 and passim: "A horizon is indeed no stiff boundary but something that

wanders along and invites to thrusting further forward (Ein Horizont ist ja keine starre Grenze, sondern etwas, das mitwandert und zum weiteren Vordringen einlädt").

29. Wolfgang Iser, *Der Implizite Leser* (Munich: Fink, 1972), p. 131, translated as *The Implied Reader* (Baltimore: Johns Hopkins University Press, 1974).

30. Hans Robert Jauss, *Literaturgeschichte als Provokation* (Frankfurt: Suhrkamp, 1970), p. 183.

31. "Das geschichtliche Wesen des Kunstwerks nicht allein in seiner darstellenden oder expressiven Funktion sondern gleich notwendig auch in seiner Wirkung liegt" (163).

32. "in den sich wandelnden Erfahrungshorizont einer Kontinuität" (169).

33. *Wahrheit und Methode,* pp. 361–466: "The horizon fusion which takes place in the understanding is the genuine achievement of speech," "die im Verstehen geschehende Verschmelzung der Horizonte die eigentliche Leistung der Sprache ist" (p. 232).

Evocations of Feeling in Renaissance Drama: Music and Religion

1. There are both strengths and limitations to Foucault's method (which is actually a loose repertoire of methods). For one discussion of these, see Albert Cook, *History/Writing* (Cambridge: Cambridge University Press, 1988), pp. 189–95.

2. John Hollander *The Untuning of the Sky: Ideas of Music in English Poetry 1500–1700* (Princeton, N.J.: Princeton University Press, 1961). Hollander gives a rich repertoire of views and reactions to music through this whole period, providing a context in which Sir John Davies' *Orchestra,* for example, could unsurprisingly connect music and dancing to the whole structure of the universe.

3. Vincenzo Galilei, *Dialogo della musica antica et della moderna* (Florence, 1582); Giovanni de' Bardi, *Discorso mandato a Caccini sopra la musica antica* (1578). The ideas of these Italian theorists were soon incorporated and extended in the writings of Thomas Morley and of Charles Butler (*The Principles of Music in Singing and Setting* [1636]). Butler provides the link between musical theory and rhetoric, since he wrote in both domains, and in widely used rhetorics he prints a chart of emotional effects (*Rhetoricae Libri Duo; De Oratoria Libri Duo* [1629]). The Ramist chart breaks down "affectus" into "simplex," which includes "voluptas," and "dolor," terms more directly evocative of dramatic interactions than Aristotle's own categorizations of emotional effects for rhetoric. Under "Compositus objecti" the chart distinguishes between objects that are aimed at a future good ("Spes," "Desiderium") and evil ("Timor," "Aversatio"). It offers thirteen others, divided as to their origin in "amor" or "ira" and as to their relation to past, present, and future. All, again, suggest reactions that are easy to correlate to actions in a play. I owe the indication of this avenue of discourse and much of the information, including the chart, to Lee Jacobus.

4. Aristotle *Rhetoric,* especially 2. 1–11, 1378a–90. An emphasis on such effects was always a staple of formal discussions about rhetoric, and notably in the abundant literature concerned with rhetoric in the sixteenth and early seventeenth centuries. In addition to the whole universe of Freudian and post-Freudian discourse, the complexity of philosophical approaches to emotion and feeling is well illustrated by Richard Wollheim's review of T. S. Eliot's doctoral thesis on F. H. Bradley in *On Art and the Mind* (Cambridge: Harvard University Press, 1974).

5. One must ultimately appeal to the experience of the auditor for the fine and haunting qualities in melody, which their very resistance to formulation gives a profound resonance of comprehensive signification. See Irving Massey, *Find You the Virtue: Ethics, Image, and Desire in Literature* (Fairfax, Va.: George Mason University Press, 1987), pp. 172–79; and Thomas McFarland, *Shapes of Culture* (Iowa City: University of Iowa Press, 1987), pp. 3–4.

6. This rationale for such categories of sign-systems in music is extended in Albert Cook, "Introduction," *Dimensions of the Sign in Art* (Hanover, N.H.: University Press of New England, 1989).

7. F. W. Sternfeld, "Shakespeare and Music," in Kenneth Muir and S. Schoenbaum, eds., *A New Companion to Shakespeare Studies* (Cambridge: Cambridge University Press, 1971), pp. 157–66.

8. In this characterization the dead Hamlet is seen to move, as always, in close adaptive touch with his direct emotional responses. In the terms of Irving Massey's fine, penetrating study of this character's employment of and response to images, Hamlet is "condemned to single vision" (*Find You the Virtue,* p. 29).

9. The polyptoton of this line, the repetition of a single word in different parts of speech ("rain," "raineth"), also contributes to the musical effect, since one element of exact repetition gets as close as words can to the exact repetition of notes that is an inescapable element of music. What Puttenham says in this regard is evocative, when he calls polyptoton "the translacer," "when ye turn and translace a word into many sundry shapes as the Tailor doth his garment, and after that sort do play with him in your ditty" (George Puttenham, *The Arte of English Poesie [1589],* eds. Gladys Willcock and Alice Walker (Cambridge: Cambridge University Press, 1936), p. 203, as cited in Sister Miriam Joseph, *Shakespeare's Use of the Arts of Language* (New York: Columbia University Press, 1947), p. 306. Puttenham's expression "ditty" names the words with a term that includes music.

10. Irving Ribner, *The Collected Plays of Christopher Marlowe* (New York: Odyssey, 1963), "Introduction"; Stephen Greenblatt, "Marlowe and the Will to Absolute Play," in *Renaissance Self-Fashioning from More to Shakespeare* (Chicago: University of Chicago Press, 1980), pp. 193–221. So Greenblatt's reading of the motives of More, for all the fine intricacy of its Realpolitik and depth-psychology inferences, is limited by his inability to handle the function in More's actual life of the allegiance to a religion that later adjudged him a saint. One could not get, through Greenblatt's reading, to More's austere but emphatic definition in his last words that he was "the King's good servant but God's first."

11. These do present an endless puzzle, as Ribner and Greenblatt insist, but it is not a puzzle that will yield by simply applying a skepticism directly to the play. The same problem obtains, somewhat less puzzlingly, with *The Jew of Malta,* where

the audience must be meant to take the utterances of this Vice ironically, and to reject them, and also to find his actions immoral in a way that the steely thrust of *Tamburlaine* is not to be taken—this even though some of Marlowe's own views and actions could be construed as similar to the Jew's. If we are not meant to register the socially negative force of the Jew's many acts of violence and fraud, they become meaningless to an audience.

"What time th'eternall Lord in fleshly slime / Enwombed was": Christian Elements in the Action of *Cymbeline*

1. The "episteme" of Foucault serves as a strong transformational principle for integrating systems of discourse into a sort of deep structure, but it is not predictive, or all-inclusive, or even consistent, as I have tried to show elsewhere. See Albert Cook, "The Wilderness of Mirrors," (*Kenyon Review,* Summer, 1986, pp. 91–111); and the chapter on the totalizing view of history in *History/Writing.*

2. Maurice Hunt, in "Shakespeare's Empirical Romance: *Cymbeline* and Modern Knowledge (*Texas Studies in Language and Literature,* 22.3 [Fall, 1980]: 322–41), relates the knotted speech initiated at the beginning of the play to questions about language, and particularly to Bacon's critique of imprecise symbols in the Idols of the marketplace. Following the present hermeneutic emphasis on linguistic indeterminacy, Hunt claims that questions of knowing are raised, by the easy proofs adduced through language from Iachimo's bedchamber observations. Yet much of what happens in the play demonstrates not the impossibility but rather the precariousness of knowing. The king's reading of the signs about the queen, instantly revised and assessed on her death, proceed not from any limits on sign systems but rather from the double edge the play exhibits in the relation between treachery and love or trust. Treachery will win, the play shows, but only in the short run.

As John W. Crawford says ("Shakespeare's *Cymbeline,*" *Explicator,* 38.4 [Summer 1980]: 4–6), "Shakespeare may be suggesting in *Cymbeline* as in *Hamlet* that the ordering of the kingdom, if it is to be effective and beneficial to all, must be made on the basis of retribution and forgiveness."

3. Alan Sinfield in "Hamlet's Special Providence" (*Shakespeare Survey* 33 [1980]: 89–98), sees a Stoic coloring in the "fall of a sparrow" speech and parallels it to a similar passage in Calvin (*Institutes,* 1.16.1). However, Stoicism and Christianity were often linked through the 1590s, and without any specific doctrinal emphasis. One example is Guillaume Du Vair (T.I), *The Moral Philosophie of the Stoicks* (London, 1598). The "Protestant," or more narrowly, Calvinist echoes can be supplemented by Catholic ones, and the religiosity of *Hamlet* cannot be confined within sectarian definitions. So Dover Wilson's intricate disentanglement of doctrines about ghosts from separate theological traditions, as all of these find expression in the play, would effectually show. (J. Dover Wilson, *What Happens in* Hamlet [Cambridge: Cambridge University Press, 1935].)

4. Roland Mushat Frye, *Shakespeare and Christian Doctrine* (Princeton: Princeton University Press, 1963), pp. 24–31. Northrop Frye briefly states the particular case for *Cymbeline* (*A Natural Perspective* [New York: Columbia University Press, 1965], p. 66): "The reason for the choice of the theme may be partly that Cymbeline was king of Britain at the time of Christ. The sense of a large change in human fortunes taking place offstage has to be read into *Cymbeline,* and as a rule reading things into Shakespeare in the light of some external information is a dubious practice." One should begin by heeding Frye's caveat, but he himself here hedges so as to have it both ways; and there is evidence, other than just doctrinal statement, for more than just the "choice of theme" in the Christian tone of this play, as I am trying to demonstrate.

5. In this connection discussions of some adequate subtlety are to be found in Wylie Sypher, "Shakespeare as Casuist: *Measure for Measure,*" *Sewanee Review,* 68 (1950); and David Lloyd Stevenson, *The Achievement of Shakespeare's* Measure for Measure (Ithaca, N.Y.: Cornell University Press, 1966).

6. See Albert Cook, *Shakespeare's Enactment* (Chicago: The Swallow Press, 1976), pp. 27–37, 151–68, 214–19. The speeches in the play tend toward skepticisms of various kinds, as William Elton demonstrates (*King Lear and the Gods* [San Marino: Huntington Library, 1966]). My discussion there concerns actions as these go against definitions in the speeches: "'The gods are just, and of our pleasant vices / Make instruments to plague us' (5.3.170–71). [This] is true only of someone who feels the justice of the remark: all vices may not be pleasant, and to the unpleasant vices of Goneril and Regan, Cornwall and Oswald, there is no instrumental handle for the gods to catch. None of these is 'plagued' in the sense of prolonged operations upon them: all die sudden deaths. A 'plague' has in fact a purgatorial value, and is instrumental in the restitution to dignity, to 'joy' as well as 'grief, for the Gloucester of whom his son is speaking." [Par.] "There is also the converse of the second proposition: the gods, of our virtues, make instruments to rescue us. The action of the play exemplifies the [quoted] proposition, and it is by the converse of [this] proposition that 'As flies to wanton boys are we to th'gods— / They kill us for their sport.' (4.1.37–38) is belied" (p. 216).

7. The tonality of the gathering where Posthumus makes his rash bet would seem to fall under St. Paul's injunction: "Let us walk honestly as in the day; not in rioting and drunkenness, not in chambering and wantonness, not in strife and envying" (Romans 13.13).

8. "Pannonians and Dalmatians," 3.1.73, following Holinshed: "And so, turning his power against the Pannonians and the Dalmatians, he left off for a time the wars of Britain." Richard Hosley, *Shakespeare's Holinshed* (New York: Putnam, 1968), from the fourth edition, 1587, 4–5 (32). Holinshed places the rule as "before the birth of the savior" and says, counter to the play that Cymbeline "refused to pay tribute." And at the same time he was "loth to break with them" and was "knighted in the court of Augustus."

9. In Holinshed, 6–7 (154–55), the Belarius trio is not correlated to Cymbeline, but are a husbandman and his two (real) sons fighting with the Scots against the Danes.

Homer Swander, "*Cymbeline* and the 'Blameless Hero'," (*ELH* 31.3 [September 1964]: 259–70): "It is clearly of the greatest possible significance that among all the versions of the cycle that include more than one kind of evidence, Shakespeare's hero alone capitulates to the relatively weak force of the token" (p. 263). Posthumus contradicts Philario's commonsense deduction (p. 264)—but still in error, though Posthumus is right about the servants, when he refuses to believe that avenue (2.5.1–35). Yet his penitence is equally conventional (p. 267).

    10. Cook, *Shakespeare's Enactment,* pp. 96–99.

    11. In Jacobean usage, as the NED shows, this word equivocates between "body (live or dead)" and "dead body," like the Latin "corpus."

    12. Meredith Skura, "Interpreting Posthumus' Dream from Above and Below: Families, Psychoanalysts, and Literary Critics" in Murray Schwartz and Coppélia Kahn, eds., *Representing Shakespeare,* 203–216: "I think, though, that what happens as we look at *Cymbeline,* even more clearly than with the other plays, is that we can see the terms conscious and unconscious as a misleading polarity. What we really experience, instead of either of these extremes is a range of different ways of being aware."

    13. Cook, *Shakespeare's Enactment* 94: "The audience . . . listens on a plane of mystery to which the characters themselves, for all their alert responsiveness, do not have access. The gallery of the capable—Imogen, Belarius, Guiderius, Arviragus, Posthumus, Pisanio, Cornelius, Philario, Lucius, and in some ways ultimately Cymbeline himself—is fuller than in any other play of Shakespeare."

    14.   Hang there like fruit, my soul,
Till the tree die.

                                  (5.5. 263–64)

    Me of my lawful pleasure she restrain'd,
And pray'd me oft forbearance: did it with
A pudency so rosy, the sweet view on't
Might well have warm'd old Saturn

                                  (2.4. 161–65)

    15. This (imaginary) kiss on the mole below the breast is arguably the strongest sexual detail in all of Shakespeare.

    16. Kenneth Muir, *Shakespeare's Sources* (London: Methuen, 1961), pp. 231–40. In addition to the stanza from Spenser and the two loci from Holinshed, Muir adduces *The Rare Triumphs of Love and Fortune* (the cave); *The Mirror for Magistrates* (Guiderius's defeat of a Roman army); Blenerhasset's "Guidericus"; the *Decameron* and *Frederyke of Jennen* (the wager on a wife's chastity); *The Rare Triumphs of Love and Fortune;* and *Philaster.*

    17. See Douglas L. Peterson, *Time, Tide, and Tempest: A Study of Shakespeare's Romances* (San Marino: Huntington Library, 1973): "From this point on in the soliloquy Posthumus concentrates upon the divine law and its satisfaction." "The liberty Posthumus seeks is a release from a tormented conscience" (p. 141). Peterson here makes much of the interchange about last things between Posthumus and his temporary Gaoler. "As his former condemnation of all wives had led to the denial of his own legitimacy and, hence, of his right to his father's

name, his forgiving of all wives, here (V.1.1–5), marks the beginning of his movement toward regaining his right to that name" (p. 138). "We have seen the gods intervene, but primarily through human agents—through men who like Posthumus and Belarius have atoned fully for their crimes against heaven and country and thus transformed themselves into agents of renewal" (p. 147).

18. Possible contemporary references are provided by Glynne Wickham: "Riddle and Emblem: A Study in the Dramatic Structure of *Cymbeline*," in John Carey, ed., *English Renaissance Studies Presented to Helen Gardner* (Oxford: Clarendon Press, 1980), pp. 94–113. Wickham relates the lion and the notion of peace in the riddle of Jupiter's tablet to the "dicton" in the frontispiece of James I's collected works (1616), as it can be traced in panegyrics and masques directed at King James from the time of his accession. If so, the reference would add a contemporary public implication to the generalities that are worked out in this play, however much they may have begun as specific references to such public facts.

19. The name, and perhaps even the person, of this Lucius is set by Spenser into close connection with the Christianizing of the Roman Empire: "And After him good Lucius, / That first received Christianity, / The sacred pledge of Christes Evangely" (*Faerie Queene*, 2.10.53. 3–5). I am grateful to Andrew Sabol for pointing out this reference.

Shifts of Tempo, Considerations of Time, and Manipulations of Theme in *The Winter's Tale*

1. There are eleven to thirteen enjambments in the first twenty-six lines of Time's speech. The speech then straightens into the more usual end-stopping of couplets for the last six lines, which have no enjambments at all.

2. For music generally in *The Winter's Tale*, particularly apposite is the formulation of James R. Andreas, "'Music Awake Her: Strike 'Tis Time': Generic Modulation in *The Winter's Tale*" (*Tennessee Philological Bulletin* of the Memphis, Tennessee, Philological Association 21 [July 1984]: 24–25): "The dramatic transitions from tragedy to comedy and from comedy to romance are analogous to the musical technique known as harmonic modulation. . . . a process of moving from one key or mode to another by means of several transitional devices. These devices include *pivot notes* (a single note, either the tonic, mediant, or dominant, becomes an important melodic degree in the new key), *diatonic pivot chords* (chords are struck common to both the established and the new key), *chromatic pivot modulation by direct leap* (sudden transition from the tonic of the established key to the tonic of the new key), and *false modulation* (a third key is momentarily introduced in passing from the old to the new key). All of these methods of modulating from one genre to another are deployed in *The Winter's Tale*, arguably Shakespeare's most musical play. There are *pivot characters*, namely Autolycus and Paulina, who are crucial to at least two of the three generic moods of the play and who catalyze the movement from one mode to the next. There are scenes that are analogous to musical chords used in modulation: *diatonic scenes* such as the famous bear chase

(III,ii) where elements common to both tragedy and comedy coalesce; *chromatic scenes,* such as the climax of the play (V,iii) where the transition from comedy to romance is more abrupt, but recalls earlier humorous moments; and brief *false modulations* where the comic equilibrium is threatened by some previous tragic complication (IV,iv)."

3. Thomas McFarland, *Shakespeare's Pastoral Comedy* (Chapel Hill: University of North Carolina Press, 1972), p. 143: "The change of stone to humanness represents a profound fulfillment of human hopes. If blood did come from a stone, then all the world would be different. Some of the deepest dreams of magic have to do with the animation of statues. Augustine in his *De civitate Dei,* attacks Hermes Trismegistus, as Frances Yates says, 'for praising the Egyptians for the magic by which they drew . . . spirits or demons into the statues of their gods, thus animating the statues, or making them into gods.' . . . So Paulina is at pains to say that the statue's 'actions shall be as holy as / You hear my spell is lawful' (5.3.104–5)."

4. The necessity of death as a prelude to the statue—perhaps so that the immobilization of the represented image will not be taken as some sort of voodoo violation of the person—is pointed up by the comic impropriety underlying Boris Vian's spoof document proposing statues of living notables in prominent Parisian locations, the first statue to be dedicated to the then living Jean-Paul Sartre. In the boundary crossing of our time, this taboo, too, has been spiritedly violated: there is, for example, a superrealistic statue of Michel Butor in a walking posture at a square in Geneva, where he teaches.

5. The case for this is made in *Shakespeare's Enactment,* pp. 221; 249–51. Antigonus makes various hypocritically exaggerated protestations, but he is alone of this trio to collude with Leontes' perverse plans for murder.

6. Othello cannot be as old as Camillo, but Desdemona is, of course, the usual marriageable age. And Sir Toby, uncle to a marriageable woman, seems merely middle-aged, but Maria, of indeterminate age, has a youthful sprightliness that suggests she too is young.

7. Albert Cook, *Prisms,* "Action," pp. 128–47.

8. Richard H. Abrams, "Leontes's Enemy: Madness in *The Winter's Tale,*" in William Coyle, ed., *Aspects of Fantasy* (Westport, Conn.: Greenwood Press, 1986), pp. 155–62.

9. Morris P. Tilley, *A Dictionary of the Proverbs in England in the Sixteenth and Seventeenth Centuries* (Ann Arbor: University of Michigan Press, 1950), M71: "As long lives a merry Man as a sad," quoted from Henry Porter, *Two Angry Women of Abington,* 1598, with eleven other examples. However, Tilley's H320a gives further examples of Autolycus's theme, "A merry heart lives long."

10. Philippe Ariès, *Centuries of Childhood* (New York: Knopf, 1966).

11. In a continuation of the theological undertone, there are references to confession, 1.2.235–38; to the sinful equivalence of slander and adultery, 1.2.284.

12. J. H. P. Pafford, *The Winter's Tale,* Arden Edition (London: Methuen, 1963), p. 166. "Center" is repeated at 2.1.102–3.

13. For the reference to "dream" here, there is a corresponding encounter at 3.2.81–82 between Hermione's "my life stands in the level of your dreams" and Leontes' "Your actions are my dreams."

14. Derek Traversi, *Shakespeare: The Last Phase* (Stanford: Stanford University Press, 1965), as cited in Kenneth Muir, ed., *Shakespeare: The Comedies,* Englewood Cliffs, N.J.: Prentice-Hall, 1965), p. 153: "The virtues which [Florizel and Perdita] are called upon to embody are an essential part, properly understood, of the life of 'grace'." "Grace" and related words occur twenty-seven times in the play. Hermione uses it most, five times. Antigonus uses none of them. Autolycus uses "grace" just once, and then in the limited sense of "courtly luxury," "have his daughter come to grace" (4.4.778).

Metaphysical Poetry and *Measure for Measure*

1. An elaboration of this idea is presented in my book on comedy, *The Dark Voyage and the Golden Mean* (Cambridge: Harvard University Press, 1949).

Seven Pillars of Wisdom: Turns and Counter-Turns

1. "I looked on *Seven Pillars* as, in essence, tragedy—a victory in which no man could take delight. In revenge you shook me for the moment. Confession is in the air. Do you remember my telling you once that I collected a shelf of 'Titanic' books (those distinguished by greatness of spirit, 'sublimity' as Longinus would call it): and that they were *The Karamazovs, Zarathustra* and *Moby Dick*. Well, my ambition was to make an English fourth. You will observe that modesty comes out more in the performance than in the aim!" From a letter to David Garnett, 28 August 1922, *The Letters of T. E. Lawrence,* David Garnett, ed. (London, 1938; New York: Doubleday Doran & Co., 1939), p. 360.

2. Jeffrey Meyers, *The Wounded Spirit: a Study of* Seven Pillars of Wisdom (London: Macmillan, 1973), p. 11. In his chapter "Composition and Revisions" (pp. 45–78), Meyers documents the elaborate work Lawrence put into this book, including references to episodes he ruled out as artistically unjustifiable. Meyers (p. 85) lists "at least ten styles" in the work: narrative, descriptive, reflective, lyric, dramatic, emotive, epic, comic, puerile, technical.

3. Page references in the text are to T. E. Lawrence, *Seven Pillars of Wisdom: A Triumph* (New York: Doubleday, 1935).

4. *Letters,* p. 514.

5. "The *Commentaries* are one of my pet books," he writes to George Bernard Shaw (*Letters,* p. 387). In another letter he couples Thucydides and Clarendon in praising Churchill's book about a phase of the same war he wrote about (p. 521).

6. *Letters,* p. 356.

7. These were written quite early, in August 1916. They are printed in John Mack, *Prince of Our Disorder* (Boston: Little, Brown, 1976), pp. 463–70. As analyses they were abundantly confirmed, Mack reports, in his much later inter-

views with the Arab principals (p. 206). Much later they were used as a military text. The data about this are given in Konrad Morsey, "T. E. Lawrence: Strategist," *The T. E. Lawrence Puzzle,* ed. Stephen E. Tabachnick (Athens: University of Georgia Press, 1984), pp. 185–203. Morsey finds Lawrence an unusually capable military strategist. It must be admitted, however, that to characterize *Seven Pillars* as history does go against the grain of Lawrence's assertion in the later suppressed introduction to that work, where he cautions lest "one mistake for history the bones from which one day a man may make history" (A. W. Lawrence, ed., *Oriental Assembly* [London: Williams and Norgate, 1939], p. 142). In "The Changing East," an article published at the time (pp. 71–102), Lawrence gives a larger overview of the historical circumstances than he does in *Seven Pillars* itself, which *in this context* he presents as a personal account only.

8. Lawrence interestingly cites Xenophon as an authority on how to conduct "diathetic" propaganda (*Oriental Assembly,* p. 117). See Jeffrey Meyers, "Xenophon and *Seven Pillars of Wisdom,*" *Classical Journal* 72 (Dec. 1976–Jan. 1977): 141–43.

9. See Albert Cook, *History/Writing.*

10. The stylistic flair, and also the concentration on linking observation to action, persists for Lawrence well beyond the time of *Seven Pillars.* When he was in the ranks and given a commission to translate the *Odyssey,* he did so in a trenchant phrasing, and one that, when it slants just a little beyond the text, does so in the direction of action. Take a passage that I literally render as:

> And in my great-hearted spirit I made a plan myself
> To go closer to him, draw the sharp sword from my thigh
> And wound him in the chest where the midriff holds the liver,
> Striking with my hand. But another spirit restrained me;
> For there we too would have perished in sheer destruction,
> Since from the lofty entrance we could not push away
> The mighty rock with our hands that he had set upon it.
> (*Odyssey,* 9.299–305, tr. Albert Cook (New York: Norton, 1966)

For this, Lawrence (Shaw) offers the following (I italicize the phrases that shade the Greek toward still more violent action in this already violent passage about the Cyclops):

> I was wondering in my bold heart whether I should *steal in, snatch* the keen sword hanging on my hip, and stab him in the body; after making sure with my fingers where was *that vital place* in the midriff, below the heart and above the liver. Yet my second thoughts put me off *this stroke,* for by it I should finally seal our own doom: *Not enough strength lay in our hands* to roll back the huge block with which he had closed *the cave.*

Here too, in the Odyssey as at moments in the Arab Campaign, waiting is a strategy, and one that stirs Lawrence to greater specification of actions than those offered by his text.

11. Charles Montagu Doughty, *Travels in Arabia Deserta* (London: Jonathan Cape, 1923 [1876]), 2: 460–61.

12. Jeffrey Meyers (*The Wounded Spirit,* p. 148) lists sixteen distinct instances in which Lawrence himself has woven a biblical quotation or allusion into his text.

13. Edward Said, *Orientalism* (New York: Vintage, 1978). In qualification of what Said says about him, among Lawrence's many tortured disclaimers is the noteworthy passage from his first chapter:

> A man who gives himself to be a possession of aliens leads a Yahoo life, having bartered his soul to a brute-master. He is not of them. He may stand against them, persuade himself of a mission, batter and twist them into something which they, of their own accord, would not have been. Then he is exploiting his old environment to press them out of theirs. Or, after my model, he may imitate them so well that they spuriously imitate him back again. Then he is giving away his own environment: pretending to theirs; and pretences are hollow, worthless things. In neither case does he do a thing of himself, nor a thing so clean as to be his own (without thought of conversion), letting them take what action or reaction they please from the silent example.
>
> In my case, the effort for these years to live in the dress of Arabs, and to imitate their mental foundation, quitted me of my English self, and let me look at the West and its conventions with new eyes: they destroyed it all for me. At the same time I could not sincerely take on the Arab skin: it was an affectation only. Easily was a man made an infidel, but hardly might he be converted to another faith. I had dropped one form and not taken on the other, and was become like Mohammed's coffin in our legend, with a resultant feeling of intense loneliness in life, and a contempt, not for other men, but for all they do. Such detachment came at times to a man exhausted by prolonged physical effort and isolation. His body plodded on mechanically, while his reasonable mind left him, and from without looked down critically on him, wondering what that futile lumber did and why. Sometimes these selves would converse in the void; and then madness was very near, as I believe it would be near the man who could see things through the veils at once of two customs, two educations, two environments. (Pp. 31–32)

14. The key insulting phrase here is a quotation from Doughty (1:95), but Lawrence does not say so. Lawrence, of course, subscribed to the notion of the equality of races and peoples among human beings: "I entirely repudiate his suggestion that one race is better than another" (*Letters,* p. 550). This statement is made in a context where the excellence of soldiers was the immediate issue, but surely Lawrence would have meant it to be taken generally.

15. For this section I am incorporating and somewhat revising my discussion of Lawrence in the "Life of Fiction" chapter of *The Meaning of Fiction* (Detroit: Wayne State University Press, 1960).

16. *Letters,* p. 414.

17. Ibid., p. 416.

18. Ibid., p. 554.

19. Ibid., p. 372.

20. John E. Mack, *A Prince of our Disorder,* pp. 283, 420.

21. R. P. Blackmur, "The Everlasting Effort: A Citation of T. E. Lawrence," *The Expense of Greatness* (New York: 1940), pp. 1–36.

22. For a different view, see Keith N. Hull, "*Seven Pillars of Wisdom:* The Secret, Contestable Documentary," in Tabachnik, pp. 96–114. Hull asserts, as against my representation here, that "Lawrence constructs a Sirhan that is the image of his inner state" (p. 107). But as distinct from writers like Mauriac and Fitzgerald and D. H. Lawrence, with whom I am contrasting him, T. E. Lawrence's details are too rugged and disjunct to be metaphoric. In a sense, they are stronger for not being so. They do not get absorbed into, or stand for, the sensibility of the writer, but resist it at every turn by calling on it for further, always receding, definition. And as Lawrence says at one point, "There the landscape refused to be accessory, but took the skies, and we chattering humans became dust at its feet" (p. 543).

23. John Mack, *A Prince of Our Disorder,* p. 28.

24. Ibid., p. 113.

25. *The Wounded Spirit,* p. 34.

26. As he says, in a typical comment, "This [waiting for word from Abdulla] was not necessary, according to book, but they knew I was a sham soldier, and took licence to hesitate over my advice when it came peremptorily" (p. 477). But again, in a more typical overview that criticizes the very detachment he has here adduced: "I complained that since landing in Arabia I had had options and requests, never an order: that I was tired to death of free-will, and of many things besides free-will . . . These worries would have taken their due petty place, in my despite of the body, and of my soiled body in particular, but for the rankling fraudulence which had to be my mind's habit: that pretence to lead the national uprising of another race, the daily posturing in alien dress, preaching in alien speech: with behind it a sense that the 'promises' on which the Arabs worked were worth what their armed strength would be when the moment of fulfilment came. We had deluded ourselves that perhaps peace might find the Arabs able, unhelped and untaught, to defend themselves with paper tools. Meanwhile we glozed our fraud by conducting their necessary war purely and cheaply. But now this gloss had gone from me" (p. 502). And even here Lawrence's references to "paper" gloss over the seriously compromising Sykes-Picot Treaty. The "paper tools" he speaks of were and could be no defense against that piece of paper.

27. "There could be no rest-houses for revolt, no dividend of joy paid out. Its spirit was accretive, to endure as far as the senses would endure, and to use each such advance as base for further adventure, deeper privation, sharper pain. Sense could not reach back or forward. A felt emotion was a conquered emotion, an experience gone dead, which we buried by expressing it" (p. 412). This is not Nietzschean. Rather it is counter-Nietzschean, though the language is reminiscent of the compacted phraseology in the later drafts of *Der Wille zur Macht.* (See Albert Cook, "The Moment of Nietzsche," in *Thresholds: Studies in the Romantic Experience* [Madison: University of Wisconsin Press, 1985]). Lawrence often ex-

presses in various forms an un-Nietzchean "heavy repugnance" for his own writing
(the particular phrase used in *Oriental Assembly,* p. 139).

28. The agonized self-scrutiny remains unabated, carrying over into the
motives of the writer that he brings forward toward the end:

> I was very conscious of the bundled powers and entities within me; it was
> their character which hid. There was my craving to be liked—so strong and
> nervous that never could I open myself friendly to another. The terror of
> failure in an effort so important made me shrink from trying; besides, there
> was the standard; for intimacy seemed shameful unless the other could make
> the perfect reply, in the same language, after the same method, for the same
> reasons.
>
> There was a craving to be famous; and a horror of being known to like
> being known. Contempt for my passion for distinction made me refuse
> every offered honour. I cherished my independence almost as did a Beduin,
> but my impotence of vision showed me my shape best in painted pictures,
> and the oblique overheard remarks of others best taught me my created
> impression. The eagerness to overhear and oversee myself was my assault
> upon my own inviolate citadel.
>
> The lower creation I avoided, as a reflection upon our failure to attain
> real intellectuality. If they forced themselves on me I hated them. To put my
> hand on a living thing was defilement; and it made me tremble if they
> touched me or took too quick an interest in me. This was an atomic repul-
> sion, like the intact course of a snowflake. The opposite would have been my
> choice if my head had not been tyrannous. I had a longing for the absolut-
> ism of women and animals, and lamented myself most when I saw a soldier
> with a girl, or a man fondling a dog, because my wish was to be as superfi-
> cial, as perfected; and my jailer held me back.
>
> Always feelings and illusion were at war within me, reason strong
> enough to win, but not strong enough to annihilate the vanquished, or
> refrain from liking them better; and perhaps the truest knowledge of love
> might be to love what self despised. Yet I could only wish to: could see
> happiness in the supremacy of the material, and could not surrender to it:
> could try to put my mind to sleep that suggestion might blow through me
> freely; and remained bitterly awake.
>
> I liked the things underneath me and took my pleasures and adventures
> downward. There seemed a certainty in degradation, a final safety. Man
> could rise to any height, but there was an animal level beneath which he
> could not fall. It was a satisfaction on which to rest. (Pp. 563–64)

29. Thomas J. O'Donnell, "The Assertion and Denial of the Romantic Will
in *Seven Pillars of Wisdom* and *The Mint*," in Tabachnick, pp. 71–95.

30. This particular triad of pairs I have taken from Jeffrey Meyers, "T. E.
Lawrence: The Mechanical Monk," in ibid., p. 124.

31. And compare: "Among the Arabs I was the disillusioned, the sceptic,
who envied their cheap belief. The unperceived sham looked so well-fitting and
becoming a dress for shoddy man. The ignorant, the superficial, the deceived were

the happy among us. By our swindle they were glorified. We paid for them our self-respect, and they gained the deepest feeling of their lives. The more we condemned and despised ourselves, the more we could cynically take pride in them, our creatures. It was so easy to overcredit others: so impossible to write down their motives to the level of our own uncharitable truth. They were our dupes, wholeheartedly fighting the enemy. They blew before our intentions like chaff, being not chaff, but the bravest, simplest and merriest of men. *Credo quia sum?* But did not the being believed by many make for a distorted righteousness? The mounting together of the devoted hopes of years from near-sighted multitudes, might endow even an unwilling idol with Godhead, and strengthen It whenever men prayed silently to Him." (p. 549)

Dialectic, Irony, and Myth in Plato's *Phaedrus*

1. Martin Heidegger, *Sein und Zeit* (Tübingen: Niemeyer, 1963 [1926]), pp. 219 ff.; *Platons Lehre von der Wahrheit* (1947) in *Wegmarken* (Frankfurt: Klostermann, 1967), pp. 109–44. This view is somewhat contested in Paul Friedländer, *Plato: An Introduction,* Princeton, N.J.: Princeton University Press, 1968), pp. 122–29, though he further qualified his observations (*Platon,* Vol. 1, [Berlin: de Gruyter, 1954], pp. 233–36). Marcel Detienne has shown Plato's continuing involvement in the archaic mythical dimensions of *aletheia* (*Les Maîtres de vérité dans la Grèce archaïque* [Paris: Maspero, 1967], pp. 114–15).

2. Friedländer (p. 151) graphically characterizes the relation between the composition of a dialogue and its failure to resolve questions: "Just as there are pictures in which the pictorial center remains vacant, and the center of attention is transferred by the arrangement of lines, colors, and light effect to one of the corners, so the dialogue, if seen as a whole, confers essential meaning on that which appeared only as means; and this meaning, in turn, illuminates and deepens even that which, as long as we did not recognize the ironic shift, appears to be its primary purpose." Aristotle's characterization of Socrates is apposite here: "Socrates asked but he did not answer; he confessed (homologei) he did not know" (*De sophisticis elenchis,* 183b 7, cited by Friedländer, p. 157).

3. See also Konrad Gaiser, *Platons Ungeschriebene Lehre* (Stuttgart: Klett, 1968), and Thomas Slezak, "Dialogform Esoterik, Zur Deutung des platonischen Dialogs Phaidros,'" *Museum Helveticum* 35 (1978): 18–32. All these written dialogues stand under the further shadow of Plato's qualification, in the Seventh Letter but also in the *Phaedrus* (276a), that oral communication is in some ways superior to written.

4. Gerhard Krüger, *Einsicht und Leidenschaft* (Frankfurt: Klostermann, 1973): "So stellt uns die Herleitung oder Philosophie aus dem Eros mit besonderem Nachdruck vor das allgemeine Problem der Beziehung zwischen *Philosophie* und *Religion* (p. 6). Das geistige Selbst in der Mania der Liebe gerade befreit (p. 12). Die Hervorhebung des Eros ist neu, und sie ist aufschlussreich für die geistige Luft in der die *Philosophie* erwächst" (p. 20). As Margot Fleischer well says (*Hermeneutische Anthropologie* [Berlin and New York: de Gruyter, 1976], p. 131), "Eros auf seiner

höchsten Stufe ist Philosophie. Philosophie ist also Eros. Sie ist Wahnsinn als Entrückung zum Wahren in der Wiedererinnerung."

5. G. J. DeVries, *A Commentary on the Phaedrus of Plato* (Amsterdam: Hakkert, 1969), pp. 18–19. Citing H. Gundert ("Zum Spiel bei Platon" in L. Landgrebe, ed., *Beispiele,* 1965, pp. 188–121) and his own earlier book (*Spel bij Plato,* 1949), De Vries lists six different senses (from Gundert's nine) in which play is used in the *Phaedrus:* "playful social conversation, playful song and dance in the service of the gods, a playful element in rhetoric and eristic, the dialectical play in Socratic irony, the general play in human existence." (One might question the last; all of the citations are from the *Laws.*) However, Plato's play among his many concepts is one procedure. An interpreter's play among Plato's given terms does not have unlimited latitude, or Plato's words make no sense at all. Jacques Derrida ("La Pharmacie de Platon" in *La Dissémination* [Paris: Seuil, 1972], pp. 69–197) rightly stresses the importance of internal "writing" to Plato, though there would seem to be no reason to enlist Plato as a supposed support for Derrida's own doctrines of absence and difference, when the *Phaedrus* argues for writing in the consciousness as a supreme *presence.* No concept of "play" will allow for so clearly erroneous a reading of Plato's text. Moreover, with respect to Derrida's title, *pharmakon* in the *Phaedrus,* every time it occurs, always means unambiguously "healing drug" rather than "poison," as Derrida himself admits (pp. 109–12). This singleness of unambiguous meaning is the more marked as, in ways I shall indicate, Plato does tend in the *Phaedrus* to play on some ambiguities in this dialogue, and to play in general. *Pharmakon* can serve only as "la différance de la différence (as it is called, p. 146) if it parts company entirely with Plato's text. (In which case why bring up Plato?) The fashionably resurrected neo-Frazerian term *pharmakos,* "scapegoat," can still less be applied to this text, or to Plato in general. The word does not occur once in all of Plato, and it does violence to much that he says to enlist it reductively under the heading of this anthropological commonplace.

As it happens, Derrida does not permit anything like such liberties with his own text, scolding those who would anachronistically translate Marx's *aufgelöst* as his *déconstruites* (*La Carte Postale* [Paris: Flammarion, 1980], p. 285). Such a translation, Derrida asserts, would "égarer le lecteur."

6. "Putting into order and adornment (*kosmousa*) myriad actions of the ancients (*tōn palaiōn*) it instructs the coming generations (*tous epigignomenous*)."

7. Of many possible citations, this from the *Laws* is especially emphatic, as befits this late work: "the god would especially be for us the measure of things, and much more than any man could say" (716c). This revises, of course, the well-known formula of Protagoras by changing the word "man" to the word "god," and then inserting "man" in a different place.

8. Dialectic here, and especially pp. 265–69, mixes its air of discriminating conclusion with an air of qualification, especially as it weaves in and out of the discourse—and Plato emphasizes the necessity to compose a discourse in a particular order. Diskin Clay ("Socrates' Prayer to Pan," in G. Bowersock et al., eds., *Arktouros* [Berlin: de Gruyter, 1979], pp. 345–53) is able to relate the prayer to Pan, Socrates' last full statement, intricately to other themes in the dialogue.

9. The distinctions and blendings about love merge into those of philosophy and poetry, as Martha Nussbaum discusses these in "'This Story Isn't True': Poetry, Goodness, and Understanding in Plato's *Phaedrus*," in *The Fragility of Goodness* (Cambridge: Cambridge University Press, 1986), pp. 200–235 = J. Moravcsik and P. Temko, eds., *Plato on Beauty, Wisdom and the Arts* (Totowa, N.J.: Rowman and Littlefield, 1982), pp. 79–124. She points out that the *Phaedrus* shares with the *Republic* the presentation of a contrast between poetry and philosophy: "A new understanding of philosophy . . . reinterprets the distinction between philosophy and poetry." As she says (p. 89), "Philosophy is now permitted to be an inspired, manic, Muse-loving activity."

10. Gregory Vlastos effectively demonstrates the presence of some physical fulfillment in the ideal Platonic love, drawing heavily on *Phaedrus* 254–56 ("Sex in Platonic Love," in *Platonic Studies* [Princeton, N.J.: Princeton University Press, 1981], pp. 38–42).

11. K. Dorter (in "Imagery and Philosophy in Plato's *Phaedrus*," *Journal of the History of Philosophy* 9 (1971): 279–88) traces contrasting patterns of imaging in the dialogues. As T. Dalfen says ("Gedanken zur Lektüre Platonischer Dialoge," *Zeitschrift für philosophischer Forschung* 29 [1975]: 169–94), "Der innere, und wohl der entscheidende Grund zur Wahl der Dialogform war eine bestimmte Auffassung vom Wesen des Philosophierens: Philosophie als ständiges Gespräch" (p. 171). This notion involves "Verschiedene Haltungen zur Philosophie" (p. 187).

12. Kenneth J. Dover, *Greek Homosexuality* (Cambridge, Mass.: Harvard University Press, 1978).

13. De Vries (op cit., p. 186) lists some of Socrates' many exuberant effusions toward Phaedrus. In addition, Socrates playfully refers to him in the third person (261, 257b).

14. The term *logismos,* judging from the lexicon (L–S), would appear to be a favorite of Lysias. The repetition of *prosekei,* "it is fitting," from Lysias's speech by Socrates (238b), may be a somewhat mocking echo.

15. Sophos = poet in Pindar O. 1.116; O. 9.38; P. 3.113; I. 1.45.

16. *Mythologema* is a rare word, possibly a coinage of Plato's, not far in meaning from the modern "mythologeme" or a group of mythologemes.

17. *Sophizomenos,* judging again from the lexicon, is a favorite word of Lysias, and also of Isocrates. The word, we may say, proleptically links the two orators who begin and end the *Phaedrus.*

18. Julius Stenzel, *Plato's Method of Dialectic,* tr. and ed. D. J. Allan (Oxford: Clarendon Press, 1940), p. 17. These are defined as "seeing them under one idea to bring together particulars that have been scattered in many places (265d) and "to be able to divide them again into separate ideas according to the ligatures they have by nature (265e). I have left *eidos* unglossed, rendering it each time as "idea," though the shift of senses is clear, and still clearer if we adduce the third use of the word in the passage, the question of Phaedrus: "What is the other idea (*eidos*) you speak of, Socrates?" (265d). *Eidos* in fact changes its meaning throughout the dialogue.

19. The antithesis between the systems of luxuries associated with Adonis

and the necessities associated with the husbandmen are substantiated in Marcel Detienne, *Les Jardins d'Adonis* (Paris: Gallimard, 1972), though he does not mention Plato there.

20. Eric A. Havelock, *Preface to Plato* (Cambridge: Harvard University Press, 1963); *The Greek Concept of Justice* (Cambridge, Mass.: Harvard University Press, 1978). In the large literature on this subject, one might signal Charles Segal, "Tragédie, oralité, écriture," *Poétique* 50 (April 1981): 131–54. See also R. Burger, *Plato's Phaedrus: A Defense of a Philosophic Art of Writing* (University, Ala.: University of Alabama Press, 1980); and P. Lacoue-Labarthe, "Typographie," in *Mimesis des articulations* (Paris: Flammarion, 1975), pp. 167–270. As Burger says, "The dialogue's reflection on its own character as a product of writing results ironically in the apparent deprecation of the activity of writing" (p. 2). "The sweet speech of the divine lover, which washes away the bitter taste of the speech of the nonlover, cannot uncover the tension within the condition Socrates lays down for the true art of speaking" (p. 69).

21. See Diskin Clay, "Socrates' Prayer to Pan," as in note 8, above.

Equanimity and Danger: The Distribution of Questions and Style of Confrontation in the Four Dialogues around Socrates' Trial

1. Nonce references to the trial, like the explicit one at the very end of the *Theaetetus*, or implied ones, like the presence and posture of Anytus toward the end of the *Meno*, do not orient those dialogues but merely import still another qualification.

2. R. Hackforth, *Plato's* Phaedo (Cambridge: Cambridge University Press, 1981 [1955]), p. 7: "The *Phaedo* is notably silent regarding political institutions and government; its ethics are wholly individualistic." This can be the case only if we ignore the situation and do not bring the argument of the *Crito*, set just hours beforehand, upon this dialogue. Socrates' situation is a public one; he is held after a trial, and his execution has been delayed because of a rule that no "public" killing can take place while the annual embassy to Delos is under way. The word for "public" "*demosiai*," is the standard word in Plato for the contrast with "private," "*idiai*." W. D. Ross, who treats doctrinal variations as a main factor in dating, well summarizes and tabulates the various views on the sequence of the dialogues (*Plato's Theory of Ideas* [Oxford: Clarendon Press, 1951], p. 2), though to see these dialogues in a dated sequence with all the others will obscure their connection with one another, and will especially reduce that of the *Phaedo*.

3. As Joseph Fontenrose says (*The Delphic Oracle* [Berkeley: University of California Press, 1978], p. 43), "the matters which the Platonic Socrates would have his ideal state refer to the Delphic Apollo were in fact those upon which he usually spoke and which the Greek states and their citizens did refer to him, 'foundations of cults, sacrifices, and other worship of gods, demons, and heroes'" (*Republic*, 427b *Laws*, 738bc, 728a).

4. They include Phaedo himself; the reported inquirer Echecrates, a Pythagorean; Cebes, who is possibly an adherent of the Megarian school, designated along with Simmias as a pupil of Philolaus; Apollodorus, associated with Socrates; Aristippus, called by Diogenes Laertius a hedonist Cyrenaic; Critoboulos and his father Crito, Euclides, Terpsion, Hermogenes; Epigenes; Aeschines; Antisthenes; Ctesippus of Paeene; Menexenus, to whom a dialogue was devoted; "and others" (59b). Aristippus and Cleombrotus should even be counted in the census, since they are named as potential auditors who happen to be absent in Aegina, and so should Plato himself, who "was sick."

5. For a discussion of Socrates' attitudes in the complex legal situation of his conviction, see Richard Kraut, *Socrates and the State* (Princeton, N.J.: Princeton University Press, 1984).

6. Indeed, like father like son. The father has also tied up a murderer, as Euthyphro is metaphorically doing to his father, whatever might be the outcome of the trial, something of which we have no hint. Euthyphro connects his situation to that of Zeus, "whom men consider best and most just of the gods," who also tied up his father who had in turn castrated *his* father (6a). (An anonymous reader pointed out this connection to me.)

7. M. I. Finley offers no evidence for his conjecture that these are not Socrates' actual words other than the fact that legends did accrue to his person ("Socrates and Athens," in *Aspects of Antiquity* [New York: Viking, 1968], pp. 58–72). But speeches were also regularly written, and regularly preserved, even in far less famous trials. Why would Socrates not have used his rhetorical skills to follow the regular routine, and why, given the fame of the trial at the actual moment, would his speech have been lost when so many trivial ones were preserved? The burden of proof for having the *Apology* be an invention of Plato's—as are all the other dialogues—would rest on those who would assert that it is not the recorded speech, even if perhaps modified along Thucydidean lines. One balanced account is offered in R. Hackforth, *The Composition of Plato's Apology* (Cambridge: Cambridge University Press, 1933), pp. 1–7. Another is offered by W. K. C. Guthrie, *A History of Greek Philosophy* (Cambridge: Cambridge University Press, 1975), 4:72–79. For its rhetorical structure, its parody of rhetoric, its essential accuracy, and its service as a later model for Isocrates' *Antidosis,* see Reginald E. Allen, *The Dialogues of Plato* (New Haven, Conn.: Yale University Press, 1984), 1:63–75.

8. This is a real back-reference, rare in the dialogues, to Socrates' connection with specific political events, where other back-references tend to be to personal involvements, like Socrates' history with Alcibiades in the *Symposium* or philosophical ones like his training under Prodicus in the *Protagoras* and the *Meno.*

9. Jean Van Camp and Paul Conart (*Le Sens du mot theios chez Platon* [Louvain: Publications Universitaires, 1956]) often trace a mythological or hyperbolic sense in the word. But in the *Phaedo,* it acquires "une étonnante souplesse" (p. 63). It is especially complicated when love is in question, in the *Symposium* (75–88).

10. L. R. Farnell lists a number of ancient references to such embassies in antiquity, most of them not so full of detail as the one here (which he includes in

his citations) (*The Cults of the Greek States* [Oxford: Oxford University Press, 1909], 4:417–19).

11. The question comes up again (83c–d). The rudimentary philosophy here keys this passage to many discussions of pleasure in the *Philebus* and elsewhere. (Hackforth gives a list, p. 49.) The general Greek context is discussed by J. C. B. Gosling and C. C. W. Taylor, *The Greeks on Pleasure* (Oxford: Clarendon Press, 1982). Their chapter "Bodily Pleasure in the *Phaedo*" (pp. 83–95), in their generally enlightening emphasis on the tradition of a physiological basis for pleasure, concentrates on the rejection of bodily pleasure and on "the attack on hedonistic calculation," rather than on what is implied by the "seeming opposites" (which they do touch on, p. 86); on *phronesis,* and on *katharsis.* Their focus cannot let Socrates' strong emphasis on the soul as opposed to the body, or his optimism and superlative language about "purity," come much into the picture.

12. In 85b Apollo is once again associated with music, this time in the swan song, which the whole dialogue is effectually declared to be. The last reference to Apollo may be conceived to be that of the last words of Socrates, "I owe a cock to Asklepius," since that god is the son of Apollo and closely associated with him. Such a sacrifice would be in a medical context the more purely pious because of no immediate use to the dead man who is having this debt discharged after his death. (With Hackforth [1981, p. 190] we may second Wilamowitz in rejecting the notion that Socrates is being cured of the sickness of life, a notion he nowhere advances.) The arresting irrelevance of this statement complicates the question about the analogies, beyond the pious act, which might bring it into relevance here. This could be the only explicit reference to a sacrifice in all of Plato, to which in general he avoids referring. (Just the Seventh Letter, the *Republic,* and the Laws use the root/sphag, in addition to a reference at Menexenus 242c7).

13. A more popular sense of singing is used metaphorically in the expanded reference to the necessity of "singing [charms to the child] every day until you have sung away [the bogey-tale that the soul also dies at death]" (77e–78a).

14. Ronna Burger states the alternatives as those between mythos and logos, though by the series of implied propositions referred to above, poetry and the logos (of philosophy) are emphatically of the same kind and so cannot in this context be given the normal contrast of opposition so common in Plato as to be a recurrent phrase. "The Aesopian mythos thus assumes what the Socratic account makes into a problem: What is the so-called pleasant or the painful? It is because it implicitly raises this question—at least once it is contrasted with mythos—that Socrates' account can be labeled a logos" (Ronna Burger, *The* Phaedo: *A Platonic Labyrinth* [New Haven, Conn.: Yale University Press, 1984], p. 27).

15. Crito's arrangements return the discussion to practice where the recommendations lead to their future, and there are, Burger reminds us (p. 115), references to law, (encapsulating the *Crito*) and to religion at the very end (a further capping answer in the *Apology*).

16. So, for example, the *phronesis* of 76c, which the souls have before birth, and which then allows them to take up "knowledges" in the plural. In 79d *phronesis* is a "reception" or "experience" of what is pure and immortal.

17. Gregory Vlastos's discussion on reasons and causes ("Reasons and

Causes in the *Phaedo*," [*Platonic Studies,* Princeton, N.J.: Princeton University Press, 1973], pp. 76–109), for all its great discrimination and sharpness, cannot cut the simplicity and ambiguity of this phrase. Further, the whole discussion of pp. 109–10, about what Socrates "has been brought to believe" about man's position in the heaven and earth of a mythical cosmology, may be taken to qualify Vlastos's argument. The *deuteros plous* is classified as only one of three levels of certainty—or better, of bearings toward solutions—and the governing posture of Socrates, as demonstrated before death, supervenes over even so clear and intricate a series as Vlastos has taught us to see. The series is irrevocably subordinate as well as toughly worked out. Further, as Julius Stenzel says (*Plato's Method of Dialectic,* tr. and ed. D. J. Allen [Oxford: Clarendon Press, 1940], p. 47): "In the Phae-do . . . the 'chorismos' . . . between experience and the Idea . . . is at its widest . . . but . . . the question what are methexis and parousia is pronounced to be entirely irrelevant" (100d). As Hans-Georg Gadamer more positively puts it (*Dialogue and Dialectic: Eight Hermeneutical Studies on Plato,* translated and with an introduction by P. Christopher Smith [New Haven, Conn.: Yale University Press, 1980]): "It is true, of course, that it is not until the *Parmenides* and the *Philebus* that the *methexis* problem is developed so radically that the participation of the many particulars in the one idea converts into the participation of ideas in one another. *However, the role played by the hypothesis of the eidos in the argument of the* Phaedo *implies this very solution.* There it is shown that 'soul' is always together with 'life' and never with 'death,' 'two' always with 'even' and never with 'odd,' 'warm' always with 'fire' and never with 'snow'" (pp. 137–38).

Index

249